THE ROOSEVELT REVOLUTION

MARIO EINAUDI

The Roosevelt Revolution

Harcourt, Brace and Company / New York

To Manon

Library of Congress Catalog Card Number: 59–7535
Printed in the United States of America

FOREWORD

This was initially planned as a book aimed at those Europeans who think and worry about modern America and are confused about its meaning: hence, as a book seeking to bridge the gap between the Great Depression and the atom bomb—the two events most firmly fixed in the minds of men everywhere—to explain what happened in the interval, and to capture the sense of drama and of history that properly belong to the years of the Roosevelt Revolution.

In writing this book—one in which the author feels a deep personal involvement, for it has grown out of his New World experience, which began at the start of the New Deal—the more urgent issues of human freedom, of economic life, and of institutional reform that are usually taken up in any discussion concerning the United States have thus been borne in mind. These are often the issues around which center the unresolved tensions and difficulties of European society.

But both America and Europe stand to gain from a candid admission of the ways in which mass industrial democracy has affected and may affect them, as well as from a re-examination of the ground covered from 1932 to 1952, and of the general historical significance of the transformations that then took place within the United States. This book, as it now appears, is clearly written with both America and Europe in mind.

It is clearly not conceived, however, either as a plea to Europe or as a defense of America. History, the changes brought about by the passage of time, the impossibility of forcing upon any country the pattern of life, or the institutions and values, of another country, do not permit any such approach to the task at hand. But two considerations remain. The first is the recognition of the claims of historical truth and the conviction that an era as laden with meaning as the twenty years of the Roosevelt Revolution should become more fully part of the remembered experience of the Western world. The second is the belief that Europe and America must realize that only a balanced and reasoned understanding of the respective grounds upon which they stand can provide an authentic basis for the solidarity so needed in their future relationships.

A tinge both of impatience and of optimism will be found in these pages. The impatience may be due to the thought that it is discouraging, at this late hour, to see the still-frequent failure to understand the essential nature of the New Deal. The optimism rests on the author's firm view that most of the changes that have occurred in the United States since 1932 have already accomplished their purpose of putting American democracy on a sounder foundation, in spite of their cost (be it money or the limitation of ancient individualistic longings). It is often forgotten that if America is paying a price for its present way of life, this is because America has dared to identify and accept some of the unavoidable conditions for the survival of a democratic community in the twentieth century.

The author's primary concern has been with the tracing of the boundary lines of the Roosevelt Revolution conceived in its broadest terms and as the event that provides the stuff and color of contemporary America.

As a result, this book—going against the most current of the prevailing interpretations—undertakes to look at the Roosevelt Revolution as a sum total of theory and practice that hangs together, as a movement that has aspired to fulfill in an orderly manner ideals of freedom, as a moral experience that can be lifted out of the morass of pragmatic expediency in which American political life is usually thought to flounder. It maintains that continuity, coherence, a vision of life in a modern democracy have all been there, in a large sense, to guide America during those two decades.

In this context, this book calls Roosevelt the leader and places him at the center of the Revolution, as a statesman having at his disposal a body of doctrine and a vivid and broadly philosophical concept of man and of his relationship to society.

Essentially, the Roosevelt Revolution is seen, in the first place, as an effort to re-establish the sense of community in a free industrial society and to come to terms with its requirements, and, in the second place, as the most important attempt in the twentieth century to affirm the validity and the central role of the political instruments of democracy in facing the crisis of our times. While democracy was being routed all over the world by the totalitarians and the technicians, it triumphed in the United States. Those who proclaim their attachment to democracy ought to consider how this was done.

I would like to state here my deep feeling of indebtedness to all those who helped me in writing this book. Fundamentally, my principal debt is to the United States. But I wish to set forth my lively appreciation for the support and criticism given me, over the years and in different ways, by so many friends, colleagues, and students. For substantial assistance not alone of a moral kind, warm thanks must go to my friend Raffaele Mattioli.

Ithaca
June 1958

CONTENTS

THE ROOSEVELT REVOLUTION

Europe's Image
of America

In dealing with many of the fundamental issues concerning the America of the Age of Roosevelt, even the well-informed European is likely to offer interpretations that are at times obsolete, often tentative or cloudy, and not seldom quite mistaken.

From Emerson to Whitman, from Upton Sinclair to Sinclair Lewis, American literature had provided Europe with a succession of dimly outlined, and sometimes contradictory, pictures. America was a giant, with a simple democratic faith. A country rapidly expanding, frontier-minded, but inhabited by childish and materialistic people. A country that had offered haven to millions of impoverished Europeans, but one that, faced with the problems of growth, did not know how to solve them.

By 1932 a certain image of America had, nevertheless, become well fixed in the European mind. America was a land of extremes, of economic success on a super-human scale, of adventure and freedom, of great industrial monopolies and ineffective government, hesitant about its internal policies as well as about its international role. Against this background, Roosevelt's accession to power took place. But, at the same time, Europeans were faced by the full flowering of totalitarianism and the imminent threat of war. How difficult it was for them to follow the Roosevelt Revolution, or to dislodge from their minds the vivid tales of disaster of the Great Depression. The stirring play unfolding on the American stage was quickly pushed

1

into the background by the rush of events of much closer im-
mediacy. Indeed, some of the echoes that were faintly carried
across the ocean waters seemed to convey the impression that
Roosevelt's New Deal was imitating totalitarian techniques in
some of its policies. Those who had time to think about the
matter at all thought it was a pity that a democratic country of
the first rank should accept fascist methods to conquer its economic difficulties.

The war and the postwar crises inevitably concentrated the
attention of Europe on the foreign policy of the United States,
on the role it played in the desperate conflict in which Europe
was engaged, and on the ideas of the American government concerning the peace. The evolution of internal American life was
deemed a matter of no particular significance. Had not Roosevelt
himself indicated that the New Deal had to yield to the exigencies
of war? Winning the war had become the purpose of American
public policy, not transforming American society. This was altogether proper, but the change, of course, underlined Europe's
views on the short duration of the New Deal and her suspicions
about the inevitability of the ultimate reassertion of the trends
that had been stopped and of the interests that had been pushed
aside by the New Deal.

Within the last ten years, the cold war and American-Soviet
relations have overshadowed everything else. The reactions of
the American government to the expansion of Soviet power
became the object of the exclusive and most intense preoccupation on the part of Europe. On the nature and direction of those
reactions much depended: the peace and the happiness of the
world, and the chances of a reconciliation of the antagonistic
positions of the two world powers. This was not the time to be
concerned about internal American policy. At best, only those
issues that bore a direct relationship to the cold war conflict
were considered meaningful. The activities of Joseph McCarthy

monopolized Europe's attention, as well as the American interpretations of the communist phenomenon and of what to do about it, especially since they appeared to be accepted by an increasingly large percentage of the American people.

Finally, in 1952, at a climactic moment of the cold war, the twenty years of Democratic rule came to an end with the return of the Republican party to the White House. Surely, if anybody still harbored thoughts of Roosevelt and of the New Deal, the time had then been reached to bury them decently. For the Republican administration soon gave indication of seeming to prepare for a return of the business community to a dominant position. The old 1929 image of America was resurrected, with variations. America was not only the country of industrial monopolies, dedicated to the realization of a materialistic and soulless prosperity. It had also become an immeasurably stronger country than in 1929, thanks to the Second World War and the atom bomb. America was now the seat of the mightiest industrial empire, ready to exploit its unique strength in a world rendered weaker and poorer as a result of a catastrophe America had not felt and had not shared.

Thus the twenty years from 1932 to 1952 were quickly written off, as far as most of their domestic implications were concerned. Few important epochs in the life of great nations have faded away more completely from the mind of those whose business it is to keep track of the course of history. Few have made a more superficial impression on the consciousness of peoples. America must always be what popular legend has decreed it has been from the beginning of time.

The temptation to let legends flourish is strong. But perhaps it is better not to surrender to it. Perhaps one should say that the present cannot properly be understood without the past, especially when the past that is forgotten is the Age of Roosevelt.

*

America and Americans have often, with disarming simplicity, exposed to the inquisitive scrutiny of the Europeans some of the weakest aspects of their interests, manners, institutions, and hopes. The boastful and crude American businessman who moves like a conquering and all-powerful master on the face of the earth is taken to represent a civilization dominated by industry, a government which is nothing more than the agent of a ruthless capitalistic society. Few outside the United States realize that the same businessman is frequently a frustrated individual at home, hemmed in by legal restraints, heavily punished by taxation, and controlled by a system of public rules that severely regulate his conduct and his decisions.

The irrepressible senator, who alone or as a member of an investigating committee, tours Europe and utters solemn and naive pronouncements on world affairs, is taken to express the official and final view of American policy. In Washington, the opinions of the same senator are often forgotten, or have to be sharply modified as they become part of a much more intricate, balanced, and slow-moving process of decision-making.

The young diplomat under pressure, or the government technician in a hurry, who for the first time in their lives are dealing with strange and unexpected situations in a world they do not as yet understand, inevitably arouse much friction, even though in the end it will be clear that no one in Washington believes that the goals of the United States are to be achieved by the systematic affronting of the legitimate rights of other peoples, or the deliberate disregard of their customs and views.

The American tourist, whose ubiquitous presence in Europe is itself proof of a large-scale social transformation back home, can and often does by his behavior shock the sensibilities of certain European classes. Few are permitted, or care, to see that what matters is not the contrast between the "uncouth" American and the "cultured" European, but the fact that large numbers of Americans can freely move about the world while few Europeans either can or wish to do so. And that the real problem, therefore, is that of dealing with groups of individuals coming in touch for the first time with a different civilization.

Surely, then, America has contributed to strengthening the mythology that every people is always ready to weave about other peoples. But how ready the Europeans have been to cultivate the garden of their imagination.

Included in the landscape is usually a belief in the all-powerful reach of American business and diplomatic agents and in the pervasively corrupting power of the American dollar. American money has been responsible for the rift in Italian socialism and for the "expulsion" of the Communists from the government of France in 1947. It is at the root of conspiracies everywhere. The devil theory of history has found in the expansion of American activities throughout the world a field of exploitation only slightly less profitable than that traditionally supplied by Soviet communism.

The persistence of a crisis atmosphere throughout the world since the Great Depression has helped to develop a fitful and partial vision of the democracy beyond the seas, and Europeans, intelligentsia and men in the street alike, have found it hard to abandon the accumulated clichés of the past. Nor is this surprising, considering the prejudices and misunderstandings that persist among European nations themselves, each a vigilant observer of the activities of the others over a long series of centuries.

The more radical or unexpected the change in the pattern of American life, the more difficult has been its acceptance in Europe. Brought up in a tradition of cynical despair concerning the possibility of reform and with the conviction that the more things are shifted around the more likely will be the continuation of old habits and sources of power, the European did not have to struggle hard to retain traditional conceptions about America.

The new was either incomprehensible or, the more astute were convinced, nothing more than a masquerade of the old.

This reaction has, again, been helped by certain habits peculiar to America, such as muckraking, one of the most widely practiced exercises in the American political and literary game. The tendency to self-examination and candid introspection, the willingness to admit shortcomings of all kinds, has been one of the more appealing and singular characteristics of American democracy. It is true that the Constitution is sacred, but the framework of freedom it provides and within which the turbulent and complex activities of American political life take place, does not rescue the men who operate under it from the reach of the most searching criticism.

Perhaps this will change; perhaps awe before big authority and helplessness before small authority will become important traits of public behavior in America as they already are in many countries of Europe. But we are dealing here with the past and the present and not with the future, and we are entitled to compare the abundance of information on the lives and doings of American politicians and public servants with the paucity of information on most of their European counterparts.

Nowhere in the world have the activities of political parties and leaders been more relentlessly exposed to public view than in the United States. The protective devices, the blackouts, or the downright lack of interest in the political processes that have for so long sheltered the doings of the members of the ruling classes in Europe, have proven ineffective in the United States. The consuming eagerness with which sociologists and their allies, flourishing as never before in the American climate, have examined the political structure and its inmates, has made doubly certain the flowering of a vast and entertaining literature of analysis, criticism, and exposure.

For the political writer and the pamphleteer, from Upton Sinclair to Lincoln Steffens, and for the press, from *The*

Nation to the Pulitzer newspapers, politics, municipal or national, have ever been the main source of public debate, an educational as well as a circulation tool, the inspiration for public-spirited crusades. To assume that in the agitated, fluid, improvised, and ever-changing American political scene, one developing amid totally novel social conditions, one that had to cope with the massive entrance of millions of immigrants, one would not uncover amusing or preoccupying examples of strange or corrupt behavior, would be absurd. Furthermore, the unusual details have shown a marked tendency to stick longer in people's minds than the boring ideological and abstract gymnastics which, with some notable exceptions, have been a staple of European politics in nontotalitarian periods. Tammany Hall and Teapot Dome make better reading than maximalism and spontaneity.

Today many, if not all, of the more picturesque elements of American political life in the decades between the Civil War and the Great Depression have unhappily disappeared. America has been moving toward better regulated and duller processes of political life. To the debunker's dismay, much of the color of the earlier periods has been lost. It has not been easy to adjust to the disappearance of Mayor Hague. Harry Hopkins was incorruptible (even though he provided good copy in other ways) and Social Security is soporific as a conversation topic.

One cannot, therefore, blame the Europeans too much for their reluctance to abandon the old-fashioned approach. By dint of a supreme effort and in spite of the obstacles the New Deal was building up against it, American politics could still be proven to be as primitively corrupt as they had been alleged to be before, the role of urban machines in American political life could be still magnified beyond reason and extended beyond its legitimate chronological boundaries and Roosevelt made to appear as their prisoner. For to understand Roosevelt's role in largely bringing to an end the old pattern of urban politics would have implied on the part of the European observer a recognition of social transformations which were not admitted to have taken place in the first instance.

Roosevelt himself is for the most part pictured as an unprincipled opportunist, as a tightrope walker who moved now right, now left, but who moved with the only purpose in mind of keeping himself from falling. This is not always necessarily meant critically, for, even in Europe, survival is recognized as a primary purpose of political leaders, but to indicate the absence of a guiding principle. Roosevelt's opportunism is after all the logical consequence of the stream of American pragmatism. Few can see that a pragmatic approach to politics need not imply the absence of firm views about the nature of political action and of the goals to be achieved over a certain period of time. There may well be incompatibility between pragmatism and the rigid planning of the Soviet Union. But there is no incompatibility between pragmatism and the acceptance of the doctrine of the general welfare and the common good to be sought through flexible means that will duly take into account changing conditions.

The greatest worry of the European intellectual is the absence of an American Left, or rather its disappearance in the recent past. The strange phenomenon is given a number of differing explanations. Sometimes it is seen as the result of terror exercised by government or by powerful private interests: the rise of the American police state having struck fear among the currents of the left and driven them underground or to extinction. At other times the European will lay the guilt at the door of American prosperity, which has blurred the perceptions and blunted the reactions of everybody, Progressives and Conservatives alike. How is it possible to have Leftist feelings in a beatific state of material satisfaction? Prosperity has done the work of reaction, and by inducing a smug sense of well-being in the masses of Americans it has removed any inclination they might have had to set up the barricades. An altogether abnormal condition of prosperity has deprived them of compassion for the rest of the world.

Political movements are grounded in social realities, and this is especially true of movements of the Left. Some of the questions about the fate of the Left that are being asked of the United States, should be asked of Great Britain. The European who is so ready to ascribe the weakness of the revolutionary Left in the United States to cowardice or to obesity, is apparently not ready to do so in the case of Great Britain, where the Left is facing a set of issues no less serious than those existing in the United States, because they arise out of the same question of what is to be done in a society that has attained so many of the objectives of the Left.

One can defend the thesis of the permanent Left, that is, of the necessity for any community, at all times, even under the most ideal conditions of peace, freedom, prosperity, and justice, to have dissatisfied, anxious people striving for something better still or for different purposes to be served by the sum total of the nation's productive efforts. But in the case of democracies that have been rapidly evolving in the last generation, like the United States and Great Britain, the question is whether the discussion can still be carried out in terms of the old distinction between Right and Left. What Europeans still refuse to see is that the difficulties the American Left has in finding itself and in coming to grips with contemporary reality may be due to a radical transformation of the underlying social conditions that have in the past tended to justify the Left.

The European critic of the weaknesses of the American Left ought to consider the probable fate of the European Left under conditions of full employment, massive redistribution of wealth, maximum possibility of realization of individual hopes and longings for change and improvement. It might well be said that, under those conditions, there would be no Left in Europe.

Certainly the Left would have to engage in a painful re-examination of the premises of its political course of action.

The inability to look at facts without preconceived and dogmatic notions has led some of the keenest European political commentators to say that American society has less mobility today than in the nineteenth century. (To the extent this is true, the decline is in part due to the necessities of a complex industrial civilization whose advent and ripening these same commentators usually consider as an inevitable part of the growth of the modern world.) Or, again, it has led them to raise the question of why the American Federation of Labor has given up the idea of class struggle to which the preamble of its statutes commits it. For it is apparently not conceivable to admit that, within a novel technological framework, the Federation can best defend the position of the American worker with methods that will try to derive the maximum advantages from an industrial system which itself is operating under novel conditions. It may take time to admit that, possibly without uttering a single time the slogan "Down with capitalism," that typical child of the New Deal, Walter Reuther, the head of the automobile workers, may ultimately succeed in bringing a more far-reaching influence to bear on the so-called American capitalistic structure and therefore on American society, than all the class-conscious and barricade-prone leaders of the European Left.

The mystery and complexity that surround the American political scene vanish when the analysis of the foreign observer shifts to economic life. Here everything is quite simple and the decisive factors of American power and success quite obvious. They are the immense single market, the wealth of raw materials, the huge underpopulated continental mass with rigidly controlled immigration since World War I. Amidst ruined human hopes, slum-infested cities, blighted forest land and natural resources, a hard-driving economic class, unchecked by any machinery of government, moves at pleasure.

The United States is the home of industrial adventurers whose names it is not necessary to repeat, for they have become part of the world's folklore. In 1927 a distinguished leader of European socialism summed up the situation simply by saying that the United States was the world's best example of capitalistic dictatorship. By 1929 the achievement of this monstrous production machinery was so impressive that its techniques and concepts had been accepted as part of the key realities of the twentieth century. Its essential parts were high wages in certain industries, mass production and the linking of the worker to the machine in new and impersonal ways, scientific management of human and technical resources, concentrated or monopolistic power, exploitation of unsuspecting consumers, unlimited drive for success, money, and ever higher output.

The picture contains a great deal of truth. As a description of the forces that stimulated the growth of the American economy, of the sentiments entertained by the dominant elements in the capitalistic society of those times, of their ambitions and their attitudes toward politics and the moral problems of society, it is uncomfortably close to reality. Of course, the so-called natural advantages of America were usually exaggerated or considered only in themselves, without taking into account the human qualities that were required to bring about such a measure of successful exploitation of the favorable natural factors available to the American producer. The qualities of self-reliance, faith in the future, belief in the mission of individuals, confidence in the effectiveness of a constitutional system based on freedom, the presence of a decentralized federal structure that did not exercise a paralyzing influence on the plans and dreams of the free enterprisers—these were factors that counted heavily in the achievement of the ultimate goals.

But if these were not always seen in all their significance, many of the unique aspects of the American economy were identified in the studies the outside world produced with awed fascination on the incredible phenomenon of American productivity, and on the freedom with which American capitalists crossed the country's widening horizons.

It was, therefore, all the more surprising to notice the failure of most of the European commentators to understand the nature of the Great Depression as well as the substance of the economic world that slowly emerged from it.

The crisis itself was interpreted in economic terms, as a failure, that is, of the system to operate successfully after some of its contradictions had brought about its inevitable collapse. Thus, 1929 was a crisis of overproduction (somewhat contradictorily for those who believed in the prevalence of rigidly monopolistic structures), or the result of the inefficiencies of an unduly intricate distribution system made up of appallingly large numbers of struggling individual middlemen.

The Great Depression was therefore not considered as at least in part the consequence of possible failures of the political system. This was due to some extent to a disbelief in the possibility of valid political action in a society dedicated to rugged individualism and "laissez faire." The state of incredulity in which the European intellectual found himself with regard to the chances of effective application in the United States of the hand of government and of the power of the community to the control of economic disorders accounted for much of the subsequent confusion. The nonpolitical approach to the Depression was also due to the conscious or unconscious prevalence in Europe of Marxian beliefs, to the conviction that only the total abolition of the underlying relationships of production could lead to democratic controls over the economic system. In a capitalistic system economics dominate politics. Hence, the utter futility of so-called public economic policy. The Great

Depression was seen, therefore, as fresh evidence of the contradictions of capitalism and what was later done about it did
not seem convincing proof of what a constitutional democracy
could do to cope with a crisis situation.

The picture of the New Deal that emerges from these premises is, not surprisingly, a curiously limited one. In agriculture,
what attracts attention is the Agricultural Adjustment Administration, with its policy of limiting crops and of paying the farmers guaranteed prices or subsidies for the negative achievement
of producing less. In industry, the National Recovery Administration constitutes the dominant reform, for it fits beautifully into
the preconceived pattern. The NRA is proof of incipient fascism
(this is particularly helpful, because fascism is the final phase
of the reaction of the bourgeoisie to the menace of working-class
revolution). It includes most of the features of a regulated, corporate structure that sanctions monopoly, even encourages it by
inviting producers to organize themselves into associations to
dominate the market, thus turning over to the capitalists the control of the economy. The power to fix prices becomes the power
to guarantee profits. The NRA is nothing but the seizure of the
state by producers threatened with collapse.

The observer writing nearly a generation later is moved to
remark that the damage done by the ubiquitous Blue Eagle and
the incomparable General Johnson is almost beyond the possibility of repair. Too many millions of words have been written,
and too many misunderstandings have been born. The impression made on the outside world by the NRA is not only out of
proportion to its effective impact on American society. It appears also to have exhausted the capacity to analyze and observe
what happened later. Since both the AAA and the NRA soon
went out of existence, in their original forms at least, they do
not deserve to be classified, in Europe's phraseology, as better
than temporary structural reforms. Triumphantly, the European
critic concludes that fundamentally no changes in economic

controls have taken place. Since the belief in private property was unimpaired, the concepts of ownership must have remained the same, for it was not to be imagined that the legal shell of property rights could be kept intact if their substance, scope, reach, and use by those who hold the title deeds had in any way been changed.

Because of this narrow vision of the New Deal, both friends and enemies of America have only an unsatisfactory view of contemporary life in the United States.

For some of the friends, today's prosperity is due chiefly to exceptional American productivity. Used in a technical sense, this is an exceedingly limited frame of reference. Productivity and prosperity are two different concepts, and even the highest measure of productivity does not in itself guarantee prosperity. The American economy has been a very productive one from the beginning, and yet it has not produced a uniformly high measure of prosperity. To take prosperity for granted, in a political vacuum and as the inevitable consequence of high productivity, leaves the Great Depression unexplained. The spirit of competition may be there to stimulate productivity, but it does not solve the riddle of the complicated realities of the American productive system. For the emphasis on the purely mechanistic and productivistic reality of the American economy could logically be followed by a belief in its vulnerability to depression and massive unemployment, or even by an expression of preference for the contemplative and relatively unproductive life of the Europeans. Why should one bother to be productive and prosperous? Perhaps the European system of mild starvation and genteel privation is better after all. But, of course, the answer is that in ascribing purely technical causes to American prosperity, one empties that prosperity of much of its substance. It is only by looking at the social and political developments that have created the conditions of today (with its good and bad aspects) that one can get a meaningful picture.

For many of the critics, the course of history is telescoped. With Truman, America was back in Harding's days; with Eisenhower, Coolidge is riding high. This establishes a satisfying sense of historical continuity and does away with the problem of trying to deal with the complexity of particular periods. In the end, nothing has happened in the past thirty years. Or, rather, something wholly external: World War II. To understand the present, we have to look, not to 1933, but to 1941. We have to look to the consequences of the war, the pent-up postwar demand for civilian goods, the artificial stimulus of Korea, the needs of a large military establishment. Thus, it is a combination of the good old days and of the bad new days that explains everything. American welfare today can be traced to the joint efforts of reborn rugged individualists and of annoying but providential Bolsheviks.

Even the rare few who realize that the present level of economic life is the result of much effort, of considerable public regulation, of a constant process of adaptation to change of the industrial machine, of a sustained acceptance by most of the business community of the relative superiority of the needs of the political community, have weakened their case by an excess of optimism. Claims of miraculous perfection and shatterproof happiness must be looked at with suspicion and doubt by those who are aware of the fresh difficulties that the Roosevelt Revolution has brought about. The United States has moved away from the pattern of the past and has shown a vitality and a sense of the requirements of democracy that are unmatched in the Western world, but the very fury of its development is accumulating serious problems for the future.

But these are thoughts too subtle for those who are convinced that the New Deal was a short appearance across the historical horizon, and that it has disappeared, leaving but few traces. They feel that, while New Deal measures have not actually been repealed, the capitalistic elite has recovered most of the lost ground in other ways. The corporate structure is more than ever a monopolistic one, and is not operated on the assumption that it is desirable to have an economy of abundance. A philosophy of scarcity, combined with techniques of mass production, inspires its actions. The deliberate restraints of the system go all the way from a failure to compete, to a withholding of inventions, to a slowing down of the rate of investment.

Under these conditions, full employment has not been achieved, and were America to approach it, there is no guarantee that it could be sustained for long if government spending were sharply reduced. The speculation of what would happen in human affairs if certain things were to occur has an irresistible fascination for the human mind and it would be churlish to deny to anyone whatever pleasure can be derived from it. It is true that if the American political system were to function in an unexpected manner, if the American people were to instruct their representatives to behave in ways radically opposed to those of the last quarter of a century, if government were to disappear, quite likely rather interesting and far-reaching consequences would come about. But one can question the seriousness of a social analysis that takes as its starting point a return to some mythical standard or norm of political action which is not there any more.

Occasionally, one even finds that some of the grimmer tragedies of the Great Depression have been kept alive as permanent adornments of the American scene. Thus, the four million destitute migratory workers and farmers of the Depression decade, America's own refugees, have been kept together and are still marching across the prairies. The fact that most of them have settled down and that the changing ranks of the still-existing migratory workers go about their work under different conditions, is not considered. One wonders whether those who write so feelingly about the hurrying American migrants really believe that the fate of some of the fast-frozen peasants of Europe is very much better.

But there is yet another vision haunting the critic of America. Even granted that the economic machine is moving forward smoothly and at full speed, that everybody is employed and spending furiously, and that millions of automobiles, tools, and gadgets of all kinds are the proud possessions of the American consumer, what follows is not a high standard of living, but an extreme state of insecurity. For the automobiles and the gadgets are the absolutely necessary tools of survival in incredibly difficult surroundings. Gadgets don't improve the standard of living of the American; they barely permit him to keep his head above water. The cities that suddenly rise in the middle of the American desert or amid the industrial jungle of the Atlantic seaboard would die in a few days if the machinery that keeps them alive were to collapse.

With this criticism we reach a new level of discourse and one that is naturally applied more frequently to American culture and civilization than to any other. But at this point the criticism is no longer directed to America as such but to the future of mankind itself, and should be offered in that spirit.

The Crisis of the State in the United States is the title of one of the most carefully documented books on American government to appear in Europe. Writing in 1951, the author is interested in the new relationships between federal and state governments, in congressional reform, executive reorganization, Supreme Court activities, and civil liberties. The volume is essentially an account of the way in which American government met the crisis of 1929 and surmounted it, and of the changes that took place over a twenty-year period. But what the title stresses is the "crisis of the state." Crisis exists where nothing is done to deal with urgent problems and not where a great deal is done successfully. But then the American constitutional system is usually seen as rigid and unyielding and incapable of meeting the requirements of emergency action, and, in any case, to suffer from the vagaries of Supreme Court interventions.

The complexities of the judicial system have proven to be a serious obstacle on the path of the interpreters. In modern times, the Supreme Court has been described as a usurper of political power; "government by judges" was the strange dead alley in which the American experiment in democratic government had ended.

When after 1937 it became clear that the Supreme Court had subjected to a careful re-examination the exercise of its constitutional powers, European critics lost their interest in the Court and shifted their attention elsewhere. With forty-eight states, and an immensely varied local, state, and federal structure, the chances of stumbling upon a decision appealing to the fervid imagination of the outsiders were very good. Why try to make sense of the many complicated, and at times incomprehensible and contradictory, decisions through which, its wheels grinding slowly and painfully, the Supreme Court has been trying in the last thirty years to fortify the guarantees of individual freedom and rights? The Hiss case, the trials of communist leaders, the passport cases, all naturally provided a much more attractive opportunity for commentary on the sad conditions of freedom in America. While earlier the judicial system had been busy destroying social legislation and defending naked property rights, it was now being used for political persecution. Serious critics found a substantial parallel between the Rajk trial in Hungary and the Hiss trial in the United States. The fact that while Rajk, who was most probably innocent, is now dead, while Hiss, who was most probably guilty of the specific charges made against him, is now free, lecturing and writing, is thought to be irrelevant and immaterial.

The truth is that all judicial systems everywhere fall short of perfection and that judicial mistakes will be made. In the case of the United States, where much of the meaning of the law, of political institutions, and of individual rights is given substance and specificity by judges, the only way to try to understand the role of the judiciary in the long-range historical growth of the country is to cast a sustained look at the highest court of the land. For its power is supreme and its influence in the long run is decisive in establishing the pattern of action of all other federal and state courts.

The psychological and moral importance of the Hiss case is immense, and the uncertainties and fears of the American people confronted by the rise in Soviet power are revealed by it with appalling clarity, but surely then the case has to be analyzed from the broadest possible point of view, in the light of problems the gravity of which is certainly without parallel in the history of the modern world. The role of those involved in it has to be judged with compassion, open-mindedness, and with the under- standing needed to see the crisis in its full course. The Hiss case cannot be separated, in these larger political terms which are the only ones of interest here, from the Lattimore case and other cases of recent years. Similarly, any conclusions on McCarthy- ism reached in 1953 and 1954 have to be revised following the reversals of official and public opinion of 1956 and 1957.

When the task is the interpretation of the long-range trends and purpose of great nations, all episodical and hurried inter- pretations ought to be shunned as carefully as possible, for institutions and peoples everywhere, considered in isolated moments of their history, usually show much that is tragic and comic, much that is a reflection of human folly and weakness.

There remains to be considered the pitiless psychoanalytical treatment of the American at the hands of the European. (Some might feel that there is an element of poetic justice in this, for nowhere more than in the United States have the practitioners of psychoanalysis multiplied or people resorted to their healing care.) As a result both of the introspective mood of many Americans and of the searching curiosity of insiders and outsiders, an overwhelming volume of evidence on the subconscious life, the inner tensions, drives, and longings of the American has become available. In scientific or pseudoscientific terms, his morality, his sex life, his anxieties and fears stand exposed to the gaze of the world. The picture that usually emerges is distressing and depressing.

Here is a brief glimpse of it. Money and a drive for power appear as chief preoccupations. The realization of these material gains is sought amid shocking trends to conformity and uniformity. The American is free in a constitutional sense, but he has been made wholly slave by the economic world he has accepted. He may believe he still has freedom of choice, while all choices are made for him by others: the manipulators and the lackeys of the capitalistic world of production.

The belief that America is approaching the state of classless society is wrong because there are depths of division unknown elsewhere. Life in the fearful expanses of slums in the American cities reaches a measure of terror and despair not to be found in any other country. Poverty in a society that is based on money values is more intolerable than in the countries where poverty is proof of acceptance of the ideals of Christian life.

The busy American who runs with a ragged look on his face in the thronged streets of the cities is not pursuing any significant purpose. Without knowing it, he is running away from himself and is expressing his fear of solitude. Solitude: the pervasive obsession of the American. To be left alone means to have to settle certain accounts with oneself and with the past that one cannot or does not like to settle. The community spirit is nothing but the confession of the terror of being left alone. The automobile is the sublimation of this fear. It is used as a means of escape and to bring about as quickly as possible the liberating encounter.

And what should be said of America's treatment of its minorities, of the condition to which the Negroes and the Puerto Ricans and many other groups are relegated? This is yet another instance of that lack of compassion and humanity that characterizes American civilization—the mass culture, the white Protestant culture, the machine-minded technological culture.

The criticism of the American economic system, the simplified understanding of the governmental structure and of political life, thus lead to a condemnation of America in terms of the human beings that compose it. Without realizing it, these critics are engaging in an autopsy of man himself. One should not forget that, if the dissecting of national traits is a pastime with a long and honorable historical past, its consequences are today much more immediate than in the past. The available tools are sharper, the concentrated attention paid to one country is unprecedented, the intensity of the social revolution of our times is such as to make these exchanges very much a part of the climate of opinion in which we live. The question that has to be asked is whether in the cruel descriptions of the American, supposing them to be true, we find reflected the unique or perverse features of American civilization, or rather the rough prefiguration of the developing characteristics of modern mass civilization.

The question is not an idle one, because most of the critics of America seem to be anxious to achieve for Europe, in many areas of public and private endeavor, the same kind of revolution that has already taken place in the United States, or at least they talk and write as if they intended to do so. Those who rush headlong in their attacks on all aspects of American life should stop for a moment and consider what it is that they are doing.

It is, indeed, not difficult to identify many of the purposes of public policy which the European intellectual considers necessary in the modern state: To recognize as desirable a further extension of human rights and dignity, the growth of a sense of community that will provide for some social reintegration at a time when individual tendencies have exceeded their legitimate boundaries, and the achievement of social justice and of security with mobility. To end the isolation that cuts off so many people from the streams of life, culture, economy, and the establishment of a greater variety of approaches to the solution of our persistent economic problems. To look to wider experimentation with so-called structural reforms, using nationalism here and supernationalism elsewhere, and both land reform and monopoly controls. To come to terms with the idea of strong government and of executive power capable of performing efficiently on different fronts and yet able to escape being called dictatorial. To use state power to achieve a reasonable redistribution of wealth and a diversity of plans for utilization of the total output, and a broadening of the educational system so that it will no longer belong to any privileged small ruling class. The increasing complexity of social relationships will gradually cause dramatic transformations in our inherited democratic and individualistic institutions. But the ultimate purpose is the realization of something called freedom, something very difficult to define and controversial and changing, yet something whose absence is quickly noted.

Let us fancifully assume that to some extent the restless scholars, writers, and pamphleteers of all the countries outside the communist world could speak this common language and perhaps even specifically agree among themselves from time to time. The purpose of this book would then be stated: In what measure and how well have the beliefs or policies just enumerated been accepted or realized in the United States from 1932 to 1952? And can we speculate on some of their consequences? The European can look at America today and like or dislike what he sees. What he cannot do is to reject America without knowing what has caused America to be what it is. This is particularly true of the European intellectual who is actively engaged in an effort to bring about a revolution on his home grounds in many of the fields which bore the main brunt of the efforts of the New Deal. There is here an element of moral responsibility which cannot be avoided.

Let us then be aware of what was done in the key areas of social life and justice, of the relationships between political power and economic interests, of the concepts of government, with which the Roosevelt Revolution was essentially concerned. One might then be free to say that there is no other example in history of a revolution of such significance that was more quickly brushed aside after its completion, or that this is a revolution that cannot be repeated elsewhere because its social consequences are intolerable. But, then, it is perhaps conceivable that one might come to recognize through it the complexity of many of the problems of our times, the revolution's persisting relevance and reality, and the need for humility and charity.

The Great Depression

The decade that ended with the Great Depression began with the end of the First World War and of the two Wilson administrations. These were the years of the ascendancy of the Republican party of Harding, Coolidge, and Hoover. These were the years in which the dream of economic plenty and of a permanent plateau of prosperity was thought to have come close to realization. These were the years of the great stock exchange boom. This was the decade that ended in October, 1929, with the thunderous crash that led to the Great Depression, and a few years later led to a new beginning—the Roosevelt Revolution.

As the attention of economists and social historians has been increasingly attracted to this fascinating period to learn the origins of the major crisis, the traditional picture of plenty, prosperity, forward movement, and steady expansion has been rather sharply modified. The twenties now appear as a period of some uncertainty, of great contrasts, of deepening wounds and injustice—not only as a time of happy adventure and uniformly growing well-being.

THE GENERAL ECONOMIC CLIMATE

The decade was ushered in by a sharp readjustment in the economy. World War I had just ended. By 1921 there were nearly five million unemployed. Most were quickly absorbed in

24

the following two years, but by 1924 there were again two million unemployed, and both in 1927 and in 1928 at least two million were still out of work. In 1929 the total had dropped to 400,000, but the pattern throughout had been one of repeated sharp swings.

The organization of workers into trade unions was lagging. The war had provided strong support for it and union membership had increased from three to five million between 1917 and 1920. But by 1929 the total was down to 3,600,000 in spite of a larger industrial population. Pressure from employers was heavy, for many of them regarded trade unions with misgivings or hostility. It was not untypical of the industrial leaders of the time to say, "The existence and conduct of labor unions in this country are inimical to the best interests of the employees, the employers, and the general public," or, "My experience is that the greatest aid in the efficiency of labor is a long line of men waiting at the gate." [1]

Available evidence shows too that the working classes were unable to improve their conditions to any substantial degree in the ten years preceding 1929. The average weekly wage of a worker in manufacturing industries went up from $22 in 1919 to $25 in 1929. The cost of living in the two years was about the same (1 per cent lower in 1929 than in 1919), so that real wages went up 15 per cent. But since the productivity of labor in that same decade went up 75 per cent, the worker had not been compensated for his greater contribution to the national output. The advantages accruing from increased efficiency and lower costs were not going to the wage earners.

No significant economic benefits could be secured by the farmers either, for between 1919 and 1929 net farm income declined by about one-third. Even if the sharp readjustment of farm prices after 1919 is written off as the unavoidable price

[1] Cf. A. T. Mason, *Security Through Freedom*, Ithaca, 1955, pp. 52–53.

of peace, the best that can be said is that the American farmers enjoyed a fairly stable level of income in the five years before 1929.

There were no strong indications of sustained and general prosperity in important fields like housing. While the total number of urban dwellings built had gone up from 400,000 for 1919 to 935,000 for 1925, the rate had dropped to half a million by 1929, when there was still no saturation of the market. There was an absence of purchasing power among those groups of the population which could have provided the necessary stimulus to construction.

On the other hand, the corporate world was booming. Net income of corporations filing income tax returns went up by about 50 per cent, or from six to nine billion dollars between 1920 and 1929. The dividends actually paid out to stockholders were about ten billion in 1929 as against seven billion in 1922, the earliest year for which reliable statistics are available. The total paid out in both years exceeded, by a substantial margin, net income after taxes. The financing of industrial investment needs was relatively simple in the optimistic atmosphere of those days and there was no impelling need to use current profits to that end. Also, there was no real problem of double taxation —first on corporate profits and then again on the share of those profits received as dividends by individual taxpayers— since the income tax rate was not heavy. As a result, no strong incentive existed to retain any large proportion of earnings for corporate purposes. Indeed, one of the principal current concerns of the federal government had been to ease the fiscal burdens on corporations. While in 1920, right after World War I, corporations showing a net income paid about 20 per cent of it in federal income tax, they were paying only 10 per cent in 1929. The effective tax load on the profitable segment of the corporate world was therefore cut in half during the "booming" twenties.

This was a rather specialized type of "boom." Government showed acute concern for the plight of the rich. Between 1921 and 1932 the effective tax rate for persons with taxable incomes of less than $5,000 did not vary. The rate was never high and much can be said, of course, in defense of small payments on the part of every citizen as proof of the solidarity of the body politic. But it is also true that even a token reduction of the tax load would have had at least symbolic value in adversity. On the other hand, the effective tax rate for a married taxpayer with two children and a net income of $25,000 went down about 12 per cent between 1921 and 1932, while the effective tax rate of a similar taxpayer with a net income of half a million dollars went down about 13 per cent.

The cumulative effect of these economic and financial policies was bound to make itself strongly felt over a period of time. John K. Galbraith's conclusion is that in 1929 the economy was fundamentally unsound—first because of bad distribution of income. Some discrepancies exist in the evidence available, but the broad outlines of the problem are beyond doubt:

In 1929 the rich were indubitably rich. The figures are not entirely satisfactory, but it seems certain that the 5 per cent of the population with the highest incomes in that year received approximately one third of all personal income. . . . This highly unequal income distribution meant that the economy was dependent on a high level of investment or a high level of luxury consumer spending or both. The rich cannot buy great quantities of bread. If they are to dispose of what they receive it must be on luxuries or by way of investment in new plants and new projects. Both investment and luxury spending are subject, inevitably, to more erratic influences and to wider fluctuations than the bread and rent outlays of the $25-a-week workman.[2]

Further details in the same vein are given in studies of the Brookings Institution. As reported by Frederick Lewis Allen,

[2] *The Great Crash,* Boston, 1955, pp. 182–83.

[In 1929] only 2.3 per cent of American families had incomes of over $10,000 a year. Only 8 per cent had incomes of over $5,000. No less than 71 per cent had incomes of less than $2,500. Some 60 per cent had incomes of less than $2,000. More than 42 per cent had incomes of less than $1,500. And more than 21 per cent had incomes of less than $1,000 a year. "At 1929 prices," said the Brookings economists, "a family income of $2,000 may be regarded as sufficient to supply only basic necessities." One might reasonably interpret this statement to mean that any income below that level represented poverty. *Practically 60 per cent of American families were below it—in the golden year of 1929!* The Brookings economists added another cautious observation: "There has been a tendency at least during the last decade or so, for the inequality in the distribution of income to be accentuated." [3]

Data on income payments collected by Simon Kuznets verify the tendency noted by the Brookings Institution.[4] The upper 5 per cent of the income groups increased its share of the total income payments from 22.9 per cent in 1919 to 26.1 per cent in 1929, while the lower 95 per cent saw their share correspondingly reduced from 77.1 per cent to 73.9 per cent. In ways that were not generally suspected, and which even today are likely to surprise many of those who summon up visions of the roaring twenties, some of the economic trends of that decade had been adding strength to the imbalances that make for economic crisis and social tension. The rosy optimism of the time concealed a static and even deteriorating state of affairs in the distribution of wealth, a condition which, in a democracy, is bound to create trouble.

Even so, trouble might have been postponed had wealth been flowing into a sound and properly managed corporate and business world.

---

[3] *The Big Change,* New York, 1952, p. 144.
[4] Cf. *National Income and Its Composition, 1919–1938,* Princeton, 1941.

THE BAD CORPORATE AND BANKING STRUCTURE

The 1920's will remain characterized in American history as a period of financial manipulations for which not even the "robber barons" of earlier times can quite provide a match. We cannot forget that many of the barons were substantial builders who left behind monuments we can still admire today, in spite of the unpleasantness that often went with their building. What the financiers of the twenties have bequeathed to posterity is at best a sense of awe at their skill in refining the use of the most subtle devices provided by our legal system.

The twenties were typified by the holding company, an institution that flowered then as never before or since. The nerve center of the American economic system, located in Wall Street, appeared to devote most of its energies to the concoction of ingenious and rarefied financial schemes, rather than to the channeling and organizing of serious productive efforts. One can today attribute a great part of the multiplier effect of the depression of 1929 to the maladjustments and weaknesses of the financial structure rather than to the malfunctioning of the machinery of production.[5] There was in 1929, to be sure, a typical overproduction and inventory crisis, but it would most likely never have developed into the Great Depression without the paralyzing influence of the collapsing financial structures that dominated so many key segments of the nation's life.

The holding company has been strongly defended as a valuable instrument in the expansion of modern industry. Its most significant use was in the field of public utilities, and it has been suggested in this connection that the holding company promoted a degree of large-scale operations and of centralized planning— a pooling of facilities, financial resources, managerial talents,

[5] Cf. Galbraith, *op. cit., passim.*

and new inventions—that no small independent operating utility would ever have been able to achieve.

It is true that by comparison with Great Britain, for instance, where the holding company was not widely used in the power field, American public utilities seemed to have reached a higher level of technical efficiency. It is even more true that the holding company method went far beyond its reasonable limits to a point where its purpose was no longer that of improving the operating level of electric or gas production, but that of making possible certain types of financial operation, wholly unrelated to any visible productive end, but such as to yield enormous benefits to the few individuals on whose behalf they were undertaken.

The experience of the Depression makes it difficult to dismiss with a casual shrug the holding company's role in the corporate world. The holding company had become an important symbol of American capitalism in the years before 1929. If its incredible intricacies added a pleasant touch of fantasy and unreality to economic life, too many important men—managers, capitalists, and lawyers—were found involved in the manipulative rather than in the productive aspects of the economy. As the twenties proceeded on their merry way, the complications of the holding company world became ever more grotesque and their reach even greater. The names of Insull, Van Sweringen, and Hobson moved into the forefront of the public stage, followed by eager hosts of bankers, anxious to seize upon the speculative possibilities of the times by using their depositors' money. Seven-layer holding companies were erected, the profit possibilities of each added layer increasing as the financial commitments and the sense of responsibility of those in command at each station decreased.

With the freedom and the immensity of the American market, stretching from ocean to ocean, the elbow-room of financial captains was unlimited. In the absence of any serious restraint imposed by public policy, the common market, created to realize the ideals of a competitive and free economy, offered instead irresistible profit opportunities to too many reckless people.

By the beginning of the Great Depression, fifteen giant holding systems controlled 80 per cent of all electric-energy generation in the United States, while twenty systems controlled 98.5 per cent of the transmission of electric energy across state lines, and eleven controlled 80 per cent of all natural-gas pipeline mileage.

When hard times started, or even when mild complications arose, any trouble at the higher levels of the holding structure would soon reflect itself in magnified form at the lower levels. To avoid disaster, pressures would be brought to bear on the lower units, which would often be required to follow policies unjustified from an operational point of view, but needed in the rescue of the controlling holding company. The protector became the exploiter, draining away the substance of its wards.

Later, when the holding companies were investigated, many serious abuses were revealed, the more significant of which were painstakingly enumerated in the Public Utility Holding Companies Act of 1935:

. . . (1) inadequate disclosure to investors of the information necessary to appraise the financial position and earning power of the companies whose securities they purchase; (2) the issuance of securities against fictitious and unsound values; (3) the overloading of operating companies with debt and fixed charges thus tending to prevent voluntary rate reductions; (4) the imposition of excessive charges upon operating companies for various services such as management supervision of construction and the purchase of supplies and equipment; (5) the control by holding companies of the accounting practices and rate, dividend and other policies of their operating subsidiaries so as to complicate or obstruct state regulation; (6) the control of subsidiary holding companies and operating companies through disproportionately small investment;

(7) the extension of holding company systems without relation to economy of operations or to the integration and coordination of related properties.

As the Securities and Exchange Commission pointed out in its 1949 Report:

> During the period from 1924 to 1930, inclusive, public utility holding companies sold approximately $4,856,000,000 of their securities to the public. The funds received from this financing were devoted almost entirely to the purchase of already outstanding corporate securities. Only a negligible portion went into the construction of plant and equipment of operating utility subsidiaries. For a period of many years up to 1928, it was the general practice of holding companies to furnish capital to their subsidiaries through the mechanism of demand notes or open-account advances. Interest was often charged on these short-term loans at rates ranging from 6 to 8 per cent and in some large systems the holding companies followed the regular practice of compounding interest monthly.

These data appear to verify the suspicion that in the years preceding the great crash of 1929 too many of the leaders of the American economic system did their best to confirm the worst assumptions that the Marxian critics had been making about financial capitalism. They were busily digging their own graves, as they were cheerfully identifying their inventiveness on the Wall Street frontier with the progress of the free enterprise system itself.

What should be remembered is not only the existence of these abuses at sensitive points in the public utility, transportation, and banking structure of the United States, but also the fact that these abuses were known to the Congress and to the federal regulatory commissions. In fact, some of these practices had been under investigation by the Federal Trade Commission since 1926. Prolonged studies and extensive inquiries, however, had failed to lead to any formulation of public policy capable of meeting the dangers inherent in the system.

By 1929 the danger had become a multiple one. The economic system was unbalanced. Its leaders were unaware of this fact and were engaging in practices which could only increase the risks of the situation. In addition, the steadying, guiding, or correcting hand of government was missing.

THE ROLE OF GOVERNMENT

As private economic interests gave every evidence of indefatigable, if dubious and unregulated, activity, the influence of public policy seemed to be vanishing. Since many of the more significant economic forces at work transcended state boundaries, public policy can be identified with federal government policy.

The Republican administrations of Presidents Harding, Coolidge, and Hoover will probably be seen by history as a rather long interlude between Wilson and Roosevelt, the New Freedom and the New Deal. Even though the passion, and even hatred, Hoover is capable of arousing is greater than that aroused by either Harding or Coolidge, there is not much that can be said to distinguish among the policies each of them followed. Throughout those twelve years, their common thread is the repudiation of much that had made the American presidency great by the time Wilson left the White House. The American Constitution itself is unique in the opportunities it offers to the Chief Executive. In addition, by 1920, the successful extension of the scope of the office had created for the President a platform of prestige, power, and influence that placed the White House at the center of American political life. Of all Western constitutional systems only the American possessed an executive power capable of handling the problems of a democracy in crisis.

But the history of the twenties is the history of a decade of fading executive leadership and of lost opportunities. As times grew more difficult, the timidity, hesitation, and paralysis of the

White House increased. The appeals to the American tradition were limited to appeals to the values of individual freedom, to the spirit of the pioneers, to the healthy role of the frontier and of Indian fighting. Had not America in its history overcome fifteen major depressions? asked Hoover. The Great Depression of the thirties could be overcome without undue interference of government power with free enterprise.

The vision and leadership of Jackson, Lincoln, Theodore Roosevelt, and Wilson, and the tools they had forged, were left idle.

In his *Economic Interpretation of the Constitution of the United States,* written before World War I, Charles Beard, that most influential of modern American historians, had analyzed the motives and economic interests of the Founding Fathers in a way that had shown the influence of Marxian philosophy in the fabric of American historical writing. But, strange though it may appear, Beard was happy with the Republican regimes of 1920–1932. The fact that the Republican administrations failed to repeal some of the major legislative items of the Wilson administration, such as the income tax law of 1913 and the Clayton Act of 1914—hence, their seeming reluctance or unwillingness to go back to the most naked primitivism of the nineteenth century—was considered by Beard as adequate proof of their social responsibility and modernity.

The Norris-LaGuardia Anti-Injunction Act of 1932 was to him further evidence of the continuity in the irreversible trend toward the expansion of the responsibility and power of the federal government. Beard was not impressed by the fact that it became law only in 1932, at the depth of the Depression, after the Democratic congressional victory of 1930 and on the eve of the electoral victory of Roosevelt.

The Republican presidents cannot be judged by their failure to destroy the legislation of the Wilsonian era or by their restraint in not always vetoing useful legislation. They are rather to be judged by their failure to use the weapons of government that had accumulated over a hundred years, and by their stubborn refusal to recognize that the safety of the Republic depended upon the full exploitation of those weapons.

Those who maintain that after their congressional victory in 1930 the Democratic Congress and party did no better than their Republican counterparts, misconstrue the essence of the problem, which is that the Constitution and American constitutional tradition have not placed in the party or in the Congress the primary responsibility for the political guidance and initiative that are essential in times of crisis.

President Hoover's inability to deal in a large way with the problems that the Depression was so steadily multiplying can be seen in a most instructive form in his veto message of March 3, 1931. After about ten years of almost continuous struggle, and after an earlier veto at the hands of Coolidge, Senator Norris had succeeded in pushing through Congress a bill providing for the establishment of a public corporation to take over the management of certain government property in Tennessee, including a chemical factory, a dam, and a power plant. The bill incorporated the views of a majority of Congress on the best public use of important facilities built during World War I and on the contribution that those facilities, modernized and expanded, could make to the welfare of one of the most impoverished sections of the United States.

The year was 1931, when the Depression had entered its most severe phase. President Hoover vetoed the bill. Unlike President Coolidge, who, following his tradition of silence, had preferred to kill the earlier bill through a "pocket veto" which did not require him to utter a single word but merely called upon him to abstain from acting, Hoover frankly went on record with a declaration of principles that provides a useful index in measuring the views on the role of government held in those years at the White House.

The bill required the President to appoint as directors of the corporation persons who professed a belief in the "feasibility and wisdom" of the purposes of the law. Since the Congress had voted to support a specific program, the directors were to commit themselves to an expression of faith in the wisdom of the policies that were to become part of the constitutional will of the American people. But, according to Hoover, this would have meant the appointing of administrators on the basis of their beliefs rather than of their experience and competence. Because economic assets must be run by businessmen and businessmen cannot believe in the validity of public operation of economic assets, therefore, it was his judgment that "three men able to conduct a hundred and fifty million dollar business can not be found to meet these specifications." To obtain from anyone an acceptance of the wisdom of the Norris bill, meant, by definition, that only the incompetent could be hired to do the job. In the light of all preceding and subsequent experience this surely must be noted as a most extraordinary belief.

But there were other and more general reasons for Hoover's refusal to sign:

I am firmly opposed to the Government entering into any business the major purpose of which is competition with our citizens. There are national emergencies which require that the Government should temporarily enter the field of business, but they must be emergency actions and in matters where the cost of the project is secondary to much higher considerations. There are many localities where the Federal Government is justified in the construction of great dams and reservoirs, where navigation, flood control, reclamation, or stream regulation are of dominant importance, and where they are beyond the capacity or purpose of private or local government capital to construct. In these cases power is often a by-product and should be disposed of by contract or lease. But for the Federal Government deliberately to go out to build up and expand such an occasion to the major purpose of a power and manufacturing business is to break down the initiative and enterprise of the American people; it is destructive of equality of opportunity amongst our people: it is negation of the ideals upon which our civilization has been based.

The specter of the breakdown in the spirit of initiative and enterprise of the American people was being raised at a time when the total of unemployed had already reached seven million and was steadily climbing in an atmosphere of deepening crisis. In the cities, the equality of opportunity still available to many was that of the equal freedom to starve. Even so, the idea that government, presented with concrete proposals of increasing community effort to replace failing private efforts, could undertake new activities within the scope of its constitutional powers, was intolerable. Hoover became eloquent:

> This bill would launch the Federal Government upon a policy of ownership and operation of power utilities upon a basis of competition instead of by the proper Government function of regulation for the protection of all the people. I hesitate to contemplate the future of our country if the preoccupation of its officials is to be no longer the promotion of justice and equal opportunity but is to be devoted to barter in the markets. That is not liberalism, it is degeneration.

Nor was Hoover impressed by the administrative precedents found in the practice of the public corporation in many lands. To him federal action meant inevitably the extension of the heavy hand of centralized bureaucracy on the lives and rights of local communities:

> The establishment of a Federal-operated power business and fertilizer factory in the Tennessee Valley means Federal control from Washington with all the vicissitudes of national politics and the tyrannies of remote bureaucracy imposed upon the people of that valley. . . .[6]

Hoover must have been pleased when he sent his veto message to Congress. He had taken a high stand on principles

[6] Cf. *Congressional Record*, 1931, vol. 74, pp. 7047–48, for the full text of the veto message quoted in these pages.

and had evoked all the terrors of tyranny and of the deadening hand of centralism. He must have felt he had saved the very idea of freedom and of individual rights. He was still to defend his views three years later, in 1934, when everything he cherished seemed to be swept away by the impact of the New Deal. The issue then could be narrowed, according to Hoover, to that of the survival of human liberty. The American people were being led either to the swamps of primitive greed or to political tyranny. If he meant that a revolution was under way, he was, of course, right.

THE SUPREME COURT

The timidity of presidential leadership in those years is all too obvious. We must now see how much the Supreme Court of the United States contributed to a climate of opinion which seemed to justify such government inaction.

The Supreme Court is a hallowed institution in American life, and its historical role has been recognized ever since the days of Tocqueville, who saw in the judicial system, with its powers of review of the constitutionality of laws, one of the strongest barriers against the tyranny of political assemblies and of popular majorities.

One should not tend to exaggerate the influence of the Supreme Court on economic, social, and political developments. Life flows on in many rivulets and streams, and in a society as mobile and expansive as the American society has usually been, changes have taken place in spite of, or without regard to, the Supreme Court. But in the period between the post-Civil War years and the New Deal, the Supreme Court did exercise a moral influence, did give its imprint and sanction to a philosophy of the state, and did define the limits of public policy in such a way that one cannot refrain from concluding that an uncomfortable part of the responsibility for the plight of the American people in the early thirties, and for the sense of frustration and rebellion caused by the impotence of government, must be laid at the door of the Supreme Court.

In a federal system which exists in reality and not on paper, and within a political tradition which relies so much on legal concepts, the principle of judicial review of legislative acts is basic. The assumption of this power by the Supreme Court is not a usurpation. Historically, in the first half-century of its existence, the role of the Supreme Court was to give substance to the powers of the newly created federal system, much as the early role of the French Parlements was that of supporting royal authority against the feudal lords.

Problems of great complexity were, unintentionally, to be created by the passage of the Fourteenth Amendment in 1868. Adopted after the Civil War, with the purpose of guaranteeing civil rights to the freed Negroes, its famous due process clause read: ". . . nor shall any State deprive any person of life, liberty, or property, without due process of law. . . ."

The language was taken from the Fifth Amendment, and the best evidence shows that its aim was to give the citizens of the United States, affected by state action, the same procedural safeguards they already enjoyed under the Fifth Amendment in the case of federal action.

Gradually—beginning with the 1880's—the *procedural* content of due process was abandoned in favor of an interpretation that saw in due process a bulwark for the protection of *substantive* property rights, and one offering the Supreme Court a chance to control social and economic legislation passed by the states. As Robert E. Cushman has stated:

> Regulations of labor and other social conditions based upon the assumption that the state ought to intervene at the expense of the individual for the benefit of a particular group or class in society were looked upon with horror by the Courts.[7]

[7] *Leading Constitutional Decisions,* New York, 1950 ed., p. 197.

During almost half a century this became the prevalent conception of the meaning and purposes of the due process clause of the Fourteenth Amendment.

On the one hand, the Supreme Court repeatedly struck down the social legislation of the states on the ground that it curtailed the citizen's property rights and freedom of contract, now deemed to be of the essence of the due process clause. That is, the states were often deprived of useful tools of economic policy in the name of an amendment that had been chiefly designed to guarantee the maintenance of procedural proprieties. At the same time, however, the states were also rebuked for undertaking to legislate in fields said to belong to the federal government. The states were hemmed in by a double set of restrictions, as set up by the Supreme Court: the restrictions imposed by the powers delegated to the federal government, and the restrictions now read into the Fourteenth Amendment.

The federal government's efforts to exercise fully its powers in the economic field—under the interstate commerce clause, for instance—were similarly thwarted. Federal legislation was voided as unconstitutional on the basis of a narrow interpretation of federal powers and of a broad assumption of surviving state powers.

Simultaneously then, and contradictorily, the Constitution was interpreted in a latitudinarian sense when substantive economic rights were placed under the protective wing of the Fourteenth Amendment in order to defend them against state regulation, and in a restrictive sense when the content of the delegated powers of the federal government was whittled down and kept within limits no longer adequate to meet the problems of the times.

A no man's land was created in the field of social and economic legislation. The states could not legislate because they could not be permitted to tamper with private property rights or with the powers of the federal government. The federal government could not legislate either, for this meant a usurpation of powers that belonged to the states under the Tenth Amendment.

This extraordinary and paradoxical state of affairs, which ended in the spectacular constitutional crisis of 1937, forms a unique chapter in the history of the Supreme Court. It has left bitter memories; it has provided a foundation for the cynical comment that the meaning of the Constitution is what the judges say it is; and it has contributed much to the demoralization of the twenties and thirties. What was more futile than the struggles of legislators and statesmen to deal with the difficult and changing problems of political life if the Supreme Court would later destroy even the most carefully contrived solutions in the name of a rigid (and, many were prepared to say, fanciful) constitutional doctrine and of an unrealistic view of the modern state? Specific references to some of the more famous cases, and to the judicial reasoning they reveal, clarify the issue.

The Lochner case of 1905 is a classical example of the Supreme Court's successful interference with state economic action through the use of the Fourteenth Amendment.[8] A New York State statute had limited to ten hours the length of the working day of bakers. The Court found the statute to be an unconstitutional interference with the right of bakery employees to work as many hours as they wished. There could be no contention, the Court said, that:

> . . . bakers as a class are not equal in intelligence and capacity to men in other trades . . . or that they are not able to assert their rights and care for themselves without the protecting arm of the state. . . . Clean and wholesome bread does not depend upon whether the baker works but ten hours per day. . . . The act is . . . an illegal interference with the rights of individuals, both employers and employees, to make contract regarding labor upon such terms as they may think best.

[8] *Lochner* v. *New York,* 198 U.S. 45 (1905).

In a dissenting opinion that contributed much to the historical significance of the case, Justice Holmes said:

> The Fourteenth Amendment does not enact Mr. Herbert Spencer's *Social Statics*. . . . A constitution is not intended to embody a particular economic theory, whether of paternalism and the organic relation of the citizen to the state or of laissez-faire. It is made for people of fundamentally differing views, and the accident of our finding certain opinions natural and familiar or novel and even shocking ought not to conclude our judgment upon the question whether statutes embodying them conflict with the Constitution of the United States.

The majority of the Supreme Court continued to cling to other views, and for thirty years Holmes was the great dissenter. Dealing with another burning social question, that of the organization of the workers into trade unions and of the extent of the legitimacy of strikers' pressures against the employers, the Supreme Court voided a Kansas statute outlawing "yellow-dog" contracts, whereby as a condition of obtaining employment a worker had to agree not to join or remain a member of a union, and an Arizona statute which permitted concerted picketing by striking workers. The constitutional grounds were, as always, impairment of freedom of contract and deprivation of property without due process of law.[9]

In 1949, a distinguished member of the academic profession who in the meantime had risen to the bench of the Supreme Court, Justice Felix Frankfurter, reviewing that remote past with the detachment of the historian, said:

> . . . unionization encountered the shibboleths of a pre-machine age and these were reflected in juridical assumptions that survived the facts on which they were based. Adam Smith was treated as though his generalizations had been imparted to him on Sinai and not as a thinker who addressed himself to the elimination of restrictions which had become fetters upon initiative and enterprise

[9] *Coppage* v. *Kansas,* 236 U.S. 1 (1915); *Truax* v. *Corrigan,* 257 U.S. 312 (1921).

in his day. Basic human rights expressed by the constitutional conception of "liberty" were equated with theories of *laissez-faire*. The result was that economic views of confined validity were treated by lawyers and judges as though the Framers had enshrined them in the Constitution. . . .[10]

These views survived the Great Depression. As late as 1936, in the Morehead case, the Supreme Court held invalid a statute passed in 1933 by the state of New York providing for a minimum-wage law for women and children.[11] Speaking for the Court, Justice Butler maintained that any minimum-wage law, regardless of its provisions, would be invalid as a denial of due process of law. Justice Stone, who to some extent had succeeded Holmes as a dissenter, noted that it was difficult "to imagine any ground other than our own personal economic predilections, for saying that the contract of employment is any the less an appropriate subject for legislation than are scores of others."

From the regulation of maximum hours, to that of minimum wages, to the outlawing of unfair labor practices on the part of business, the Supreme Court took a stand which, even though not always consistent or continuous, dealt a hard blow to the effectiveness of one of the most useful aspects of American federalism: the experimental value of forty-eight different approaches to legislation supplied by forty-eight states. Even if mistakes and rash experiments were made by the states, their consequences were kept within the limits of the state boundaries, while the other states could learn much from the process of trial and error. In imposing a rigid uniformity of views, the Court dried up some of the wellsprings of political action.

The other side of the history of this period is found in the decisions of the Supreme Court that limited federal legislation through a narrow interpretation of the powers delegated to the

---

[10] *American Federation of Labor* v. *American Sash Co.*, 335 U.S. 538 (1949).

[11] *Morehead* v. *New York ex rel. Tipaldo*, 298 U.S. 587 (1936).

federal government. Again legislation dealing with trade unions, child labor, and minimum wages became the target of the Court's opinions.

In 1908, the Court voided a federal statute penalizing a railroad for discharging a worker because he belonged to a labor union.[12] The interstate activities of the railroad were not deemed sufficient reason for federal intervention, in itself condemned as a violation of the liberty of contract guaranteed by the due process clause of the Fifth Amendment. Both the alleged deficiency of federal powers and the barriers set up by the substantive content given to due process helped the Court slow down federal policies in the labor field.

Even more famous were the two child-labor decisions.[13] In 1916, the Wilson Congress had passed the Child Labor Act, which sought to use the interstate commerce clause of the Constitution to bar interstate commerce of goods produced in mines or factories employing children in violation of the Act. The Congress was trying to solve the problem of child labor, not by direct intervention, that is, by prohibiting it—for no constitutional authority could be found for such interference in intrastate production processes—but indirectly, by making it impossible for goods produced by child labor to move across state boundaries. This was an effective approach, for it would have deprived the producers of those goods of most of their markets. It was this very concept, representing the core of congressional intent, that the Supreme Court struck down by saying that what could not be done directly could not be done indirectly. As a further obstacle, the Court added the Tenth Amendment, which reserves to the states powers not delegated to the federal government. The fact that the states were not doing anything to stop child labor did not worry the Supreme Court.

---

[12] *Adair* v. *United States,* 208 U.S. 161 (1908).
[13] *Hammer* v. *Dagenhart,* 247 U.S. 251 (1918); *Bailey* v. *Drexel Furniture Co.,* 259 U.S. 20 (1922).

As Justice Holmes said in 1918 in his Dagenhart dissent:

. . . if there is any matter upon which civilized countries have agreed,—far more unanimously than they have with regard to intoxicants and some other matters over which this country is now emotionally aroused,—it is the evil of premature and excessive child labor. I should have thought that if we were to introduce our own moral conceptions where, in my opinion they do not belong, this was preeminently a case for upholding the exercise of all its powers by the United States. But I had thought that the propriety of the exercises of a power admitted to exist in some cases was for the consideration of Congress alone, and that this Court always had disavowed the right to intrude its judgment upon questions of policy or morals. It is not for this Court to pronounce when prohibition is necessary to regulation if it ever may be necessary— to say that it is permissible as against strong drink, but not as against the product of ruined lives. The act does not meddle with anything belonging to the states. They may regulate their internal affairs and their domestic commerce as they like. But when they seek to send their products across the state line they are no longer within their rights.

In spite of this persuasive criticism on both moral and constitutional grounds, the Court again reacted negatively when confronted by another legislative effort to deal with child labor, this time through the power of taxation. The Revenue Act of 1919 had imposed a 10 per cent excise tax on the annual net profits of industrial and mining establishments employing child labor. In the Drexel case, the Court decided that, since the tax was not levied for revenue purposes but had been imposed to regulate the production of goods, the use of federal taxation powers in this instance was unconstitutional. This was all the more surprising since the Court had in earlier decisions approved the use of taxing power for nonrevenue purposes when it could be established that what was being sought was the attainment of some significant social purpose. But it took until 1941 to modify the Supreme Court's position.

In 1918, Congress had passed an act fixing minimum wages

for women workers in the District of Columbia. In 1923, the Court held the law invalid as a denial of due process of law under the Fifth Amendment.[14] Now the purpose of the Fifth Amendment is to see to it that Congress shall not deprive any person of his freedom or property without due process of law. There were no objections in the Adkins case to the procedures by which federal regulations were being enforced. The objection was to the substantive requirements of the Act. The Court denied that there was any connection between the wages women receive and their health, morals, or welfare. The liberties guaranteed by the Fifth Amendment became the contractual liberty to do as one pleases even in the most delicate fields of social welfare.

Going back again to the historical meditations of Justice Frankfurter, we read in a letter addressed to Chief Justice Stone on May 27, 1940:

> After all, despite some of the jurisprudential "realists" a decision decides not merely the particular case. Just as *Adkins v. Children's Hospital* had consequences not merely as to the minimum wage laws but in its radiations and in its psychological effects, so this case would have a tail of implications as to legislative power that is certainly debatable and might easily be invoked far beyond the size of the immediate kite. . . .[15]

These psychological effects, Frankfurter recognized, were indeed among the most important, even though not immediately visible, consequences of Supreme Court decisions rendered on critical social and economic issues. As American industrial

---

[14] *Adkins* v. *Children's Hospital*, 261 U.S. 525 (1923).

[15] See the letter in A. T. Mason, *Security Through Freedom*, Appendix, pp. 217–20. The allusion to the "tail of implications" of "this case" is to the questions raised by *Minersville School District* v. *Gobitis*, 310 U.S. 586 (1940). In this case, in an opinion written by Frankfurter himself, the Court had validated a Pennsylvania statute requiring school children to salute the flag in spite of religious scruples. Stone's dissent had provoked the letter. The Court overruled the Gobitis case in *West Virginia State Board of Education* v. *Barnette*, 319 U.S. 624 (1943).

civilization began to show serious weaknesses, the Supreme Court could not hope to escape its share of responsibility.

After 1923, when four of the nine justices (Sutherland, Butler, Sanford, and Taft as Chief Justice) were Harding appointees, the Supreme Court's interpretations of the Constitution stiffened. Edward S. Corwin writing at a turning point in the history of the Supreme Court, said:

> Within recent years . . . an increasing rigor is to be discerned in the Court's standards, especially where legislation on *social and economic* questions is concerned. Prior to 1912 the Court had decided 98 cases involving this kind of legislation. "In only six of these did the Court hold the legislation unconstitutional. From 1913 to 1920 the Court decided 27 cases of this type and held seven laws invalid"; while between 1920 and 1930, out of 53 cases the Court held against the legislation involved in fifteen.[16]

This is the period in the history of the Supreme Court that Corwin elsewhere calls one of judicial review, pure and simple:

> The Court, as heir to the accumulated doctrines of its predecessors, found itself for the time being in possession of such a variety of instruments of constitutional exegesis that it was often able to achieve almost any result in the field of constitutional interpretation which it considered desirable. . . . Senator Borah, in the Senate debate on Mr. Hughes' nomination for Chief Justice, in 1930, declared that the Supreme Court had become "economic dictator in the United States." Some of the Justices concurred in these observations, especially Justices Holmes and Brandeis. Asserted the latter, the Court has made itself "a super-legislature" and Justice Holmes could discover "hardly any limit but the sky" to the power claimed by the Court to disallow State acts "which may happen to strike a majority [of its members] as for any reason undesirable." [17]

[16] *The Constitution and What It Means Today,* Princeton, 1937 ed., p. 376. Corwin is quoting from an article by Felix Frankfurter, "The Supreme Court and the People," *Forum,* June 1930.

[17] Corwin, ed., *The Constitution of the United States of America,* Washington, 1953, p. xxvii.

Taken all together, the deficiency of congressional action, the absence of presidential leadership, the stubborn defense by the highest court in the land of untenable constitutional theories, and the headlong rush of financial manipulators toward what turned out to be only a lawyers' paradise—all these had shattering consequences. The result was an atmosphere of irresponsible trust in the forces of nature, which would automatically take care of the future, if that future happened to turn sour.

THE GREAT DEPRESSION

There is much discussion concerning the exact moment when the Great Depression ended. The pessimists, or those who accept the theory of capitalistic stagnation, are convinced that the depression is still here and that it is only military spending that maintains the appearances of prosperity. Others will say that it was not the New Deal but the outbreak of World War II which ended the Great Depression, proving the futility of eight years of Roosevelt acrobatics and confirming the theory that only the intervention of an external and extraordinary factor such as war could end the crisis.

But some will say that the number of the unemployed had been cut in half by 1937 and that the gross national product (measured at 1953 prices) had in both 1936 and 1937 reached about the same volume as 1929, claiming these figures as proof of substantial recovery and of the notable success of New Deal policies. While 1938 brought about a sharp relapse, recovery was once more under way early in 1939, when the Federal Reserve Board index of industrial production for the first three months of that year was only 7 per cent below that of the corresponding period of 1929. There was no war then. But nearly nine million workers were still unemployed.

What these conflicting views on the end of the Great Depression show is the sharpness of the disputes created by the crisis and the immensity of the issues left in its wake. There is, however, no controversy as to when the Depression began. Its beginnings are linked in the memories of man to the unprecedented chaos and panic of the New York Stock Exchange during the month of October, 1929.[18] A few weeks of uncontrollable fear shattered the illusions, hopes, and beliefs of generations of Americans, fixed with awesome precision a turning point in American history as great as any in the past, and set in motion as if by chain reaction the forces that determined the character and depth of the events that were to follow.

October, 1929, belongs to the mythology of American life. It possesses all the elements of drama, of personal crisis, of concentrated symbolic value needed for the creation of the folklore and legends which decorate the life of nations.

The Wall Street crash was important in itself, for it destroyed the fortunes of millions of people. It was important for what it revealed of the behavior, activities, intentions, and larcenies of a class of financiers, bankers, bond salesmen, their allies and front men who had in the previous decade assumed a commanding position in American life. It was also an admirably effective device for showing up the weaknesses of the American corporate structure, as Galbraith has shown. The super-holding companies, suffering from maximum vulnerability to the changing winds of fortune, dragged down into ruin the mere holding companies. The holding companies in turn forced the consequences of their disaster on the operating companies. The operating companies, which in their limited productive landscape might still have found justification for near-normal activities, were in turn led to take drastic restrictive steps in the light of the precarious conditions of their financial masters.

The Depression deepened rapidly with the inexorability of fate. Between 1929 and 1932, the gross national product declined from 104 to 58 billion dollars, wage payments from

[18] Cf. Galbraith, *The Great Crash*.

45 to 25 billion, and corporate profits of 10 billion became losses of 3 billion. Factory employment declined by one-third, and the number of unemployed shot up from 400,000 to nearly twelve million. The production of durable manufactures decreased by more than 70 per cent between June, 1929, and June, 1932, and even output of nondurable manufactures decreased by one-third.

The Great Depression revealed brutally for the first time some of the problems of a young society that had been able to achieve continuous and rapid expansion until that point and had been ready to assume great risks because of the promise of the rewards to come. It showed some of the burdens imposed on a society in constant turmoil and one subjected as well to heavy pressures from the outside world ever since 1842 (when for the first time more than 100,000 immigrants landed on American shores in any one year), but particularly since the beginning of the twentieth century (when yearly arrivals had exceeded a million people in six out of twenty-nine years, never falling below 300,000 a year except during a brief wartime period). It exposed, that is, some of the consequences of America's open frontiers, exacting an awful price for the country's contribution to the realizations of mankind's dream of freedom. For the millions who converged on America in the fifty years before the Great Depression, America represented the supreme goal of freedom from want and fear, a chance to do and be what few could do and be in the Old World.

No country had ever been faced with such a difficult task, even if one takes for granted the existence of the so-called unlimited possibilities of the American continent. It was not surprising to see that such a task was unfinished in 1929, that the position of many of the newly arrived Americans remained marginal, their roots in the new soil shallow, their exposure to economic risks very high.

But some members of the older strata of American society

also suffered the consequences of the modern and efficient way in which life had been organized in the New World. For much of this so-called efficiency seems to depend on an infinite division of the productive process, an unlimited readiness on the part of everyone to rely on the efforts of somebody else for the satisfaction of 99 per cent of his needs. Self-sufficiency is deprecated as a primitive and expensive remnant of feudalism. Social mobility and progress mean not only a mass transfer of population from the land to the cities; they also mean that the surviving dwellers on the farms will consider themselves authentic members of a modern community only if they eat for the most part food which they do not produce. They lead to the permanent cutting off of the masses of urban dwellers from their last ties with the land. These arrangements look, and often are, neat, progressive, and economic. They also multiply the consequences of calamity and decrease the ability of man to cope with disaster.

There are thus peculiar reasons, part and parcel of the "American dream," which contributed to the immensity of the Depression. On the one hand there were millions of newcomers who were not yet sufficiently strengthened economically and were therefore buffeted wildly by the sudden tornado. On the other hand, millions of old-timers, fully committed to the working of an impersonal and automatic production system, were left helpless when the system stopped functioning.

It is true that the American Depression was part of a worldwide depression, but it is true, too, that nowhere else did the crisis assume the extreme characteristics it did in the United States. It was the very inefficiency of the older European industrial countries that spared them the worst. A slow decline from not very impressive heights had been underway in France since 1925. A measure of social security already existed in such countries as Great Britain which had found it impossible to share in the unlimited optimism of America. Often the viscosity of the economic system, or the ancient reliance on government intervention as a built-in feature of an unreliant capitalistic system, narrowed the difference between normalcy and crisis. The ties that many urban people had maintained with the countryside opened up avenues of retreat which in many instances made the difference between starvation and survival. Only in Germany did the crisis attain some of the acuity it reached in the United States, and there the political consequences were very grave indeed.

The Great Depression was not only a traumatic experience from which some have not yet recovered. It was also the cause of a far-reaching reorientation of the thinking of the American people. It provided the opportunity for a reassessment of accepted values and of the order of social priorities. It set in motion trends and released forces that have had and are still having incalculable consequences on the structure and aspirations of American society and government.

The business and financial communities, the bankers and brokers who had paraded as the *avant garde* of the American people, suffered most. Theirs was the immediate and direct responsibility for a great deal of what was happening. Theirs was the incompetence and inability to deal with the problems they themselves had created. The solemn marchings of serious and black-frocked gentlemen to and from the Corner ("the House of Morgan is intervening at 12 o'clock") soon stopped. There was nothing that Wall Street could do that would make any difference. Wall Street itself, as the Depression lengthened, became the object of inquiry and investigation, the most famous of them all being the investigation of the Stock Exchange started by the Senate Committee on Banking and Commerce in April, 1932. The examples of human folly and greed, of breach of faith, and of sheer stupidity revealed by that investigation are perhaps not more numerous or shocking than would have been found in a similar investigation of other important centers of human power in times of great temptation and crisis. But the facts are that the Senate did investigate the Stock Exchange and that a midget did sit on Mr. Morgan's lap. The verdict of history has been pitiless and the loss of power and influence by Wall Street irretrievable.

The moral and intellectual poverty, thus revealed, produced hard thoughts on the substance of the values that the discredited Wall Street society had for so long propounded. A true prophet, Stuart Chase, had as far back as 1929 raised some question about American prosperity and had doubted its reality when so much of it seemed to hinge upon the wildly extravagant use of two diabolical gadgets—the radio and the automobile. Could a lasting prosperity be built on the mere multiplications of machines suddenly invented and thrust across the human land-scape? Could America witness for much longer the reckless squandering of its wealth and beauty? Could it see its forests killed by arsenic fumes, its land eroded by uncontrollable waters, with dust covering the plains?

What were the elements of a prosperous nation? Could it be that these included a sense of communal responsibility and solidarity, of readiness to assume burdens needed for the sake of society as a whole? If these were some of the new values, or, better still, of the recovered values of the past that would go into the building of the American welfare of the future, based on the satisfaction of duties shared and on the pride coming from the contemplation of a well-tended domestic garden, who was to assume responsibility for leading the country toward the realization of these goals, and what were the necessary policies?

It was at this point, in the gloomiest and darkest days of the Depression, as the third and fourth winter came along, that the thoughts of the more sensitive and restless turned to the Soviet Union. This was the time of the discovery of the Soviet Union, the age of Stalin's communism. The machinery of production had not stopped in the Soviet Union. The five-year plan was beginning to succeed. As Edmund Wilson, representing the mood of a whole generation of intellectuals, wrote:

> With a businessmen's president in the White House, who kept telling us, when he told us anything, that the system was perfectly sound, who sent General Douglas MacArthur to burn the camp of the unemployed war veterans who had come to appeal to Washington, we wondered about the survival of republican American institutions; and we became more and more impressed by the achievements of the Soviet Union which could boast that its industrial and financial problems were carefully studied by the government, and that it was able to avert such crises. We overdid both these tendencies; but the slump was like a flood or an earthquake, and it was long before many things righted themselves.[19]

These longing glances were cast in the direction of a country about which very little was known. The harsh realities of Stalinism either were not admitted or were lost in the babel of languages used by the intellectuals. It was possible to compound admiration for Soviet realism and planning with the bitter memories of Sacco and Vanzetti and of Gastonia, especially since the purges and trials of Moscow were still to come.

But this confusion did not last long. The crisis gave a sense of power and direction to the intellectuals and the politically minded, even if it prompted some of them to look to the Soviet Union. The hold of the Soviet Union on their interests and thoughts was never real or prolonged. What was real and prolonged and ultimately fruitful was the kind of mental gymnastics that the Depression forced on the educated elite of the country. If everybody else had failed, if the businessman admitted bankruptcy and if the government admitted to a frightful shortage of ideas and of courage, could it not be that the previous relationships of power should be reversed, so that people whose stock in trade was ideas, a readiness to experiment, and

[19] *The Shores of Light,* New York, 1952, p. 499.

a regard for the entirety of the historic past would at last be able to come into their own?

It has often been noted that the Great Depression, for all its extreme and tragic features, did not end in a revolution of the kind that brought Hitler to power in Germany. It is beyond dispute that there was no revolution on that pattern in America. Everywhere the victory of the totalitarians was the victory of those who denied the supremacy of politics and of ideas, who violently pushed the political world into the background to promote the triumph of the technocrats and the experts, of the dialecticians of historical materialism, of the defenders of inevitability. The totalitarians claimed they were rescuing societies which had lost themselves in the vague world of the liberal age, and that a way had to be opened for the efficiency experts and the central planners and for the believers in the one-way direction of human traffic and human destiny.

There was, however, in the United States a revolution of the politically minded, of those who were supporting the supremacy of the political decision, of successive political decisions, tentatively reached after discussion, of those who defended the right of political leaders to speak in the name of the general welfare. It was the revolution of men with ideas, confused and contradictory, yet applicable, even if only in piecemeal fashion, to the problems urgently confronting the American community. It was the triumph of the nonplanners and of the "inefficiency experts," who, nevertheless, brought a sense of order and direction to the collective effort.

The "efficiency" of the business world had brought about all too visible results. The uncertain steps of those who had never met a payroll might prove to be a steadier guide for the future. Their economic innocence made them look with astonishment at the fact that between 1929 and 1932 annual purchases of goods and services by federal, state, and local governments had *decreased* from 8.5 to 8.1 billion dollars. On the face of it, with the economy at a standstill, this did not make much sense. A time had arrived, perhaps, when public economic decisions had to be taken as a result of overriding political considerations.

In the fall of 1932, politics started to rise in the United States to a position of unprecedented splendor though its influence was sinking rapidly elsewhere in the world. And Franklin Delano Roosevelt was the leader and interpreter of this political revolution.

2

Roosevelt

THE LEADER

Franklin Delano Roosevelt must stand at the center of the Roosevelt Revolution. He was its leader and its voice. He was the driving force that gave a sense of direction to one of the major transformations of a modern democratic and industrial society.

This claim is made despite the historian's knowledge that events occurred of which Roosevelt was not aware, that legislative decisions which were later rightfully viewed as major achievements of the New Deal were taken without any obviously direct participation by Roosevelt (witness the National Labor Relations Act). The claim can be sustained even though sociologists and economists might point out that a number of developments would have occurred—such as changes in the social pattern and perhaps even in the balance of economic power in the United States—without Roosevelt. It can be supported notwithstanding Roosevelt's failures and contradictions and the important roles played by the many political leaders who crowd the stage of the New Deal.

Among the opinions of scholars and of intellectuals, of contemporaries and of historians, on the character of the Roosevelt leadership, certain judgments appear with unusual frequency. Here are the very people who almost by definition

57

were committed to the New Deal, for the New Deal represented the victory of ideas over matter, of action over inaction, of change against the status quo, of experimentation over rigidity. Yet many of them, even though unable or unwilling to repudiate Roosevelt and ready to praise him as one of the great men in the history of the American republic, get fussy about the qualities and content of his leadership. Roosevelt was Machiavellian, a pragmatist, an opportunist. Roosevelt was no theorist, no political philosopher, no economist. One begins to doubt whether anybody was at the helm from 1933 to 1945 and to wonder how, in the face of such striking deficiencies, certain persistent lines of public policy could be sustained over so many years.

Others will seek to give weight to concepts of leadership which only with difficulty can be housed within the American framework of democratic constitutionalism, and maintain that the creative leader can only be the leader who stands apart from society and assumes roles only tactically to realize his long-range strategic aims. Roosevelt mirrored American society. He therefore took roles which in the ultimate analysis imply the absence of leadership.[1]

It should be said at the outset that, apart from theoretical problems, many of these charges are not true and cannot be reconciled with the evidence that really matters. Roosevelt was a skillful administrator, if by that we mean the capacity to excite in first-rate minds and at moments of crisis a devotion to duty and a creativeness of thought that will on balance achieve the needed goal. Roosevelt was a political philosopher, if by that we mean his intellectual and emotional commitment—over a

---

[1] These are the views of James M. Burns, in *Roosevelt: The Lion and the Fox,* New York, 1956; see his note on the study of political leadership, pp. 481ff. Burns writes that "the modern executive may be willing to risk endangering the integration of his followers in trying to improve their position. . . . The essence of my estimate of Roosevelt as a political leader is that he fails to exercise creative leadership in this sense" (p. 487).

very long period of time, embracing virtually his entire life—to basic notions concerning the nature of man and of the group, the relationship of man and of the group to the state, and a keen awareness of all the complexities that the idea of the state entails in a federal system.

To deny the central position of Roosevelt throughout the Roosevelt Revolution indicates a readiness to go all the way either with a wholly chance view of the nature of history and of the affairs of nations ("What happens in Washington or anywhere else doesn't really matter very much. Fate is in charge of mankind.") or with a deterministic view of history ("Not fate, but iron laws of history are in control. Men in power are their puppets.") or with an elite theory of history ("Why should we look at the formal leaders of our democratic system when we know that the real decisions are taken elsewhere in the shadowy and informal realms where men of power meet and decide?").

Even if one is tempted to yield in part, or from time to time, to the despair of fate, or to the illusory and relaxing comfort of riding the wave of the future, or to the delight of a conspiratorial search for our authentic and hidden masters, the temptation should be checked before too much damage is done. For the danger is that of destroying the foundations of a democratic and constitutional society in which painfully and slowly policies do unfold and in which leaders do occasionally rise to the top capable of expressing the aspirations of that society in an original, fresh, and impelling way.

Leadership within this context cannot mean the lifting of the leader above and outside the society. The democratic leader is the man who is able to express the urge of his society to achieve common and deeply felt needs. The failure of democratic leadership is the failure of the leader to identify those needs and realize them.

In this sense, Roosevelt has been the supreme democratic leader of our time, and the qualities he brought to the immensely difficult task of bringing the most powerful community of the Western world out of the depths of the Great Depression and out of the ordeal of war to a higher plateau of welfare and freedom are of a very high order. They are not all easy to single out and describe, and some of them are more in evidence than others.

There was, first of all, a quite exceptional intelligence at work. Roosevelt showed a quick grasp of public affairs, a retentive memory, a capacity to draw on very short notice on remote and half-forgotten sources of information, a skill in using the level of discussion and of analysis that was best suited to the interests and the level of information and of intelligence of the groups to which he was addressing himself. He moved with imagination and with the skill of a "creative artist" among the tangle of conflicting and confusing views and interests.[2]

There was Roosevelt's unique sense of identification with his land. His words in 1932, "we have reached the last frontier," may have conveyed the impression that Roosevelt thought the game was up and the end in sight. But despite the fact that there was perhaps no mystery left in America once the continent had been spanned from ocean to ocean, this was still a land of wonder and magnificence, and few men could describe it as

[2] Frances Perkins, *The Roosevelt I Knew,* New York, 1946, p. 163. Miss Perkins, who is one of the key sources for an understanding both of Roosevelt and the New Deal, offers the following example of F.D.R.'s imaginative mind: "Illustrative of these qualities is the way in which, after one or two interviews, he accepted the abstruse and almost incomprehensible report of Dr. Albert Einstein on the possibility of developing an atomic bomb from the theories and slender accumulation of knowledge of nuclear physics and fission. Roosevelt had a meager scientific education and could not possibly have understood and followed Einstein's scientific arguments. But Einstein is also a warm, human, imaginative personality, and the sympathy that sprang up between them made it possible, in part, for Roosevelt to accept his theoretical explanation. He gave the signal to go ahead on the exploration and development of the atomic bomb because of his hunch that Einstein, like his fellow scientists, was truthful and wise. He had seen him on Henry Wallace's recommendation, and he knew Wallace, a man of scientific understanding, was also truthful and wise."

well as Roosevelt. The winding rivers, the cities and the plains, the relationships of one region to another, the ties that kept together families and communities, the development of the Hudson River and that of the South, Hyde Park and Warm Springs, the spoliation of the forests and the wasting of waters, these were ever-recurring themes that over a period of forty years gave vivid and concrete meaning to Roosevelt's utterances and to his faith in man and in the United States. The last geographic frontier may have been reached, but within the fully explored country there were a thousand mistakes to be righted and the theme of the essential communion between man and the land was one to be endlessly kept alive and refined.

Land, water, and trees were not the entire picture. The spiritual and historical vision of the United States as a nation and as a member of the community of nations was always present. It is of the essence of democratic leadership to possess a sense of history, for without it the leader can too easily become the rabble-rouser. This sense of history Roosevelt had in the highest degree. It bore fruit in two ways.

The first was in restoring the idea of community to its proper role. Roosevelt was convinced that the idea of communal effort was a basic idea of the American past. The history of America had been a history of pioneers and of individuals moving within a framework of civic responsibility. The New Deal was an effort to restore as fully as possible the sense of community and of duty.

In the second place, it bore fruit by relating to the contemporary happenings of other countries the internal struggle of the United States to regain control over its future. Roosevelt has been called an isolationist up to his "quarantine" speech. This can be said with justification, perhaps, from the narrow and specific point of view of his initial prudent reluctance to committing the United States to exceedingly risky positions in the menacing European conflicts at a time when the country had still not recovered from its internal distress. But from the larger historical point of view, Roosevelt cannot be classified as an isolationist, for constantly and consistently he had the clearest idea of what American democracy had to do in order to be true to itself and to keep afloat in the face of the crisis of democracy throughout the world.

The sensitive reaction of Roosevelt to the crisis of totalitarianism in the twentieth century stands in memorable contrast to the obtuse and dull reactions of nearly all other leaders of the democratic nations. A shrewd recognition of the dangers to democracy in the modern world enabled him to identify the key elements of a positive democratic government. Fascism, communism, and national socialism were concrete realities of decisive importance; his understanding of their decisive importance enabled Roosevelt to suggest the proper course of action at home. The task confronting American democracy never appeared to him as that of leading a crusade against communism. The first duty was that of creating within the country the conditions at home that would make communism in America impossible.

Roosevelt's skill and ease in conveying his thoughts was one of the important sources of his success. He had an amazing virtuosity in coining memorable phrases and slogans and summaries of policies that would remain for long in the imagination of the people and would describe vividly, if not always accurately, the core of the problem ("horse-and-buggy," "economic royalists," "one-third of a nation," "we have only begun to fight"). Rereading after twenty years his radio addresses, fireside chats, and more formal speeches, one is struck by the variety and richness of expression, the precision of the language when precision was needed, its sweeping generality when a mood had to be transmitted. He could harass and excite, soothe and encourage, drive to anger and to hopeful effort in a way that made the country conscious of the presence of meaningful leadership at the top. With Congress he could use threatening language and resort to ultimatums with fixed deadlines that would leave no doubt as to where the President stood. He could as well by the use of enticing and flattering language freely obtain from the legislature the kind of co-operation he needed.

He lifted his relations with the press to a level that in its substantive meaning has never been matched before or since. Much has been said of the steadily widening influence of the press conference as an instrument in the operation of the American system of government. The presidential press conference is unique as the American system of government is unique. As a result of its use, the President has gained a platform on which he stands to communicate his thoughts to the people. The President has also to submit to the discipline of the press conference and to the risks that may come from its reckless and unskilled use. The press conference has in recent years become more formalized, as its reach has been extended by the intrusion of radio and television. But the press conference has also to some extent deteriorated since 1952, because on balance the President has tended to become a passive participant in it, since he merely reacts to the questions of newspapermen and follows the general drift of the questions put to him.

Not that Roosevelt could or would escape the kind of insistent and often malicious probing by journalists which has become such an important part of the press conference of the fifties. Yet he held the initiative in his hands most of the time. To an extraordinary extent he used the press conference as an outlet for his own thoughts and reflections on great questions of state and dominated it. The press conference under Roosevelt was not the equivalent of the question period in the House of Commons. It was often the equivalent of a solemn declaration of executive policy.

As their transcripts appear in his *Public Papers and Addresses,* the conferences are wonderfully revealing of the mind

of Roosevelt at work in transmitting his thoughts and difficulties to an able and suspicious group of journalists. The content might vary, from a concise statement of a new government
policy to musing and speculative glances at the future. The tone
might vary, too, mild or aggressive, humorous or angry, according to the circumstances. But always the press conferences
provided important, even if at times tricky, expressions of
presidential policy and hopes. They show the seriousness with
which Roosevelt took the tasks of presidential leadership and of
supplying information to the press in a free society. The frequency of the press conferences, their length and substance, the
careful unfolding of complex issues confronting the President
(witness the press conference of May, 1935, after the Supreme
Court decision invalidating the NRA)—everything underlines
the fierce intensity of the attempt by Roosevelt to do well something that he considered of paramount significance.

Roosevelt added an element of drama and suspense that
made politics fascinating and vital. One can see him at work
in the early days of the New Deal, presiding over the meetings
of the National Emergency Council, watching the activities of
innumerable department heads, worrying about their relationships with the press, eager to present a co-ordinated administrative front to the outside world. One sees his awareness of the
usefulness of sustained publicity through the "dosed" release
of information so that the maximum advantage could always be
extracted by any announcement of public policy. One sees him
scornful of the opposition press and fully capable of measuring
the extent and quality of the influence of the *Chicago Tribune*
and of the *New York Sun,* persistently coming back to the conclusion that in spite of all the difficulties the administration was
having with a largely hostile press, his task was that of giving
the American people, through the press, the biggest possible
budget of news.

As a leader, Roosevelt was never one to conceal his enjoyment of power. His verbal trick—"you and I know"—so annoying to his enemies and taken as an example of prideful egotism, was a reflection of his belief that a President is bound at all times, but particularly in moments of crisis, to use in full the powers that the Constitution makes available to him. The Presidency must be the source of ideas and of programs, the powerhouse from which are administered the policies of the government. Power in a democracy cannot be left idle and it is only through its proper exercise that democracy can be strengthened.

Power can be used in many different ways, none of them to secure the position of the leader, all of them to permit the leader to do his job. To the confusion of many later or even contemporary observers, Roosevelt used power in a soft-spoken, circuitous, and subtle way, just as he could also be utterly ruthless and outspoken in the pursuit of given policies.[3]

Regardless of its quality, Roosevelt's exercise of power was never separated from the world of reality and of the possible. As a democratic leader, Roosevelt knew that public opinion, propriety, constitutional requirements, and historical traditions all fixed limits to the exercise of power. He saw a sense of ex-

---

[3] Burns, *op. cit.*, p. 373, suggests an intriguing and unexpected parallel between Roosevelt and Stalin: "The problem, from Roosevelt's standpoint, was one of power rather than of narrow efficiency. His technique was curiously like that of Joseph Stalin, who used the overlapping delegation of function, a close student of his methods has said, to prevent 'any single chain of command from making major decisions without confronting other arms of the state's bureaucracy and thus bringing the issues into the open at a high level.' Roosevelt, like Stalin, was a political administrator in the sense that his first concern was power—albeit for very different ends." The usefulness of the parallel is not immediately apparent, for the overlapping of Stalin's delegations of power had the main purpose of paralyzing any attempt at deviation from a rigidly fixed policy goal. As he moved toward the fulfillment of the Plan, Stalin used overlapping as insurance against treason. On the other hand, Roosevelt's administrative "confusion" was induced by an experimental mood, tentatively seeking out the best way of achieving a flexible purpose. And to say that Roosevelt's first concern was power, without identifying the ends for which power was to be used, leaves the question unsettled.

pediency, of quest for the shifting terms of the problems to be
solved, as important aspects of the exercise of democratic power.
Roosevelt knew what the limits of the New Deal were. Within
those limits, he drove forward unafraid, unmoved by the most
adverse odds, and, in 1937, quite ready in a seemingly casual
way to confront that most sacred of American institutions, the
Supreme Court. His was a revolution that recognized the binding framework of tradition and of constitutionalism. But within
the framework, the battle was open and as strongly pursued as
circumstances warranted.

Very little of this strong yet constitutional exercise of power
would have been possible had Roosevelt been left without the
sustenance of certain ideas and beliefs and had he been unable
to express them with reasonable continuity. One wonders how
much "theory" is needed to make a man a "theorist." Roosevelt didn't know who Kierkegaard was until late in his life, and
John Maynard Keynes has been described as quite disappointed
at the failure of Roosevelt to understand his *General Theory*.
The apparent childish delight with which Roosevelt listened to
the proponents of wild ideas and schemes is taken to suggest
a theoretical frame poorly and loosely put together and therefore unable to resist successfully the onslaught of the intellectual
crackpot. His hesitation on the scope and purpose of economic
planning and his inability to give up a mild obsession about
budget balancing are listed as black marks that no proper
theorist should have on the debit side of his speculative ledger.

These gaps, weaknesses, contradictions, and areas of ignorance nevertheless did exist side by side with a strongly con-
structed theoretical whole which included many of the essential
ideal elements of leadership needed by American society in the
1930's. What is more, it can be shown that Roosevelt had come
to these conclusions about the common good and the nature of
democracy over a long period of time and that the growth of his
ideas has an essential continuity, the progressive militant of

Theodore Roosevelt's era and of Wilson's "New Freedom,"
merging via the governorship of New York into the leader
of the New Deal.

The test of democratic leadership is to be found in the sum
total of effective achievements secured in a climate of freedom.
The leader has failed if at the end of his tenure democracy has
been lost and constitutionalism has been abolished, if the crisis
has not been solved and no measures are on the statute books
that will make it possible to cast a reassured look at the future.
By this pragmatic test, Roosevelt has been a great leader. By
1952, America was in many decisive ways a new country, yet
one still cherishing many of the traditions of the past and living
under the protecting shelter of an ancient Constitution. No man
can be held responsible for the ultimate unfolding of all the
consequences that may flow from the decisions in which he
played a vital initial role. The time may come when an appraisal of the dangers of the new organized mass democracy into
which the United States has moved will have to be made.
It is idle to speculate on a still distant future which is in any
case going to be influenced by other factors, both new and
imponderable. No historical appraisal of Roosevelt can go
much beyond the frame of reference imposed by the events
and conditions that belonged to his times. From this point of
view, Roosevelt's leadership in peace and in war, at home and
abroad, was successful. Roosevelt must be placed at the core
of the Roosevelt Revolution.

THE NATURE OF DEMOCRACY

The only two great countries among the Western democracies
not blessed by a Christian-Democratic party are Great Britain
and the United States. These are also the only two countries
whose leaders, in times of revolutionary transformation, chose
to call themselves Christian and democratic. Roosevelt's ad-

mission is less well known than that of the British Labor party leader, Clement Attlee. It took place in a brief exchange with a newspaperman and is related by Francis Perkins:

> A superficial young reporter once said to Roosevelt in my presence, "Mr. President, are you a Communist?" "No." "Are you a capitalist?" "No." "Are you a Socialist?" "No," he said, with a look of surprise as if he were wondering what he was being cross-examined about. The young man said, "Well, what is your philosophy then?" "Philosophy?" asked the President, puzzled. "Philosophy? I am a Christian and a Democrat—that's all." [4]

It is certainly true that the two Protestant Christian-Democrats, acting wholly outside the framework established by Christian-Democratic parties and within the historical tradition and climate of opinion of non-Catholic countries, tried to realize the substance of what on the continent of Europe is still only a vaguely outlined ideal program of Christian democracy. This could be described as a redefinition of the meaning of democracy and of the role of democratic institutions, such that the fundamental inheritance of Western individualism could be reconciled with the new requirements of social and communal life in an industrial age.

Roosevelt's conviction was that this redefinition was needed because democratic values were being threatened by economic disorder. No easy assumptions could be made about the survival of democracy in the United States, because of the world-wide spreading of dictatorship and totalitarianism, and of the internal menace represented by the flowering of pressure groups, the uneven distribution of power, the excessive atomization of a society eager to go back to some commonly felt experience.

The views of Hoover and Roosevelt on the relevance for the United States of the European political and economic crisis are quite significant in this connection. Hoover was convinced that totalitarianism had developed in Europe because of the

---

[4] *The Roosevelt I Knew*, p. 330.

excessive tampering by governments with individual freedoms and the traditional economic order. Crisis and coups were due to specific "mistakes" that governments better guided by the proper notions of right and wrong could have avoided. The ensuing economic and political chaos had led directly to the worsening of conditions within the United States. Ultimately, the Great Depression was due to the mess in Europe. Therefore, the task was that of immunizing and isolating the United States against the spreading of the disease. Here was in essence an earlier version of the "fortress America" doctrine Hoover was to expound many years later. This interpretation of Hoover's views holds generally true, even though during the last six months of 1932 Hoover tended to ascribe the deteriorating condition of the country to the Democratic party, to Roosevelt, and to the impending threat of the New Deal: as the enemy had entered the gate, the responsibilities of Europe were forgotten.

To Roosevelt, the dislocations abroad proved instead that a big job lay at hand in the United States. "Conditions congenial to Communism were being bred and fostered throughout this Nation up to the very day of March 4, 1933. Hunger was breeding it, loss of homes and farms was breeding it, closing banks were breeding it. . . . Discontent and fear were spreading through the land" (PPA, 1936, 386).[5]

[5] The abbreviated reference in parentheses is to *The Public Papers and Addresses of Franklin D. Roosevelt,* in this case the 1936 volume, p. 386. The same abbreviated references will be used henceforth, and usually, for simplicity's sake, in the text. This is the major printed collection of official Roosevelt papers, covering the seventeen years, as Governor of New York and as President, from 1928 to 1945. The compiler, collator, and annotator was Judge Samuel I. Rosenman, one of Roosevelt's close friends and advisers. Thirteen uniform volumes in all have been published, in New York, in three different series and by three different publishers, under conditions less favorable than might have been expected for an undertaking of this importance. Five volumes were published in 1938: *The Genesis of the New Deal, 1928–1932; The Year of Crisis, 1933; The Advance of Recovery and Reform, 1934; The Court Disapproves, 1935; The People Approve, 1936.* Four others followed in 1941:

Communism was a manifestation of social unrest which flourished along with widespread economic maladjustment and as the result, for the most part, of internal conditions and not of external factors. Roosevelt set out to prove that American democracy could work if it took due notice of its needs. The call was for the operating room, not for the isolation ward.

A sense of urgency was present, even after the initial dramatic one hundred days of the first Roosevelt administration had receded into history. In 1937, Roosevelt felt that the situation of the civilized world had been for several years "at a point of extreme danger" (PPA, 1937, 307). Dictators have recognized the need of speed in government action. "They keep the conveyor belt moving—but at a terrible price to the individual and to his civil liberty" (PPA, 1938, 588). To say that strong government leads to dictatorship is wrong. "History proves that dictatorships do not grow out of strong and successful governments, but out of weak and helpless ones" (PPA, 1938, 242). Four years after the famous struggle over the Supreme Court, Roosevelt wrote of his decision of 1937 to demolish the roadblocks set up by the Court against the New Deal, justifying it on the grounds of the decisiveness with which a beleaguered democracy must deal with its dangers. "To stand still was to invite disaster. Across the seas, democracies had even then been yielding place to dictatorships, because they had proven too weak or too slow to fulfill the wants of their citizens. Social forces in our day gather headway with ever-increasing speed" (PPA, 1937, introduction dated June 3, 1941, lix–lx).

If world conditions made speed in handling the difficulties of democracy unavoidable, internal conditions had created a

The Constitution Prevails, 1937; The Continuing Struggle for Liberalism, 1938; War and Neutrality, 1939; War—and Aid to Democracies, 1940. The final four volumes, published in 1950, are: *The Call to Battle Stations, 1941; Humanity on the Defensive, 1942; The Tide Turns, 1943; Victory and the Threshold of Peace, 1944–1945.*

no less pressing state of affairs. What Roosevelt saw was a government deprived of community spirit. The task, he told a press
conference, was to get people "to think about the rounded
problem of government and of all the people of the country,
instead of just thinking along their own special line of business." He was to be against "small groups coming down here
with great vociferation." He was hoping that "we will get
away, more and more, from what we call the pressure groups"
(PPA, 1938, 133).

The very concept of the nature of party in a democracy
might have to be changed, so that a party worthy of assuming
government responsibilities would demonstrate that it could
rise above the politician's level of discourse and, by developing
ideas and standing firmly for certain ideals, would appeal to
the voters who were going to support the party not because of
its label, but because of its program. "I do believe in party
organization. . . . But the future lies with those wise political
leaders who realize that the great public is interested more
in Government than in politics, that the independent vote in
this country has been steadily on the increase" (PPA, 1940,
28).[6]

This was an appeal from "lower" politics to "higher"

[6] One of the features of the Roosevelt mythology is the belief that
Roosevelt played up to the traditional city bosses in Newark and New
York and Boston and Chicago and elsewhere, thus lowering the level of
morality of American political life and undoing the work of the reformers, the progressives, the muckrakers, the fighters against Tammany Hall
and corruption. Of course it is true that in the beginning Roosevelt
sought with apparent unconcern the support of urban "machines." He
saw no reason to risk offending powerful political leaders capable of
influencing substantial blocks of voters. To do otherwise might mean
to incur the risk of re-electing the Republicans. But the inescapable fact
is that it was Roosevelt and not the progressives, the "clean government"
crusaders, or the League of Women Voters who destroyed, or drastically
weakened at their roots, the traditional political organizations of the
cities. The Roosevelt Revolution altered the underlying conditions upon
which many of them had been built, by transferring to the government
the social responsibilities which many of them exercised, in part at least,
for the welfare of their followers.

politics, to the liberating political decision taken on the broadest basis, away from the narrow vision of the municipal scene, that classical stage for the activities of "politicians." It was not an appeal from political life to the rule of the technocrats. It was a summons to party interests to respect the dividing line between factionalism and the operations of democratic government.

Both external and internal issues therefore required a fresh look at the substance of democracy and at the purposes of democratic government. The error of his immediate predecessors had been that, under changing conditions, they had continued to think that the role of government was an unchanging one. For the first one hundred years of the nation's life, an abundance of land, timber, and minerals had led the federal government to assume as its duty that of "promoting business and relieving depression by giving subsidies of land and other resources." From the beginning, private enterprise had been assisted by government. "But today the government no longer has vast tracts of rich land to give away and we have discovered that we must spend large sums to conserve our land from further erosion and our forests from further depletion" (PPA, 1938, 243). Thus the terms of the equation had been reversed. In the past, the natural resources of the country had been distributed to permit the development of a great industrial and financial civilization. Today government must intervene to help the existing economic system and to protect the remaining public assets.

It is the role of democratic institutions to serve the needs of democratic society. This could be done, according to Roosevelt, by recognizing once more the need of collective action. The collective spirit had never been absent from the American past, and the rugged individualism of the twentieth century was a travesty of its true meaning. For individualism in American history had never been equated with the egoistic, coldly calcu-

lated, antisocial spirit of the enterpriser of the 1920's. The
time had come to return to the origins in order to remedy the
deviations from the concept of solidarity which had developed
in the recent past. As Roosevelt defined the problem, in the
inimitable language that is at the root of the Roosevelt legend,
"The spirit of the frontier husking bee is found today in carefully drafted statutes. . . . The cavalry captain who protected
the cabins of the Northwest is now supplanted by legislators
. . . toiling over the drafting of . . . statutes and over the
efficiency of government machinery to administer them" (PPA,
1938, 430).

The central notion of Roosevelt's doctrine of democracy was
that of community. His efforts throughout were aimed at demon-
strating the compatibility, indeed the essential identity, between
the community's concern for the general welfare and the
survival of the traditions of individual freedom and dignity.

Roosevelt, the wealthy Hudson Valley aristocrat and *grand
seigneur,* found intolerable the idea of "little tin gods on wheels
up at the top who have got some kind of heavenly right to rule"
(PPA, 1928–1932, 71). He poked fun at the unhappy Hoover
who in his incautious way had, in *American Individualism,*
written in pejorative terms about "the crowd." This was an
elite theory of society placing "at the top of our social system
in this country a very limited group of highly able, highly
educated people, through whom all progress in this land must
originate." As against this there is "the definite fact that the
mass of humanity does think, that it can make up its mind on
the pros and cons of all public questions; that it often originates,
and that there is a very definite relationship between what Mr.
Hoover calls the crowd and the continuation of modern progress" (PPA, 1928–1932, 69).

Avoiding theories both of atomistic individualism and of
an elite, modern democracy must focus on the idea of the
common good. Roosevelt felt confident that his government was

"being run less for political purposes and more for the general good" than had been true for some time.[7]

A definition of the content of the common good and of the way in which the common good was identified and realized proved no less baffling to Roosevelt than to the long series of political philosophers who have tried to give body to that idea in terms that could be reconciled with the survival of a free society made up of autonomous and moral human beings.

To realize the common good means to satisfy the fundamental needs of a given society. "In the long run the instincts of the common man, willing to live and let live, work out the best and safest balance for the common good" (PPA, 1938, 39). The common good is something that can be realized over a period of time, provided all the members of the community are free to judge, are equally brought within the scope of the deciding process, and are relieved from the excessive pressures of small and partial pressure groups. There is a wisdom of the community, of the people itself, which will assert itself if the proper conditions of freedom and welfare are maintained. What is important is the elimination of class rule, "for rule by class takes counsel from itself and fails to heed the problems and, therefore, the good of all kinds and conditions of man" (*ibid.*).

Twelve years after the campaign of 1928, Roosevelt goes back to his conviction "of the superior ability of the whole of the voters to pass upon political and social issues in free and unhampered elections, as against the exclusive ability of a smaller group of individuals at the top" (PPA, 1940, 437). The tasks of a society which wants to retain its democratic nature and to be free from the anarchy of extreme individualism and the deadening tyranny of totalitarianism, must be that of

---

[7] Unpublished minutes of the joint meeting of the Executive Council and of the National Emergency Council, June 26, 1934, p. 20, in the National Archives, Washington.

ascertaining the "aggregate judgment of all the people." Roosevelt speaks of "aggregate judgment" or "aggregate opinion" to indicate the final sum total of views on any given problem. The "aggregate judgment" is the judgment of the community, and Roosevelt implies that a democracy is successful as it ascertains the aggregate judgment of its members on as many questions as possible, and then proceeds to act on it.

With these words, Roosevelt seems to be pushing aside the disputes of majority or minority rule and to be groping toward some concept of a general will of the community which will reflect the views of all, stress the ties of solidarity among the members of the community, and identify the things that have to be done regardless of the special interests involved. There is a merger here of the individual with the community. The aggregate opinion emerges as the valid one, and Roosevelt reminds us that "it is well to remember that the individual citizen contributes most to the good of this largest group [the people of the United States] only when he or she thinks in terms of the largest group. Only if the spirit of that is carried out can democracy . . . succeed" (PPA, 1936, 148–49).

Having reached this point in the development of a theory of democracy—a point which frankly states that only as he thinks and behaves as a member of the group can a citizen fulfill his mission and then only to the extent that an aggregate view satisfies the needs of the community—Roosevelt is anxious to show that such discipline is imposed only for the sake of the individual. "Our common life . . . our laws and our basic Constitution, exist primarily to protect the individual, to cherish his rights and to make clear his just principles" (PPA, 1935, 406). There are to be no "forgotten men" and no "forgotten races" in America, and the goal of a properly oriented and organized democracy still is in the end the protection of the rights of men, the multiplication of their energies, the full flowering of their dignity, their complete participation in the processes of democracy.[8]

Roosevelt's democratic society then appears as a society based on co-operation and a continuous effort to achieve its shifting goals. There are no supermen or heroes or great engineers in it; there are no fixed goals that have to be reached regardless of the cost. It is a society humble in its ways and ready to be inspected by the inquiring eye of the outside world.

THE NEW DEAL

The New Deal was the attempt to translate into concrete political action some of the ideas about the new democratic community. Roosevelt was the leader, yet he was not alone, and in the exceptional success he had in calling forth from many imaginative minds a complete dedication to the task of reconstruction of the American government, we find one of the elements of his greatness. The pattern of the New Deal

[8] At a special press conference for Negro newspaper publishers, on February 5, 1944, Roosevelt told this story: "I always think of two or three years ago—not an election trip—I was down in Chattanooga. A very interesting thing happened. I was going all around to the points of interest in Chattanooga—I think I dedicated one of the dams—and I drove with Governor Cooper through the streets, the southern end of Chattanooga, through the Negro section.

"And there was tremendous enthusiasm to see the President. And suddenly we came onto this broad avenue that was running south, we came to a place where all the enthusiasm quit and stopped; and there were a good many colored people on the streets, but they just stood there, they were completely apathetic.

"And I turned to Governor Cooper. I said, 'What's the matter with these people?'

"He said, 'You are not in Tennessee any longer, you are in Georgia' [laughter].

"That is a very interesting thing. Now in Tennessee the great majority of Negroes in Chattanooga are voting: they can take part in the life of the community. You get across this invisible line, you pop over into the State of Georgia, not one of them can vote. Now that is just a plain fact. It's an interesting fact. Just, as I said, hands down—[demonstrating]—no enthusiasm at all; and a block further back everybody saying, 'Hello, Mr. President' . . ." (PPA, 1944, 67).

emerged out of the swelling, noisy, and confusing chorus of many voices. Roosevelt's voice, however, stood out.

Twenty years before his 1932 acceptance speech, Roosevelt already had spoken of the struggle for "liberty of the community rather than liberty of the individual" and of the responsibility of the modern state for the realization of the purposes that can be achieved only in common. Taking up the issue of the conservation of natural resources, and thus underlining at this early stage what was to be one of the major purposes of his political life, Roosevelt said:

> There are, however, many persons who still think that individuals can do as they please with their own property even though it affects a community. The most striking example of what happens in such a case that I know of, was a picture shown me by Gifford Pinchot last week. It was a photograph of a walled city in northern China. Four or five hundred years ago this city had been the center of the populous and prosperous district, a district whose mountains and ridges were covered with magnificent trees, its streams flowing without interruption and its crops in the valleys prospering. It was known as one of the richest provinces in China, both as a lumber exporting center and as an agricultural community.
>
> Today the picture shows the walled town, almost as it stood 500 years ago, but there is not a human being within the walls, and but few in the whole region. Rows upon rows of bare ridges and mountains stretch back from the city without a vestige of life. Everything is in a dilapidated condition, and this is all due to the liberty of the individual. This is what will happen in this very State if the individuals are allowed to do as they please with the natural resources to line their own pockets during their life. With them the motto is "After us the deluge." They do not care what happens after they are gone and even do not care what happens to their neighbors. . . .[9]

The United States was not going to be another China. In

[9] Speech to the People's Forum, March 3, 1912, in *Franklin D. Roosevelt, Selected Speeches, Messages, Press Conferences and Letters,* ed. by Basil Rauch, New York, 1957, pp. 14–15.

1920, in accepting the Democratic vice-presidential nomination, Roosevelt defined in a few striking anticipatory words the twelve years of inaction and crisis that lay ahead: "We oppose money in politics, we oppose the private control of national finances, we oppose the treating of human beings as commodities . . . we oppose a mere period of coma in our national life." And, in January of 1929, he looked to the end of the stock market boom and to a time when the Democratic party would be "sanely radical enough" to be swept into power with the votes of all those who would have suffered as a result of the collapse.[10]

If the New Deal had no firm program at the end of 1932, its leaders knew what action was needed on the part of government and what direction the new administration would have to take: it would have to accept a sweeping increase of its responsibilities; it would have to intervene at critical points in the economy; it would have to take care of those who had been reduced to helpless conditions by the Depression. Fundamentally, the general welfare clause of the Constitution was to be given its broadest interpretation, and through it the attempt would be made to break the deadlock of private interests and the vicious spiral of a shrinking economy.

The New Deal began in the blackest period in the history of the republic since the end of the Civil War. In his acceptance speech, Roosevelt hopefully noted that "The great social phenomenon of this depression . . . is that it has produced but a few of the disorderly manifestations that too often attend upon such times" (PPA, 1928–1932, 649). But the time was short and, unless the people of the country got "work and security," a serious threat would be posed to the constitutional structure of the United States. Roosevelt pledged himself to a New Deal for the American people.

The main theme of Roosevelt's presidential campaign in the summer and fall of 1932 was that the country would now

[10] *Ibid.,* pp. 34, 60.

try to do through co-operative action what single individuals and groups had failed to do by themselves. What concretely this action would be could not be clearly stated in advance. The specific responsibilities of governments, the range of possible alternatives confronting them, could become evident only after they were in power. What Roosevelt could say was that prices would be stabilized, employment would be increased, public works and relief would be gotten under way; and he could say that government would assume a far greater role in the management of key areas of the nation's welfare, such as natural resources and power.

As Roosevelt surveyed the national landscape, a grim view stretched before his eyes. The greatest industrial plant the world had ever seen lay nearly idle, and extraordinary fear and anxiety for the future pervaded the country. The concern uppermost in the mind of Roosevelt was that of bringing back to life the complex existing structure. Even if only this could be done at first, the country would be restored to a high level of well-being.

Surely those were the thoughts of Roosevelt and of his advisers in the course of the preparation of the San Francisco address, the most famous of the 1932 campaign. This was the speech of the "last frontier." America had come a long way since its beginnings. Throughout the nineteenth century, the forces of the industrial revolution were released and a new dream created. So great were the advantages of the industrial revolution that the United States "accepted the bitter with the sweet. It was thought that no price was too high to pay for the advantages which we could draw from a finished industrial system." Things were possible then that are no longer possible today and policies of government which seemed right then are no longer applicable today. "Our industrial plant is built. . . . Our last frontier has long since been reached, and there is practically no more free land. . . . There is no safety valve in the form of a Western prairie to which those thrown out of work by the Eastern economic machines can go for a new start. We are not able to invite the immigration from Europe to share our endless plenty." A reappraisal of values is needed: "I feel that we are coming to a view . . . that private economic power is . . . a public trust as well. I hold that continued enjoyment of that power by any individual or group must depend upon the fulfillment of that trust." [11]

The reappraisal induced Roosevelt to say that the reckless speculative gambling that had characterized much of the recent economic life of the United States had to be stopped. The new task was "the soberer, less dramatic business of administering resources and plants already in hand. . . . The day of enlightened administration has come" (PPA, 1928–1932, 751–52). These words, reread after a quarter of a century and at the end of an era of notable expansion and renovation, of inventiveness and of new nongeographic frontiers, offer a tempting opening to those critics of the New Deal who have seen in it chiefly the reflection of a negative mood denying all the traditional values of the American dream. The truth is that the chore of making the American economic system, such as it was then, run again through enlightened administration and reforms was indeed the most urgent requirement. It could not be otherwise. Fresh advances could be possible only after the primary problems of normal life had been faced and solved.

[11] See the text of the San Francisco speech in PPA, 1928–1932, 742–56. According to Arthur M. Schlesinger, Jr. (*The Crisis of the Old Order,* Boston, 1957, pp. 425–26), the speech reflected more the views of one of Roosevelt's principal advisers, Professor Adolf Berle of Columbia University, than those of Roosevelt; that is, rather the influence of the academician than the boundless optimism and buoyancy of the candidate himself. But Schlesinger adds that the speech "provided impressive reasons for enlarging the role of government. For Roosevelt, who was more interested in results than in systems, this was probably more important than the basic framework of interpretation." It should not be forgotten, however, that the basic framework was justified by the conditions of the country at that time.

To the extent that the New Deal was confronted by a gravely ill economic system, its approach to the responsibilities of government had perforce to represent a radical departure from other American manifestations of the philosophy of reform since the end of the nineteenth century.[12] The task of earlier reformers had been that of redirecting or controlling, or breaking up a tidal wave of economic progress. Bryan, Theodore Roosevelt, and Wilson were preaching and acting in the midst of prosperity and were moved by a defense of the interests of those members of the community who felt themselves by-passed and discriminated against or actually damaged by the forward march of the business system.

Roosevelt, on the other hand, had to use the tools of government and the ideas of progressivism in the midst of a bankrupt economy. The farmers did not have to be protected against the exploitation of the railroad companies, nor the consumers against the monopolistic practices of the steel industry. The problem now was to get worthless wheat off the farmers' hands and induce the monopolists to start producing steel again.

The atmosphere of crisis explains the substance of one of the major initial actions of the Democratic administration which the elections of November, 1932, had triumphantly sent to Washington. The National Industrial Recovery Act (NIRA) cannot be understood except in terms of the emergency of the spring of 1933. If we look at it against the long American history of trust-busting, it does appear as a curious deviation from it, but the point that cannot be dismissed is that the NIRA supported the trustification of comatose and not of healthy and aggressive producers. And whether it did even that is far from certain. The issue is considerably more complicated.

The NIRA is significant on two closely related counts. It is significant, first, because of the grant it made to business to

---

[12] See on this point the analysis of Richard Hofstadter, *The Age of Reform,* New York, 1955, pp. 300ff.

organize itself, according to manufacturing categories, in order to revive production. This grant of self-government included as well certain price-fixing rights and the acceptance of controlled competition which could possibly have led to no competition at all. Secondly, in exchange for this grant of autonomous organization and pricing embodied in codes to be drafted for each separate industry, industry was to recognize the rights of labor to organize in freedom and to abide by the wage and employment standards fixed by the President.[13]

In substance, then, the NIRA was a charter of freedom for business and labor, under the auspices of the government. For the period of two years (for this was the limit established by the Congress), industry was to show what it could do to restore maximum production, to mend what industry itself considered one of the major reasons for the depression—destructive competition—under the benevolent eye of a government ready to admit that an increase in prices would be beneficial to the American economy.

On the other hand, labor was to be freed from the harassing conditions of the past which had slowed down or stopped its organizing efforts. The working man received the right to bargain collectively through representatives of his own choosing and was fully protected in his choice of a trade union. And he was told that, in all industries governed by codes, the President

[13] The famous Section 7A of the Act provided: "(1) That employees shall have the right to organize and bargain collectively through representatives of their own choosing, and shall be free from the interference, restraint, or coercion of employers of labor, or their agents, in the designation of such representatives or in self-organization or in other concerted activities for the purpose of collective bargaining or other mutual aid or protection; (2) That no employee and no one seeking employment shall be required as a condition of employment to join any company union or to refrain from joining, organizing, or assisting a labor organization of his own choosing; and (3) That employers shall comply with the maximum hours of labor, minimum rates of pay, and other conditions of employment approved or prescribed by the President." See a discussion of these points in Merle Fainsod and Lincoln Gordon, *Government and the American Economy,* New York, rev. ed., 1948, pp. 173ff.

would intervene to fix maximum hours of labor, minimum rates of pay, and other satisfactory conditions of employment.

The National Recovery Administration (NRA) which acquired the responsibility of administering the NIRA, has often been portrayed as the American version of the fascist corporate state. The only possible ground of comparison is the fact that both the corporate state and the NRA had a shadowy and unreal life. The corporate state never did what in theory it was supposed to do and its shell was used for quite different purposes. The NRA went out of existence in the spring of 1935 as a result of an adverse decision of the Supreme Court.

On the grounds of principle, no similarities can be found. The corporate state was a system in which the power of the totalitarian state was dominant. Both trade unions and employers were brought under the control of the fascist dictator and deprived of all freedom. The workers were compelled to join the one official trade union recognized by the State. The corporate system itself made no effort to fix minimum wages and standards of work. The whole mechanism was contrived purely for the purpose of mobilizing the national economy so that the fascist dictatorship could make adequate preparations for war.

The NRA was, on the other hand, an attempt to strike a bargain between government and business, whereby business acting under the fairly remote control of government would try to increase production, while at the same time it would give better working conditions to the worker and the utmost freedom of organization to trade unions.

The NRA shows, that is, the extent to which the New Deal remained within the framework of what has been loosely called the capitalistic system. Free enterprise was to acquire as much freedom as possible, provided it recognized its social responsibilities. The proviso was so clear it is hard to see the NRA as a surrender of traditional controls of government over business conduct, or as a weakening of antitrust policies. When Roosevelt decided in the spring of 1933 to incur the risks of the NRA, he was aware that the free hand business had received was to be kept in check in other ways. And not only through the increased power of worker's organizations. The idea of future controls was certainly present in his mind when in his annual message to Congress on January 3, 1934, he pointed to the need of encouraging "the slowly growing impulse among consumers to enter the industrial marketplace equipped with sufficient organization to insist on fair prices and honest sales."

If a concluding comment is still needed on the discredited parallel between the NRA and the corporate state, it could be this: The NRA tried to achieve the very ends that fascism succeeded in stifling—it sought to promote in organized fashion a balanced relationship among key competing groups in the economic order and to give to private interests of all kinds a meaningful role to play.

The NIRA was the last of the great legislative measures of Roosevelt's "one hundred days," which included the Agricultural Adjustment Act to raise the farmer's purchasing power, the Civilian Conservation Corps to help reforestation and the employment of young people, the Federal Emergency Relief Act, the first of the Investment Securities Acts, and the Tennessee Valley Authority Act.[14]

In the seeming confusion and contradictions of the legislative program of those months, a common purpose was becoming visible: the great retreat of government was to be brought to an end. In one of a series of "fireside chats" to the people early in 1934, Roosevelt looked back at the turmoil and haste of the preceding months and said, "A few timid people, who fear progress, will try to give you new and strange names

[14] Burns, *op. cit.,* pp. 168–71.

for what we are doing. Sometimes they will call it 'Fascism,' sometimes 'Communism,' sometimes 'Regimentation,' sometimes 'Socialism.' But, in so doing, they are trying to make very complex and theoretical something that is really very simple and very practical" (PPA, 1934, 317).

With the passage of time, the common purpose, the continuity and the persistence of Roosevelt's New Deal have become more visible. It is hardly possible for anyone to deny the uninterrupted link that—over a span of more than twelve years—ties together the campaign of 1932 and the promise to maintain full employment after the war made in Roosevelt's last message on the State of the Union on January 6, 1945. Too often, initial hesitations, temporary lack of interest, a shifting of attention under the pressure of other issues (quite apart, of course, from the major preoccupation with World War II that became F.D.R.'s dominant thought in the last six years of his life), have been construed as denials of the principles of the New Deal. But fitfulness and occasional stumblings and variations in the weights given in the political balance to this or the other New Deal measure cannot affect the overall judgment of the historian. In the beginning and at the end, Roosevelt stood firm on the New Deal and took major risks in holding to his views and in leading the Congress and the country along the path of decisive transformation. The New Deal was a continuing revolution, from which there was no turning back as long as Roosevelt lived.

A very good example of this can be found in F.D.R.'s support of the National Labor Relations Act (the so-called Wagner Act) in 1935. The President's cool detachment during the initial stages of discussion of the bill by Congress concealed in effect a commitment of long standing. As he had told the National Emergency Council on March 30, 1934, he was under no illusions concerning the labor policies of American industrialists:

I had the National Manufacturers Association in this afternoon and I asked them five questions. They were talking about Section 7-A and objections to the Wagner Bill. I said, "I have been in touch with you people now for about 23 years. So far as I know, the National Manufacturers Association has never made a study or taken a stand on minimum wage during that entire period; has never made a study or taken a stand on lowering hours which were excessive during that entire period; you have never made a study or taken a stand on child labor; you have never made a study or taken a stand on workmen's compensation, except adversely; you have never made a study or taken a stand on unemployment insurance, except adversely. That is a very simple record of your association for the past 23 years. Correct me if I am wrong." They said, "No, you are right." I said, "What do you think of the concentration of more people in big centers?" They said, "We have never studied that." I said, "Why the hell haven't you." They said, "We are, in the main, in favor of decentralization of industry." I said, "Why don't you study it?" They said, "All right, we will go out and study that."

That has been the attitude of the National Manufacturers Association and the United States Chamber of Commerce during all the time they have been in existence. I believe we can get them to come along with us on this. It is a great bunch, but you have to "talk turkey" to them.[15]

The problem was: effective freedom of choice for as many citizens as possible. The enemies of the New Deal spoke of regimentation. Roosevelt felt that those guilty of regimenting the American people were the supporters of great economic interests and monopolies. The New Deal saw itself freeing those who had been the victims of excessive economic pressure. The Wagner Act, replacing the National Industrial Recovery Act, which had been declared unconstitutional, would do just that by giving to the working class new rights of freedom of association.

Roosevelt, as Governor of New York, had supported un-

[15] Proceedings of the National Emergency Council, March 30, 1934, pp. 12–13.

employment insurance. Social Security was a logical development of that position. And he had been thinking for a long time of the "largest mass of the American population," of

> the people . . . in un-American surroundings and conditions. . . . The question comes up, are we licked in trying to help them in their living conditions? A good many real estate people consider we are; and they say the Government should not help them. We say, will private capital help them? They say, No, it can't, but we don't want the Government to help them. Are we licked in trying to help these people—40,000,000 of them, men, women, and children? Their answer is, Yes, we are licked; we must not do anything to help them, because we might interfere with private capital. The answer is, No, we are not licked. We are going to help them! [16]

In introducing the Social Security program to Congress in 1935, Roosevelt said that the country needed to achieve a proper balance between security and wealth. The needs of security were great, and action was required on three fronts: security of livelihood, security against the major vicissitudes of life, security of decent homes.

As the re-election campaign of 1936 approached, the tempo of the polemic increased.[17] On the eve of the elections, Roosevelt told America that the New Deal had just begun to fight; the fight would continue until many of the hazards of industrial society were eliminated from its midst.

The word "security" was to be used not in the limited sense of pensions and insurance:

[16] Proceedings of the National Emergency Council, December 11, 1934, p. 29.

[17] In 1935 and 1936, Roosevelt's support of the Wagner Act and of Social Security and the severity of his language against "economic royalists" gave the impression of a radical Roosevelt rather suddenly embracing extreme views. But, as has been pointed out (Burns, *op. cit.,* pp. 225–26), he was reacting to the extremity of the attacks against him from certain business and political quarters. Adapting himself to circumstances, he was fighting back with the utmost vigor.

I use it in the broader sense—confidence on the part of men and women willing to carry on normal work, and willing to think of their neighbors as well as themselves, confidence that they will not have to worry about losing their homes, about not having enough to eat, about becoming objects of charity. Add to that one more objective: that all Americans may have full opportunity for education, for reasonable leisure and recreation, for the right to carry on representative Government and for freedom to worship God in their own way (PPA, 1936, 460).

Early in 1937, Roosevelt prepared for the fight he saw ahead to undo the damage that the Supreme Court had been inflicting on the New Deal. In a strong message to Congress, he outlined the issue as follows:

I see a great nation, upon a great continent, blessed with a great wealth of natural resources. Its hundred and thirty million people are at peace among themselves; they are making their country a good neighbor among the nations. I see a United States which can demonstrate that, under democratic methods of government, national wealth can be translated into a spreading volume of human comforts hitherto unknown, and the lowest standard of living can be raised far above the level of mere subsistence.

But here is the challenge to our democracy: In this nation I see tens of millions of its citizens—a substantial part of its whole population—who at this very moment are denied the greater part of what the very lowest standards of today call the necessities of life.

I see millions denied education, recreation, and the opportunity to better their lot and the lot of their children.

I see millions lacking the means to buy the products of farm and factory and by their poverty denying work and productiveness to many other millions.

I see one-third of a nation ill-housed, ill-clad, ill-nourished (PPA, 1934, 4–5).

The most difficult years of the New Deal were probably 1937 and 1938. In some respects these were years of failure for Roosevelt. They offer the acid test of F.D.R.'s commitment to a policy that would, as far as was in his power, bring about lasting changes in the economic and political framework of the United States.

The period opens with the historic fight of the President against the Supreme Court, a conflict treated in some detail below and recalled here only to say that no charge of opportunism or of "foxy cleverness" can properly be leveled at Roosevelt in this connection.[18] At a turning point in the struggle for the survival of the New Deal, Roosevelt took a stand against extreme odds and in spite of the weight of American institutions and history arrayed against him.

The year continued with a worsening of economic conditions, and as 1938 got under way the mood of the country was still a gloomy one. Roosevelt has been charged with paying little attention to the strong advice that came then from John Maynard Keynes in favor of a bolder plan of public spending.[19] It is easy after the event to suggest that the adoption of the views of the British economist would have ended the Depression, or at least provided an ideal test of their validity. It is also possible to maintain that by driving hard for the passage of the Fair Labor Standards Act, which became law in 1938, Roosevelt was building upon a platform that would have provided a better foundation for improving standards of living for the American working class than Keynes's quite novel and hotly debated theories.

One cannot, in analyzing the Roosevelt Revolution, ever forget the President's deliberate intention to remain within the framework of the existing order. The order was to be radically modernized and improved, glaring gaps had to be

[18] Apart from the somewhat ingenuous way in which the Court reform proposals were drafted. But, then, no one was really taken in by the bland assertion that the new plan had been introduced out of solicitude for the personal health and strength of the justices. The fundamental elements of the debate were clear to everyone who cared to see them.

[19] Most of Keynes's letter is reproduced and its significance discussed in Burns, *op. cit.*, pp. 329ff.

filled, and public responsibilities had to be assumed. Hence the enforcement of wage-and-labor standards and of controls over the activities of Wall Street, the development of new instruments of government in the field of holding companies and power, the support of syndicalist freedom, the adoption of painfully higher taxes to meet the new obligations, the setting up of Social Security. The New Deal had come to life in a house in which the defense of the moral responsibility of free citizens was still the one purpose of the democratic community. Just as the wholesale take-over of industries was never contemplated, so no sweeping adoption of Keynesian policies was deemed feasible. Let us remember that the 200 per cent increase in the civilian expenditures of the government—from two to six billions of dollars—between 1933 and 1939 was a daring and large-scale exercise of the government power to spend. In refusing to proceed headlong in the direction a few among his advisers were advocating, the President was bringing into a fresh balance of mutual responsibilities the elements of a system that had been wonderfully productive in the past and that had nurtured ideals of freedom and social mobility.

Roosevelt's concern for the proper functioning of the system, as it was, is again reflected in another well-remembered episode of these years, the attempted purge of his enemies in the conservative wing of the Democratic party. Writing three years later about it, the President was convinced that the great measures debated in this period—reorganization of government, fair labor standards, monopoly reform, water-power development—had by then become more or less accepted as part of the American way of life. And yet bitter opposition to them was coming from some Democratic members of Congress "who had been elected in 1936 and in earlier years on liberal platforms, and who had pledged themselves to support the great objectives and social measures enunciated in those platforms" (PPA, 1938, introduction of 1941, xxvii).

What Roosevelt tried to do was to "nationalize" Democratic party politics, and on this national platform build a liberal, progressive movement capable of overriding local conditions and attitudes that were no longer compatible with the necessities of the times. In this he was in some way anticipating the views expressed after the war by one of the more idealistic members of the New Deal team, Henry Wallace, anxious for his part to give reality to a new political party system which, starting with a coherent and meaningful program, would proceed to secure the election of members of Congress all equally committed to the defense of that program and indeed bound by it in all their activities.

It is most probable that Roosevelt and Wallace were moved by different considerations in their approach to party politics. Roosevelt was thinking in terms of old-fashioned morality and of old-fashioned political rules. People should do what they have said they would do, and it would be helpful to have to fight a reduced congressional opposition. Wallace (who was not in favor of the 1938 purge) may have been dreaming of a "systematic" coherence to be introduced in the disorderly game of parties: ideas, conceived at the loftiest level of thought, filtered through debate, accepted by the elected party representatives, kept pure in the ark of the covenant, and carried out by congressmen who had no other selfish or different policies of their own.

Whatever the justifications used by Roosevelt before the war and by Wallace after the war to enforce political discipline, they ran against deeply rooted traditions of independence, of local autonomy, of the rights of a congressman to do as he pleased vis-à-vis his electors, his party, and the government. American democracy cherished the freedom of its ablest members too much to wish its elected representatives to be mere slaves of programs and of party whips. Those who are concerned by the massive transfer of constitutional powers to party organizations taking place in Europe will certainly not complain that this transfer did not take place under the New Deal. One can, nevertheless, understand Roosevelt's resentment in seeing people who had been returned to Congress only because they had exploited his name and his program do their very best to nullify the main legislative consequences of that program.

The purge of 1938 did indeed fail, personal and state loyalties proving stronger than Roosevelt's appeal. To the extent that F.D.R.'s intervention made possible the breakup of rigid situations and encouraged the participation in political life of new men convinced of the importance of issues and of clarity in the operation of a constitutional system, the purge was not a wasted fight.

Preoccupation with the present did not rule out thoughts about the future. Roosevelt's message of April 29, 1938, containing his recommendations to curb monopoly and the concentration of private power, is evidence of continuing concern for the very structure of the economic system. An able historian of the period thinks that the investigation of the Temporary National Economic Committee (TNEC) moved in a direction opposite to that of the National Recovery Act; instead of the codifying and trust-supporting legislation of 1933, we now have the antimonopoly slogans of 1938.[20] As we have seen, the 1933 legislation was nothing more than a temporary grant of freedom to business in exchange for heavy and novel responsibilities in the field of wages and labor organization. The 1938 inquiry was, on the other hand, a long-range move aimed at analyzing the American economy in all its aspects—another instance of the restless probing of the American system typical of the New Deal. Its forty-three volumes are still to be considered a major study of the legal and economic entities, such as the corporation, which have altered the life of twentieth-century men beyond

[20] Hofstadter, *op. cit.,* p. 311. But Hofstadter himself has to admit that already in 1935 the New Deal had moved against trusts in a substantial way with its legislation on the public utilities holding companies.

recognition by asserting sweeping and all-encompassing powers over the individual that in past centuries had been claimed only by the state and the church. From a purely documentary point of view—and the TNEC in the end was nothing more than the organizer of a successful and large-scale undertaking to collect data—the inquiry was not one of the least significant measures in the long series of government endeavors to bring public controls, order, and light to the corporate world.

If the TNEC leads us chiefly to hypotheses and might-have-beens ("What would have happened had war not broken out?"), the Fair Labor Standards Act of the same year was a major proof of what Roosevelt called the New Deal's concern for the common man. Within a few months of its passage, the Act had placed under its jurisdiction more than twelve million workers and had established maximum working-week standards (forty hours a week beginning with 1941), with overtime at one and one-half times the regular wage for work in excess of the maximum hours. Minimum wages were to reach forty cents an hour by 1945, with a forty-five-cent maximum payable sooner on the recommendation of industrial committees. Employment was prohibited for children under sixteen years of age, or under eighteen years in the case of hazardous occupations. Roosevelt could well say of the Act that "except perhaps for the Social Security Act, it is the most far-reaching, far-sighted program for the benefit of workers ever adopted here or in any other country" (PPA, 1938, 392).

The final period of the history of the New Deal coincides with World War II. From 1939 to 1945, "Dr. New Deal" was said by Roosevelt to have retreated in favor of "Dr. Win-the-War." It is curious to see how often this slogan has been interpreted as meaning the end, that is the demise and defeat, of the New Deal. What it really signified was that—leaving untouched the achievements of the New Deal until that moment —higher military priorities were to control the national effort.

In any case, as defense and armaments enter the picture with the message to Congress of January 4, 1939, Roosevelt could proudly say that, as a result of the work done since 1933, the United States has forged instruments better suited to meet the problems affecting national strength. The American people have been made "conscious of their interrelationship and their interdependence. They sense a common destiny and a common need of each other" (PPA, 1939, 6).

"Dr. New Deal" may have been on leave, but it was a purely temporary one, forced by events. Roosevelt never repudiated it and even from time to time used the war for the furtherance of his peacetime program. And in the last year of the war we catch a final glimpse of the thoughts Roosevelt was thinking as he planned for the future.

The difficulties of democracy tend to increase once the tensions and the common purposes of war are past. Roosevelt did not wait beyond the winter of 1944 to remind the United States of what was to be expected in the days ahead and of the national commitment to a new Bill of Rights, "under which a new basis of security and prosperity can be established for all." These rights were the right to a job; the right to adequate food and clothing; the right of every business to an atmosphere of freedom; the right to a decent home, to medical care, to protection from the economic fear of old age, sickness, and unemployment; and finally, the right to a good education.

These rights, which had played such a large role in the legislation of the New Deal, would be further strengthened after the war. In his last re-election campaign, at the end of 1944, Roosevelt promised the country he was not going to turn the clock back. "To assure the full realization of the right to a useful and remunerative employment, an adequate program must, and if I have anything to do about it, will, provide America with close to sixty million productive jobs." And to Congress, on January 6, 1945, he repeated his belief in the duty to maintain full employment and to give work to all those willing and able to work. Once more the magic figure of sixty million jobs was indicated, together with programs for the proper use of natural resources and for the support of productivity and mass purchasing power (PPA, 1944–1945, 41, 504, 505).

The New Deal can therefore hardly be seen as a brief parenthesis in the twenty years of American history from 1932 to 1952. If by New Deal we mean the systematic development of new government responsibilities, to be carried out within the framework of a free society, then the history of the New Deal is the history of those twenty years. There was never any going back, and, of course, even after 1952 continuity of policy has been maintained as the norm in many areas. Starting at a moment of deep crisis, the United States has accomplished the transition toward the full expression of the concepts of the modern state with remarkable and sustained success. The method has been pragmatic, the confusion has been high, the achievements have been substantial. No one can doubt that America owes the change to Franklin Delano Roosevelt.

If this is true, then the following summary of the policies of the New Deal and of the role of its leader by an American historian will appear startling:

> Within the nation in these twelve years was developed a distrust of the basic democracy of the republic, as well as a social philosophy that included within its practices, if not in its pronouncements, many of the primary leveling objectives of communism. A whole generation of youth was cut off from the past by an eloquent proponent of revolutionary change.[21]

It is never simple to settle problems concerning differences of ideologies. It has sometimes been tempting for idlers toying with schemata to equate the New Deal with communism,

---

[21] E. C. Robinson, *The Roosevelt Leadership, 1933–1945,* Philadelphia, 1955, p. 376.

even though from a doctrinal point of view they are totally incompatible and even though communism rejected the New Deal and rallied to it only on the basis of the sheerest expediency. It was not unusual to have on the periphery or even near the heart of the New Deal, people who were not only intellectuals, but who had in the past flirted with Marxism. The overriding fact went unobserved that in most instances these intellectuals threw their Marxist baggage overboard as soon as they could find something specific to do within a system that was so productive of reform and improvement. Therefore, the New Deal was proclaimed guilty of including communist objectives in its practices because it was deviating from the practice of the recent past, or because it was embarking on bold experimentation, or merely because it was dusting off the Constitution to see what was the authentic meaning of that document.

Roosevelt's attitude toward communism was always the disenchanted one of the skeptic, the rigorous one of the believer in the soundness of the American tradition, the negative one of the statesman aware of its totalitarian character. It was also the practical one of the man of common sense who, in the interest of freedom of thought, is able to distinguish between spying and sabotage and mere belief in abstract doctrine or generic support of an idea.[22]

As far as the New Deal was concerned, its only relation to communism was that it had been an effort to remove the elements of weakness that might breed communism. The crisis of 1933 Roosevelt saw as "a crisis made to order for all those who would overthrow our form of government" (PPA, 1936, p. 385). If the years from 1929 to 1933 did not in the end result in a collapse, it was because of what the American government did after 1933. Roosevelt had said in the campaign of 1936 that "to meet by reaction the danger of radicalism is

---

[22] See Roosevelt's distinctions, made at the press conference of November 26, 1940, PPA, 1940, pp. 577–79.

to invite disaster. Reaction is no barrier to the radical, it is a challenge, a provocation. The way to meet that danger is to offer a workable program of reconstruction" (*ibid.*). This workable program in its concrete application did not contain any trace of Marxist or communist influence. It was rather the most serious effort to go beyond the irrelevancies of a Marxist critique that had become obsolescent in the context of American society.

The historical importance both of the contents and of the success of the New Deal lies in the fact that the New Deal and its aftermath are the central factors forcing the communist world today to a reconsideration of the fortunes and fate of the capitalistic system. Far from being a derivation from an alien ideology, the New Deal is one of the root causes of the ideological insecurity of contemporary communism.

SOME NEW INSTRUMENTS OF GOVERNMENT

With great rivers crossing the land in all directions and carrying immense masses of water to the sea and with federal ownership of many of the most strategic power sites, the role of government in the use of energy resources has been a major issue throughout the modern history of the United States. As Governor of New York, Roosevelt, in the tradition of the supporters of public development of publicly-owned natural resources, backed the public development of the St. Lawrence River and of other water resources belonging to the people.[23] His plans extended beyond the borders of New York State and he saw the need of a policy to check the utility holding companies, and to establish a "yardstick" to help in controlling prices of electric energy.[24]

[23] See for instance his first address as Governor, January 1, 1929, PPA, 1928–1932, pp. 75ff.
[24] Schlesinger, *The Crisis of the Old Order*, p. 390.

In the 1932 campaign, Roosevelt outlined his ideas concerning power in a speech at Portland, Oregon, at the center of some of America's more important, and as yet untamed, water resources. Three main thoughts deserve attention:

First, to have a meaningful power plan it is not necessary for the government to nationalize all public utilities:

> I do not hold with those who advocate Government ownership or Government operation of all utilities. I state to you categorically that as a broad general rule the development of utilities should remain, with certain exceptions, a function for private initiative and private capital (PPA, 1928–1932, 738).

This was a concept to which Roosevelt was to remain true during the entire New Deal. We have the testimony of one of his closest advisers, Miss Frances Perkins, the Secretary of Labor in the New Deal Cabinet, on how Roosevelt "always resisted the frequent suggestion of the Government's taking over of railroads, mines, etc., on the ground that it would be unnecessary and would be a clumsy way to get the service needed." [25] There was no need to destroy private property in order to force private property to accept its social functions. The power of government should not be underestimated, nor the complexities of the tasks of economic management which a mere transfer of property titles could not possibly solve. Needed were fruitful and flexible ideas, not legal or ideological ones.

Secondly, the role of government in the field of electric power had to be selective. By a *few* carefully chosen geographic areas of intervention one could reach wide national objectives:

> Here you have the clear picture of four great Government power developments in the United States—the St. Lawrence River in the Northeast, Muscle Shoals in the Southeast, the Boulder Dam project in the Southwest, and finally, but by no means the least of them, the Columbia River in the Northwest. Each one of these, in each of the four quarters of the United States, will be forever a

[25] *The Roosevelt I Knew,* p. 330.

national yardstick to prevent extortion against the public and to encourage the wider use of that servant of the people—electric power (PPA, 1928–1932, 740).

But, as the third main thought, financial controls over *all* public utilities holding companies were needed in order to do away with the dangers inherent in unregulated monopoly practices. Here selectivity had to yield to general rules imposed in the name of financial morality and freedom.

An immediate chance for the development of the yardstick principle lay at hand at Muscle Shoals on the Tennessee River. After his election, but before his inauguration, Roosevelt traveled through the Tennessee Valley in the company of Senator George W. Norris, the staunchest supporter of the public development of water resources. Speaking in Alabama on January 21, 1933, Roosevelt outlined his vision for the future.

> My friends, I am determined on two things as a result of what I have seen today. The first is to put Muscle Shoals to work. The second is to make of Muscle Shoals a part of an even greater development that will take in all of the magnificent Tennessee River from the mountains of Virginia down to the Ohio and the Gulf.
>
> Muscle Shoals is more today than a mere opportunity for the Federal Government to do a kind turn for the people in one small section of a couple of States. Muscle Shoals gives us the opportunity to accomplish a great purpose for the people of many States and, indeed, for the whole Union. Because there we have an opportunity of setting an example of planning . . . (PPA, 1928–1932, 888).

Planning was to lead to the co-ordination of scattered efforts and to the study of the possibilities offered by the growth of the use of power. Planning did not mean the imposition of a plan. It meant the exploration of ideas and the selection of certain instrumentalities to achieve varying goals. Power, for instance, could be used to achieve other purposes. Power was at the core of so many of the aspects of modern economic life that its proper regulation and exploitation had become a primary function of government.

Roosevelt saw the belief in the public use of power as a twentieth-century complement to the nineteenth-century liberal doctrine of the duty of the state to fix the rules of the game. Most of those rules had been procedural, and they were to be kept. They could be kept better and for a longer period of time if the liberal tradition could be made to accept the addition of certain substantive rules of the game: power, for instance, used to create the fresh opportunities and conditions within which a free democracy will grow. These were the ideas that moved Roosevelt, in his message to Congress, April 10, 1933, to recommend setting up the Tennessee Valley Authority.

> It is clear that the Muscle Shoals development is but a small part of the potential public usefulness of the entire Tennessee River. Such use, if envisioned in its entirety, transcends mere power development; it enters the wide fields of flood control, soil erosion, afforestation, elimination from agricultural use of marginal lands, and distribution and diversification of industry. In short, this power development of war days leads logically to national planning for a complete river watershed involving many States and the future lives and welfare of millions. It touches and gives life to all forms of human concerns (PPA, 1933, 122).

The long-range social objectives were paramount in Roosevelt's mind. In 1934 he said: "TVA is primarily intended to change and improve the standards of living of the people of that valley. Power is . . . a secondary consideration" (PPA, 1934, 467). Speaking in the privacy of the National Emergency Council on December 11, 1934, Roosevelt was even bolder:

> There is a much bigger situation behind the Tennessee Valley Authority. If you will read the message on which the legislation was based you will realize that we are conducting a social experiment that is the first of its kind in the world, as far as I know.[26]

[26] Proceedings of the National Emergency Council, December 11, 1934, p. 30.

Six years later he was openly telling Congress that "it is time that people should understand that power development was only a part—and ultimately only a relatively small part—of a great social and economic experiment in one of our major water sheds" (PPA, 1940, 38).

What mattered were not only the objectives that the integrated policy of the TVA would achieve. The method, too, was equally important, and it was to be as far removed as possible from any forceful imposition of rigid directives that the people affected had not had a chance to consider. Planning in the Valley was to be achieved through the pooling of the energies of the different levels of government to be found in the complex federal structure of the United States, through a fuller realization of that difficult democratic ideal of participation in government by as many citizens as possible. In an address delivered at one of the dams that were rapidly altering the landscape of Tennessee, Roosevelt said, on September 2, 1940:

> These fine changes we see have not come by compulsion—for . . . thousands of townspeople have met together in the common effort. They have debated it and discussed it. Participating in the processes of their Government—State Government, local Government, Federal Government—they have altered the looks of their towns and their counties. They have added fertilizer to the soil. They have improved their industries. No farmer was forced to join this conservation movement. No workman was compelled to labor here under onerous conditions, or for less than a rightful wage. No citizen has lost a single one of these human liberties that we prize so highly in this democracy. This is a demonstration of what a democracy at work can do, of what a people uniting in a war against waste and insecurity can and propose to do (PPA, 1940, 362–63).

One of Roosevelt's ambitions remained, to the very end, that of creating other independent authorities on the pattern of the TVA. He kept coming back to the image he had of the seven great regions into which nature had divided the nation.

"I hope that in time we will get seven different Authorities," he said on November 14, 1944, a few months before his death at a press conference largely devoted to this question (PPA, 1944–1945, 422). Nothing happened then, just as the war had prevented the realization of his earlier proposal of 1937. Nothing has happened since, and the promise of more TVAs remains one of the unfulfilled promises of the New Deal.

As the TVA was to be the prime example of what the direct role of government should be in the use of energy, the elimination of the public utilities holding companies was to achieve the same end in the demonstration of what indirect government intervention could achieve.

As a New Yorker and, therefore, one close to the financial center of the nation, Roosevelt had long been aware of the expanding influence of that typical Wall Street creation, the holding company. Applied to the public utility field and conceived perhaps at first as a mere extension of the idea of the investment trust, it had led to spectacular abuses and was to prove a major source of weakness for the American financial system after 1929.[27] Roosevelt was soon committed to a policy of strict control of these instruments of financial power. As Governor, he had criticized the feeble efforts of the New York legislative bodies to control them: "I wish to emphasize my belief that they are entirely inadequate." The legislature had not touched on a chief cause of inflation of consumer expenditures, that of the excessive capitalization of the holding company. "The speculative interests, which have been magnified in the utility industry by holding company operators, are diametrically opposed to the interests of both legitimate investors and consumers" (PPA, 1928–1932, 248).

These words were to prove prophetic in the years to come. Early in 1935, Roosevelt sent to Congress his legislative plans for the dissolution or sweeping regulation of public utility hold-

[27] See Introduction.

ing companies. The principles inspiring his recommendations were the same. The government will not take over an industry that has been mismanaged and is bankrupt. It will rather seek to recreate the conditions under which an authentically private utility industry can flourish. For the characteristic of the utility holding company system, with its stranglehold over most of the electric, gas, and water industry of the United States, is that it has created monopolistic self-contained areas of private control from which government agencies are in effect excluded and within which the operating and producing companies are exploited to the disadvantage of consumers. Alone to benefit are a few manipulators who have secured control of vast economic empires with exceedingly small investments of their own.

Regulation has small chance of ultimate success against the kind of concentrated wealth and economic power which holding companies have shown the ability to acquire in the utility field. No Government effort can be expected to carry out effective, continuous, and intricate regulation of the kind of private empires within the Nation which the holding company device has proven capable of creating.

Roosevelt felt that the disappearance, within the proposed time limit of five years, "of those utility holding companies which cannot justify themselves as necessary for the functioning of the operating utility companies of the country, is an objective which Congressional leaders I have consulted deem essential to a realistic and farsighted treatment of the evils of public utility holding companies." This was the famous "death sentence," to be carried out in all cases except where a holding company could continue to operate on a geographically integrated basis.

Roosevelt was conscious of increasing conservative attacks against the New Deal in the name of the American tradition, property rights, and the defense of freedom against socialism. But he was quite clear in his mind that the holding company "does not belong to our American tradition of law and business." The violators of the American tradition were the Wall Street lawyers who had invented intricate patterns of corporate control in defiance of the principles of a free economy. Showing his mastery of language and his skill in dealing with the political concepts used by his opponents, Roosevelt counterattacked, suggesting:

> it is time to make an effort to reverse that process of the concentration of power which has made most American citizens, once traditionally independent owners of their own businesses, helplessly dependent for their daily bread upon the favor of a very few, who, by devices such as holding companies have taken for themselves unwarranted economic power. I am against private socialism of concentrated private power as thoroughly as I am against government socialism. The one is equally as dangerous as the other; and destruction of private socialism is utterly essential to avoid government socialism (PPA, 1935, 98–103).

Not only was Roosevelt in the main stream of American history in making this appeal. He was ready to do battle with the weapons he hoped Congress would give him, in order to defeat the monopolists and to create the basis of what Roosevelt's successors were to call a "people's capitalism."

Even more important, he was indicating by his use of the words "private socialism" that he was conscious of the problems that would be raised by the continuing extension of the scope and reach of the private corporation, of the fact that, left to their own devices, the champions of rugged individualism and the mortal verbal foes of socialism would be the first to create their own brand of collectivism, to force on their "subjects" the rigidities and compulsions of socialism. He would not sit idly by and in name of free enterprise allow the free enterprisers to destroy freedom.

THE CONSTITUTIONAL SYSTEM

In briefest summary, Roosevelt's position was one of un-reserved acceptance of the constitutional system inherited from the past, provided that the lack of balance that had been evident for a long time in the distribution of powers could be remedied and that the Constitution itself could be interpreted with the flexibility and courage required by the crisis facing the country.

Roosevelt was both ready and driven by circumstance to accept new tasks for the federal government. If this extension of power seemed to militate against the survival of local and state governments, he felt that the change was due to the necessities of the times. The simple life of the past "has vanished and we are each and all of us, whether we like it or not, parts of a social civilization which ever tends to greater complexity." In spite of this, "self-government we must and shall maintain." Let no one imagine that if state and local governments are unable to act, the federal government shall refrain from action because of a restrictive interpretation of constitutional powers. The processes of government represent a continuum and the United States cannot admit the existence of a no man's land where the influence of government is not felt:

> Whether it be in the crowded tenements of the great cities or on many of the farm lands of the Nation, you and I know that there dwell millions of our fellow human beings who suffer from the kind of poverty that spells undernourishment and under-privilege. If local government, if State Government, after exerting every reasonable effort, are unable to better their conditions, to raise or restore their purchasing power, then surely it would take a foolish and short-sighted man to say that it is no concern of the national Government itself (PPA, 1936, 201).

In its essential aspects, Roosevelt's conception of the constitutional system began with strong ideas concerning the role of the Presidency.

In describing his conception of the role of the President, room must first of all be made for his pride in the history of the United States and in the part played by great presidents at decisive moments in that history. As a vice-presidential candidate in the years immediately following the end of World War I, Roosevelt chose the quiet of a New Hampshire village to say:

> As I recall history, most of our great deeds have been brought about by Executive Leaders, by the Presidents who were not tools of Congress but were true leaders of the Nation, who so truly interpreted the needs and wishes of the people that they were supported in their great tasks. Washington would not have led us to victory in the Revolution if he had merely followed the actions or lack of action of the Continental Congress. Lincoln would not have issued the Emancipation Proclamation if he had heeded the leaders of the Senate. Cleveland would not have maintained the Monroe Doctrine in the Venezuela affair if he had first asked the advice of mere party leaders. [Theodore] Roosevelt would not have kept the Government out of the clutches of predatory interests if he had bowed to Mark Hanna and Foraker and Boss Platt.[28]

This was sound history. All great Presidents had exercised their powers to the fullest extent and had not subscribed to the notion that strong executive leadership properly carried out within the constitutional framework was dictatorship. Woodrow Wilson, under whom Roosevelt had served as Assistant Secretary of the Navy, had said in his *Constitutional Government:* "The President is at liberty, both in law and conscience, to be as big a man as he can. His capacity will set the limit. . . . The Constitution bids him speak, and times of

---

[28] Campaign speech in Manchester, New Hampshire, September 13, 1920, *Roosevelt's Selected Speeches,* ed. by Rauch, p. 37.

stress and change must more and more thrust upon him the attitude of originator of policies." [29]

On the eve of his election, Roosevelt told Anne O'Hare McCormick of the *New York Times:*

> The Presidency is not merely an administrative office. That's the least of it. It is more than an engineering job, efficient or inefficient. It is pre-eminently a place of moral leadership. All our great Presidents were leaders of thought at times when certain historic ideas in the life of the nation had to be clarified. . . . The objective now, as I see it, is to put at the head of the nation someone whose interests are not special but general, someone who can understand and treat with the country as a whole.[30]

Later, having twice been given the leadership of the country by the American electorate, Roosevelt added to his general views on the Presidency the particulars experience had shown him were essential. On the President falls the responsibility of recommending national objectives. The primary obligation for determining the general policy of the administration naturally lies with him. The President needs also to have at hand modern and improved tools of executive action, and the administrative machinery of the White House must be modernized (PPA, 1936, 636; 1937, 308; 1938, xxviii).

This vision of the role of the President implied a flexible view of the Constitution: "Our Constitution is so simple and practical that it is possible always to meet extraordinary needs by changes in emphasis and arrangement without loss of essential form" (PPA, 1933, 15). These words of Roosevelt's first inaugural address offer a clue to the nature of the constitutional crisis that began to build up in 1935 and led to the conflict with the Supreme Court. No change in emphasis, no practical

---

[29] P. 70.

[30] *New York Times,* September 11, 1932, quoted in Schlesinger, *The Crisis of the Old Order,* p. 494.

shifting of certain powers to the President, not even, in the end, any broad exercise of the legislative function would be possible under a rigid construction of the Constitution. The Supreme Court provided a final test of Roosevelt's conception of the duties of the modern state and of the meaning of the American Constitution.

The opposition by the Supreme Court to many of the more important New Deal measures had been gathering strength since the beginning of 1935. In January, it had struck down the powers of the President to control the flow of oil in interstate commerce granted to him under the NIRA, as unconstitutional delegation of powers to the Executive. The states were unable to halt the practices that were demoralizing one of the vital economic activities of the country, but the Court felt the President could not, on the basis of the powers given him by Congress, deal with the problem. A little later, the Supreme Court invalidated the Railroad Retirement Act, which provided for the payment of pensions to railroad employees. In a 5 to 4 decision, the Supreme Court refused to recognize that in establishing pension plans for railroad workers the Congress was exercising its commerce powers under the interstate commerce clause. Several other decisions in May of the same year led to the most important—and, it should be noted, unanimous —decision of the Supreme Court invalidating the NIRA on the two fundamental grounds that the legislation contained a purely discretionary and therefore invalid delegation of powers to the President and that the act was based on a loose definition of interstate commerce that failed to discriminate between the direct and indirect aspects of that commerce and therefore intruded upon economic activities that were to be regulated by the states themselves.[31]

At this point Roosevelt expressed his views on the larger

[31] *Panama Refining Co.* v. *Ryan,* 293 U.S. 388; *Railroad Retirement Board* v. *Alton Railroad Company,* 295 U.S. 330; *Schechter Poultry Corp.* v. *United States,* 295 U.S. 495.

problem of the role of the Supreme Court within the framework of constitutional government. At his 209th press conference held on May 31, 1935 (PPA, 1935, 200–222), the
President began by saying that he would outline some of the
central thoughts of the Supreme Court NRA decision as well
as some of the consequences that would flow from it. The
Supreme Court, in its search for the proper constitutional
balance, refused to recognize the nature of the emergency
facing the United States. "Extraordinary conditions do not
create or enlarge constitutional power," the Court had said,
but the President thought otherwise; the emergency of the
Depression was as great as the emergency of war, and some of
the World War I legislative measures had conferred upon the
Executive far greater power over human beings and property
than anything that was done in 1933, Roosevelt said. The Supreme Court had also been distressed by the thought that NRA
codes could be imposed upon an industry if the industry itself failed to agree on a code. Nearly all the codes had been
voluntary ones, and the President could remember only one
that had been imposed—the alcohol code.

The really important thing was the failure of the Court
to redefine the content of federal jurisdiction over interstate
commerce in the light of twentieth-century needs. The Constitution had been written in the "horse-and-buggy age," when
independence and not interdependence was the rule, when fair
business practices had never been discussed, the very words themselves unknown in the vocabulary of the Founding Fathers. The
indirect influences on interstate commerce are so great that
they must be included in any realistic discussion of how it affects
the country's welfare. Yet the Court had quoted with approval
its earlier decisions that described building as a local activity,
as mining, manufacturing, or growing crops. To take a narrow
view of interstate commerce means to deprive the national
government of essential powers over the national economy at

the point where the tensions and the issues of modern life really arise. It is hopeless to believe that in the great industries of oil, coal, steel, the states can alone remedy serious crisis conditions.

With the NRA decision, the Supreme Court was casting grave doubts over other important aspects of the New Deal. It raises doubts about the Securities Act of 1933, since the activities of the stock exchange can be said to take place in one building in one city. It also undermines the validity of the Agricultural Adjustment Act, for the raising of crops is a local affair. The issue is not a partisan one:

> Don't call it right or left; that is just first-year high-school language, just about. It is not right or left—it is a question for national decision on a very important problem. We are the only Nation of the world that has not solved that question. We have been relegated to the horse-and-buggy definition of interstate commerce.

The entire statement is a reflective and deeply felt analysis of the problem of the responsibilities of government, undertaken by a strong political leader, conscious of his power but determined to stay within the constitutional tradition, a leader faced by the baffling obstacle created by a judicial interpretation of the Constitution not in harmony either with the history or with the current predicament of the country. Looking beyond the Schechter case, Roosevelt saw increasing difficulties arising from it and threatening his entire program of government. His duty, he felt, was to inform the country of the terms of the issue, and not to run away from it. The problem will have to be solved: "I don't mean this summer or winter or next fall, but over a period, perhaps, of five years or ten years we have got to decide: whether we are going to relegate to the forty-eight states practically all control over economic conditions." [32]

[32] This moderate and wise statement was described by the *New York*

Roosevelt's anticipation of the future trend of Supreme Court decisions was quickly fulfilled. On January 6, 1936, the Court declared the Agricultural Adjustment program unconstitutional. The Court held that the AAA processing taxes were void because they were to be used to support a system of federal regulation of agriculture which was outside of the powers that the Constitution had delegated to the Congress. The Court held, too, that the clause in the federal Constitution "to provide for the general welfare" was not an independent grant of power but was linked to taxation. Finally, subsidies paid to farmers who voluntarily agreed to reduce crops were coercive in character. The minority of three dissenting justices characterized the majority opinion as a "tortured construction of the Constitution." In May, 1936, the Court, again in a 6 to 3 decision, set aside congressional legislation concerning the coal industry (which had provided for price-fixing, minimum wages, and other conditions of work), on the ground that coal mining was a purely local matter. Finally, in what must have appeared to Roosevelt the supreme irony, in June, 1936, the Supreme Court denied to the state of New York the power of doing some of the very things that the same Court had already denied to the federal government. In a 5 to 4 decision, the Court nullified a New York statute fixing minimum-wage standards for women in industry.[33]

As Roosevelt comments:

Since the Court had already held that the federal government could not provide for such minimum wages, there seemed to be a complete "no-man's land," in which no power in government could protect laboring women from the oppressive sweatshop wage scales which had been traditionally forced upon them in the past.

Times of June 1, 1935, as an "imprudent speech," betraying "pique" and "bitterness," "temper" and "hopelessness."

[33] *United States* v. *Butler,* 297 U.S. 1; *Carter* v. *Carter Coal Co.,* 298 U.S. 238; *Morehead* v. *New York, ex rel. Tipaldo,* 298 U.S. 587.

The language of the opinion was so broad and inclusive, that it seemed hopeless for any state to try legislation of this kind in any form.

By June, 1936, the Congressional program, which had pulled the nation out of despair, had been fairly completely undermined. What was worse, the language and temper of the decisions indicated little hope for the future. Apparently Marshall's conception of our Constitution as a flexible instrument—adequate for all times, and, therefore, able to adjust itself as the new needs of new generations arose—had been repudiated. Apparently the physical conditions of 1787 in farming, labor, manufacturing, mining, industry, and finance were still to be yardsticks of legal power for dealing with the wholly different world of one hundred and fifty years later. Those of us who had been taught by the great exponents of the Constitution that it contained enduring principles of wisdom and justice which could be applied to any new set of conditions, had apparently been listening to false prophets (PPA, 1937, lvii, Introduction written in 1941).

Roosevelt spent the second half of 1936 pondering a variety of plans with which to meet the emergency created by the Supreme Court. That it was a serious emergency he had no doubt, and his concept of executive leadership made it equally clear he would have to do something about it. His concern was increased because sooner or later the Supreme Court would have had to rule on a number of other New Deal measures—the Social Security Act, the National Labor Relations Act, the Public Utilities Holding Companies Act. He felt that "to stand still was to invite disaster." The Supreme Court could declare unconstitutional the New Deal legislation; still the problems which had prompted the legislation would have to be faced.

Early in 1937, after his triumphant victory at the polls in 1936, he was ready. In his message to Congress of January 6, he opened the debate by saying that the Constitution of the United States was a document with which little fault could be found, and that what was needed was chiefly its enlightened interpretation so that it could be used "as an instrument of progress, and not as a device for prevention of action." He quoted Edmund Randolph, a member of the 1787 Constitutional Convention in Philadelphia, who said that it was the purpose of the Convention to write a constitution that would deal with essential principles only, "lest the operation of government should be clogged by rendering those provisions permanent and unalterable which ought to be accommodated to times and events." The country could not permit a "prolonged failure to bring legislative and judicial action into closer harmony. Means must be found to adapt our legal forms and our judicial interpretation to the actual present national needs of the largest progressive democracy in the modern world. . . . We do not ask the Courts to call non-existent powers into being, but we have a right to expect that conceded powers or those legitimately implied shall be made effective instruments for the common good" (PPA, 1936, 639–41). Again this was a moderate statement, deeply imbued with a sense of history and of respect for the spirit of the Constitution. But it was at the same time a firm restatement of the way in which constitutionalism had to be made to work.

The message gave no hint of what the President planned. Light came less than a month later, on February 5, 1937, when a special message to Congress called for a general reorganization of the judicial branch of the federal government. The real purpose was hidden behind the alleged primary purpose of helping an overburdened judiciary to meet the increasing pressures laid upon it. The plan was a complex and detailed one, much of it of no interest here. Its core, however, was to be found in this recommendation:

> I, therefore, earnestly recommend that the necessity of an increase in the number of judges be supplied by legislation providing for the appointment of additional judges in all federal courts, without exception, where there are incumbent judges of

retirement age who do not choose to retire or to resign. If an elder judge is not in fact incapacitated, only good can come from the presence of an additional judge in the crowded state of the dockets; if the capacity of an elder judge is in fact impaired, the appointment of an additional judge is indispensable (PPA, 1937, 55–56).

In practice this would have meant the appointment of several new judges to the Supreme Court bench. With Roosevelt making the appointments, the anti-New Deal majority would have been broken) Roosevelt concealed this real purpose by speaking of the incapacity of elderly justices, who should, in their enfeebled condition, be helped along by younger and more vigorous ones. The truth, of course, was that the conservative majority of the Supreme Court, well represented by McReynolds and Van Devanter, was far from being feeble and incapacitated. It was made up of hard-working justices, skillfully battling for the defense of their own conception of the Constitution. Roosevelt did not want to increase the output of the Supreme Court; he wanted to alter the substance of its thinking.

The public storm aroused by Roosevelt's proposals, which were quickly seen for what they were, was overwhelming. The warmth of the reaction showed a strong attachment to the existing formal structure of the Supreme Court. Its "packing" would have done violence to a tradition that had to be respected, even though a majority of the people was in favor of the goals sought by Roosevelt and denied by the Supreme Court. Here was one of the problems of constitutional democracy: the cleavage between the legitimate aspirations of a people burdened by the weaknesses of its economic system, and the regard that must be kept alive for the forms and procedures of strongly cherished institutions. The people wanted Roosevelt to give them the cake, but they sided with the Supreme Court which refused to allow it to be baked.

Roosevelt remained unperturbed on the surface and got ready to do battle. The American government could not continue to be paralyzed in its future planning, he told a Democratic victory dinner of March 4, 1937:

> I defy anyone to read the opinions concerning AAA, the Railroad Retirement Act, the National Recovery Act, the Guffey Coal Act, and the New York Minimum Wage Law, and tell us exactly what, if anything, we can do for the industrial worker in this session of the Congress with any reasonable certainty that what we do will not be nullified as unconstitutional (PPA, 1937, 119).

He saw the entire New Deal threatened by the refusal of the courts to sanction it.

> The language of the decisions already rendered and the widespread refusal to obey law incited by the attitude of the courts, create doubts and difficulties for almost everything else for which we have promised to fight—help for the crippled, for the blind, for the mothers—insurance for the unemployed—security for the aged —protection of the consumer against monopoly and speculation— protection of the investor—the wiping out of slums—cheaper electricity for the homes and on the farms of America. You and I owe it to ourselves individually, as a party, and as a Nation to remove those doubts and difficulties (PPA, 1937, 120).

More than that, he saw a threat to the entire democratic way of life as a result of the stubbornness of the Supreme Court in defending obsolescent constitutional interpretations. Decisive values of freedom were at stake, and the United States could not forget the experience of other countries suffering from communism or dictatorship:

> We do not deny that the methods of the challengers—whether they be called "communistic" or "dictatorial" or "military"—have obtained for many who live under them material things they did not obtain under democracies which they had failed to make function. Unemployment has been lessened, even though the cause is a mad manufacturing of armaments. Order prevails, even though maintained by fear, at the expense of liberty and individual rights. So their leaders laugh at all constitutions, predict the copying of their own methods, and prophesy the early end of democracy throughout the world (PPA, 1937, 360).

The United States was fortunate in its system of government, because the Constitution used specific language when dealing with "eternal verities, unchangeable by time and circumstance," as in the Bill of Rights. When the Founding Fathers

> . . . considered the fundamental powers of the new national government they used generality, implication and statement of mere objectives, as intentional phrases which flexible statesmanship of the future, within the Constitution, could adapt to time and circumstance. For instance, the framers used broad and general language capable of meeting evolution and change when they referred to commerce between the States, the taxing power and the general welfare (PPA, 1937, 363).

As the debate unfolded, it became obvious that Roosevelt was using the opportunity to seek clarification of much larger problems on freedom, dictatorship, and the Constitution. His words to the country on the subject of the Supreme Court contrasted sharply with his words to the Congress. The cunning, indirect, and partially concealed approach was discarded in favor of a direct confrontation of basic issues, of an appeal to the origins, and of a sober warning about the dangers of the present. This proved to be a winning technique, just as that of his message to Congress proved to be a losing one.

The Supreme Court's position began to undergo a "seachange." The "odd man" on the Court's bench shifted his views, and what had been a 5 to 4 majority against the New Deal became a 5 to 4 majority for the New Deal. Though Roosevelt lost the battle of the Congress, for his judicial reform plan had to be abandoned, he won the war. The Supreme Court, beginning with a decision issued on March 29, 1937, not even two months after F.D.R.'s message, completely reversed itself on the question of the rights of the states to fix minimum wages for women. The freedom of contract which barely a year earlier the Court had said prevented any kind of government interference in the establishment of wages, now was defined as "liberty in a social organization which requires the protection of law against the evils which menace the health, safety, morals and welfare of the people." [34]

Well could Roosevelt in a lengthy introduction written on June 3, 1941, to the 1937 volume of his *Public Papers* (PPA, 1937, xlvii–lxxii), claim victory for the New Deal. He lists the many decisive opinions of the Supreme Court during 1937 which represented a historic change in the Court's philosophy, and this without the appointment or the resignation of a single justice. The Court had sustained the National Labor Relations Act, something it could have refused to do on the basis of the Schechter decision on the NRA. The Court had found that labor disputes and strikes could affect interstate commerce and could therefore be regulated by federal action. In addition, before the 1937 court term was over, the Social Security Act had been validated, on the ground that unemployment and old-age dependency were matters of federal concern.[35] The accuracy of Roosevelt's conviction that "it would be a little naive to refuse to recognize some connection between these 1937 decisions and the Supreme Court fight," must be accepted by any unbiased observer.

The new trend continued. Writing in 1941, Roosevelt could say that the Court "has given continuous and consistent approval to the policies of government action which have motivated most of the reform measures of the New Deal." Indeed, the "retreat of the Court," in the words of Robert H. Jackson, was complete.

Twenty years after it began, no visible alterations in the lines of the retreat can be detected. Surely the Court fight of 1937 was not alone responsible for the change, and not even Roosevelt made that claim. The issue was broader. The elections

[34] *West Coast Hotel* v. *Parrish,* 300 U.S. 379 (1937).
[35] Cf. Chapter IV, for a detailed discussion of the "constitutional revolution" of 1937.

of 1936 had much to do with the soul-searching of Justice Roberts, the "odd man" of the old majority. The Court would perhaps have soon realized the trap into which it had fallen and the impossibility of maintaining for long its fixed positions. Of course, the elections of 1936 revolved largely around the personality of Roosevelt and the political philosophy of the New Deal. Their outcome and their meaning could not be lost—even on the lonely men at the apex of the American constitutional pyramid.

From a historic point of view, and in weighing the role of Franklin D. Roosevelt in the process of evolution of American society, the Supreme Court struggle is both an important and a decisive event. It is important, because of its part in bringing about a fresh set of constitutional interpretations. It is altogether probable that without Roosevelt's Supreme Court plan the process of adjusting the doctrines of the Court to the needs of the country would have been more protracted and painful and likely to lead to increased domestic difficulties.

It is decisive, because it gives the full measure of the man at the center of the Roosevelt Revolution. It was a courageous act, consistent with Roosevelt's beliefs and with his views on the pattern of growth of the American government, and in keeping as well with his convictions concerning the risks of democracy in a world of totalitarianism.

With it, we can leave Roosevelt, his somber warnings and his lifting promises, and turn from the broad issues that have been discussed so far to the specific narrative of the new tools of government and of the new men, of the dismantling and the rebuilding, of the functioning of institutions and of the social changes—the stuff of the Roosevelt Revolution and the elements that give it meaning.

3

New Tools
for the New State

THE PRESIDENCY

In his book, *A Citizen Looks at Congress,* Dean Acheson, a former Secretary of State and himself a model of the administrator and public servant brought to the fore by the New Deal, reminds us of the changing views on the role of the President in the American system of government held by one of the great American presidents, Woodrow Wilson.

Contemplating the American political scene in 1884, Wilson concluded then that the Congress was bound to become the dominant force in the federal system, since the Presidency had "fallen from its first estate of dignity" and stood silent in the shadow of congressional power. By 1900, Wilson began to change his mind. In the preface to a new edition of his *Congressional Government,* he shows his awareness of the growth of the Presidency as a result of the Spanish-American War. Due to the increasing weight of foreign affairs, the President now occupied the center of the stage:

> Much the most important change to be noticed is the result of the war with Spain upon the lodgment and exercise of power within our federal system: the greatly increased power and opportunity for constructive statesmanship given the President. . . . When foreign affairs play a prominent part in the politics and policy of a nation, its Executive must of necessity be its guide: must utter every initial judgment, take every first step of action,

119

supply the information upon which it is to act, suggest and in large measure control its conduct. The President of the United States is now, of course, at the front of affairs, as no president, except Lincoln, has been since the first quarter of the nineteenth century, when the foreign relations of the new nation had first to be adjusted. There is no trouble now about getting the President's speeches printed and read, every word. Upon his choice, his character, his experience hang some of the most weighty issues of the future.

By 1908, in his *Constitutional Government,* Wilson could not ignore the presence in the White House of Theodore Roosevelt. The Presidency had become the vital center in the nation's affairs. The President represented the interests of the entire community and his was the conscience of the whole country:

> His is the only national voice in affairs. Let him once win the admiration and confidence of the country, and no other single force can withstand him, no combination of forces will easily over-power him. His position takes the imagination of the country. He is the representative of no constituency, but of the whole people. When he speaks in his true character, he speaks for no special interest. If he rightly interpret the national thought and boldly insist upon it, he is irresistible; and the country never feels the zest of action so much as when its President is of such insight and calibre.[1]

By 1913, Woodrow Wilson himself had moved to the White House, in a position to show what could be done to use the Presidency as a modern tool of government. His demonstration was striking proof that he knew how to interpret the powers of the President and how to use them effectively. This was true of his first administration, before the entry of the United States into World War I, when Wilson's major concerns were in the domestic field. It was also true later, during the war

---

[1] See the entire second chapter, "The President," in Dean Acheson, *A Citizen Looks at Congress,* New York, 1957, pp. 47–60. For the "history and analysis of practice and opinion," Edward S. Corwin, *The President, Office and Powers, 1787–1957,* New York, 4th ed., 1957, remains the indispensable work.

and until the signing of the peace treaties. The conflict with the Senate over the Treaty of Versailles and the League of Nations Covenant dealt a bitter blow to Wilson's aspirations and programs and also to the position of the President. For Wilson's defeat toward the end of his second term not only played havoc with the foreign policy of the United States but also helped to incline people to the belief that it was best for America to see the powers of the President reduced and those of the Congress enhanced. It is certain that the twelve years from 1920 to 1932 saw a wasting in the power of the American government as the influence of the President faded and as the Congress was unable to replace it.

Coming to power after such a long lapse of presidential power, Franklin D. Roosevelt can be called the creator of the modern Presidency.[2] Taking an office which lay as a useless ruin in the midst of the most severe crisis the American government had seen since the Civil War, he made it into a most effective and at the same time responsible instrument of executive power. And since the powers and privileges and responsibilities that he did gather around the White House have remained there, one can speak of the permanent nature of the transformation wrought by Roosevelt.

In the years after 1952, the occupant of the White House has not seemed anxious to exercise fully all of the powers that have been placed at his disposal. Time and again, General Eisenhower has appeared reluctant to follow in the path marked by his two predecessors. This is, in some way, an understandable attitude, for in a democracy a change in government must signify to some extent a change in policy. And since most policy of the twenty years from 1932 to 1952 had borne the imprint

[2] Clinton Rossiter, *The American Presidency,* New York, 1956, p. 119: "Roosevelt's influence on the Presidency was tremendous. Only Washington, who made the office and Jackson who remade it, did more than he to raise it to its present condition of strength, dignity, and independence."

of the White House, change could properly mean a lightening of the sharply etched outlines of that imprint. But it is unlikely that present and future presidents will refuse—in the final showdown—to do what the modern President has to do. No permanent return to the past, no substantial weakening of the powers of the President are possible, without risking the survival and the stability of the republic. It is hardly conceivable to think of a President prepared to take that risk. In any case, the performance of the American Executive Office will be measured in the future largely against the standards established from 1932 to 1952 by both Roosevelt and Truman. It is well to recall what the principal ones are.

Roosevelt was eminently successful in making of the Presidency the chief source of political leadership and of legislative ideas, in translating into reality from his dominant position the broad views on the community and on the Constitution whose examination has just been concluded.

The Congress was not regarded by Roosevelt as a distant and perhaps superior entity, to be regarded with awe. It was a constitutional branch of the federal system to be brought into immediate contact with the Executive and into substantial concurrence with the views on the legislative needs of the country, as identified and defined by the Executive.

Roosevelt used startlingly different techniques in his dealings with Congress. He resorted to personal appearance to deliver the more important messages, so as to give physical reality to the abstract idea of Presidential leadership. He played up the elements of drama and contrast that were present in such abundance in the events of those years. By singling out one objective for separate treatment in a special message, he facilitated the concentration of public attention on the issue he had chosen, and made it more difficult for Congress to avoid its responsibilities.

His pressure on Congress was relentless. It was the friendly pressure of the master politician, exercised in intimate and repeated meetings, singly or collectively, with important members of Congress. It was the pressure of the manipulator of public funds and the pork barrel who knew in a thousand practical ways how to keep the legislators happy and how to obtain at the same time what he wanted. It was the "shock" pressure exercised through a direct appeal to the people over the heads of the members of Congress.

The people could be reached, apart from the press conference, through the "fireside chat," used by Roosevelt to inform the country of the thinking of the White House on important policy matters, and to clarify public opinion before going to Congress with specific legislative recommendations. In the twentieth century we have often seen the exploitation of mass-communication technology by political leaders as either the harbinger or the evidence of dictatorship. But during the New Deal, the fireside chat came to be accepted as a proper, if new, exercise of presidential influence justified by the serious conditions of the times, and not as a maneuver designed to facilitate the carrying out of unconstitutional goals. It served the purpose of asserting the primary role of the President in the order of American institutions and of giving him a platform from which could be presented the problems before the people and the plans for legislative action.

Nor did the advance of the Presidency during the Roosevelt administration translate itself into a weakening of the Congress. It will be hard for the historian of the future to speak lightly of the Congresses that sat between 1932 and 1952 and that approved, and often improved, the basic program of the New Deal. The truth of the matter is that the growth of the Presidency was accompanied by a similar growth in the stature of the Congress as a parliamentary body. Without the assertion of the powers of a strong executive, the Congress itself could not have survived, but Roosevelt never wished to deny its basic functions.

This was true even when the President applied an almost intolerably brutal pressure on a recalcitrant Congress. One classical example is to be found in his wartime message on price controls, which amounted in effect to an ultimatum:

> I ask the Congress to pass legislation under which the President would be specifically authorized to stabilize the cost of living, including the prices of all farm commodities. The purpose should be to hold farm prices at parity, or at levels of a recent date, whichever is higher.
>
> I ask the Congress to take this action by the first of October. Inaction on your part by that date will leave me with an inescapable responsibility to the people of this country to see to it that the war effort is no longer imperiled by threat of economic chaos.
>
> In the event that the Congress should fail to act, and act adequately, I shall accept the responsibility, and I will act.
>
> At the same time that farm prices are stabilized, wages can and will be stabilized also. This I will do.
>
> The President has the powers, under the Constitution and under Congressional Acts, to take measures necessary to avert a disaster which would interfere with the winning of the war.
>
> I have given the most thoughtful consideration to meeting this issue without further reference to the Congress. I have determined, however, on this vital matter to consult with the Congress.
>
> There may be those who will say that, if the situation is as grave as I have stated it to be, I should use my powers and act now. I can only say that I have approached this problem from every angle, and that I have decided that the course of conduct which I am following in this case is consistent with my sense of responsibility as President in time of war, and with my deep and unalterable devotion to the processes of democracy.[3]

The fact that the message was delivered during the war is not the most significant part of it in trying to understand the

---

[3] PPA, 1942, 364. See Rossiter's comments, *op. cit.*, pp. 115–16; and also Edward S. Corwin and Louis W. Koenig, *The Presidency Today,* New York, 1956, pp. 57–59.

legislative methods of President Roosevelt. The important themes are those of urgency (the message was sent on September 7 and the ultimatum it contained expired twenty-three days later), of the reality of the presidential powers which the President was determined to use, and of the requirements of the democratic process. Roosevelt's ability to exploit in varying combinations these appeals to speed, which was of the essence of adequate government action, to the central position of the Executive in the modern state, to the job of rescuing democracy from the temporizing and uncertainties which appeared to beset it everywhere—in this is the explanation of his repeated triumphs over the confused counsels of legislators. On balance, Roosevelt had his way in all major legislative issues and even where he failed in his immediate objective, as in his attempted reorganization of the Supreme Court, he got the substance of what he wanted just the same.

The New Deal legislative approach pioneered by Roosevelt was continued, though not so successfully, by Truman in the seven years of his Presidency, from 1945 to 1952. Truman's legislative balance sheet is an impressive one because of his sustained effort to take the initiative and to fight hard for the kind of legislative action he wanted.[4] Both Roosevelt and Truman proved, to the general benefit of the country, that legislation is not the business of legislative bodies alone. It is

---

[4] On Truman's legislative record, Richard E. Neustadt has this to say: "In the first place, it is clear that Truman managed to obtain from Congress means for modernizing, bringing up to date, a number of outstanding New Deal landmarks in social welfare and economic development among them: social security, minimum wages, public health and housing; farm price supports, rural electrification, soil conservation, reclamation, flood control and public power. Not all of these were strictly New Deal innovations, but all gained either life or impetus from Roosevelt in the thirties. And in the new circumstances of the post-war forties they were renewed, elaborated, enlarged upon, by legislative action urged in Truman's Fair Deal program; even their underlying rationale nailed down in law by the Employment Act of 1946." ("Congress and the Fair Deal: A Legislative Balance Sheet," *Public Policy*, vol. v, 1954, pp. 378–79.)

also very much, and in the first place, the business of the Executive.

What Roosevelt and Truman did in revitalizing the Presidency as the fountainhead of legislative ideas and as the spearhead of executive pressure on the Congress, is only part of the story. Democratic government needs complicated instruments of administration to carry out the legislative measures that have been entered in the statute books. The American Constitution vests in the President the executive power and asks him to ensure the faithful execution of the laws. This has become an immense burden in the twentieth century. But while the Constitution is clear on the President's responsibilities, no effective administrative machinery under the President's command existed when Roosevelt was elected. This machinery was to a large extent created by Roosevelt with his Executive Order 8248 of September 8, 1939.[5]

The immediate result of the Executive Order was to give the President an enlarged staff including, for the first time, a number of administrative assistants who, endowed with a "passion for anonymity," furnished the unseen arms and brains of the President.

In the second place, as a result of the 1939 Executive Order, the Bureau of the Budget was made part of the Office of the President. With a staff of only 430 employees in 1955, the Bureau of the Budget became under Roosevelt and Truman the central agency for the planning of the national accounts of the country.

When that capstone of the New Deal philosophy, the Employment Act of 1946, was passed by the Congress, the only

---

[5] This Executive Order has been described by Luther Gulick, a member of the Presidential Committee on Administrative Management, appointed by the President in 1936 to look into the problem of the adequacy of the President's office, as a "nearly unnoticed but none the less epoch-making event in the history of American institutions." Cf. Rossiter, *op. cit.,* pp. 99ff.

place where the Council of Economic Advisers created under the Act could legitimately be sheltered was the White House, for the President had by then become the co-ordinator and the leader of federal economic policies; the instruments to be used in the future to give direction to those policies could not be placed at the disposal of anybody else.

When the National Security Council was established in 1947 "to advise the President with respect to the integration of domestic, foreign and military policies relating to the national security," it too became part of the Executive Office of the President. Finally, both the Office of Defense Mobilization (created in 1953) and the Central Intelligence Agency belong to the Executive Office.

Thus we find in the White House a vast accumulation of new tools of government and a whole range of fresh responsibilities that have since 1933 become part and parcel of the American system. The powers are there. The agencies that are needed for their exercise have been established.

Some might say that the Roosevelt Revolution has made of the President the prisoner and victim of an office that now exceeds in its scope the capacity of any single person. It is certain that no President can hope to escape today from the performance of the duties which have been turned over to him. His constitutional mandate has acquired much clearer and better defined contours. His burdens are infinitely greater. He is the visible embodiment of the tragic nature of democratic government today.

Let us pause to consider the Employment Act of 1946 and what it seeks to do. The Act is important for two reasons: it sets forth the responsibility of the federal government for the economic welfare of the country, and it specifically makes the President of the United States the chief agent of that welfare.

The Act's initial statement of purpose is carefully qualified. The recital of provisos is detailed. The implementation of the

Act must be consistent with the other obligations of the federal government. The views of industry, agriculture, and labor, as well as of state and local governments, must be taken into account. The aim of fostering free and competitive enterprise is kept in sight. The government will not upset the economic applecart and will make no move to take over private industry, nor in any way do violence to the prevailing relationship of interests, both private and public.

Once these conditions are remembered, the ultimate obligation of the government under the Act emerges as a continuing duty to use all practicable means for the purpose of creating and maintaining conditions under which those willing, able, and seeking to work will be afforded useful employment opportunities and to promote maximum employment, production, and purchasing power. These are far-reaching, if generalized, goals. They are more important as an acceptance of responsibility than as a precise statement of economic policy. What we have here is a declaration of intent, pledging the federal government, for the sake of the general welfare, to sustain the highest level of economic activity so that no member of American society shall go without work.

Many will consider such language a more prudent and realistic declaration of intention than the abstract "right to work" commitments found in postwar European Bills of Rights. It promises economic policies on the part of the federal government that will seek the attainment of the objectives of the Act. It identifies the federal government with the promotion of production and of full employment as required by the general welfare. It is the final repudiation of the views so stubbornly maintained by Hoover, who, even as he was preparing to leave the White House, kept repeating that the deepening crisis was brought about by the fear of what the New Deal might do to private enterprise and to the American economy.

The Act itself in its final declaration of policy flatly commits the government to the promotion of maximum employment and production without reference to a free competitive enterprise system. And it is quite likely that when any intervention of the federal government will take place, it will be either because private enterprise will have failed in the particular instance or because the question of private enterprise itself will be irrelevant. We live in dangerous times, amid a rapidly changing economy which moves toward relationships and structures whose nature is in effect unknown to us. We can be grateful to legislators who have sanctioned the use of economic machinery which, we must hope, may be useful in times of crisis. Let us not quarrel with them because in doing the right thing— creating the machinery that will help maintain freedom itself— they appear to give initial pride of place to the "free enterprise" system.

The Employment Act goes beyond generalities and looks at the ways in which implementation can be secured. It places the President at the center of the economic stage. Section 3a requires of the President the annual transmission to the Congress of an Economic Report which must embody a review of current conditions in all their aspects, and "a program for carrying out the policy declared in Section 2, together with such recommendations for legislation as he may deem necessary or desirable." The Economic Report cannot limit itself to a more or less theoretical appraisal of the current or foreseeable trends of economic events, but must lead to suggestions for legislative action. Thus the Employment Act has become the source of all major White House recommendations on economic policy since 1946.

The President is not left to his own devices or to scattered and inconsistent advice in arriving at the conclusions reached in the Economic Report. Section 4 of the Act sets up the Council of Economic Advisers as part of the Executive Office of the President. Its three members are chosen by the President even though, as for all major appointments to policy-making positions, the Senate has to consent to the appointments. They must be persons who as a result of experience and attainments are "exceptionally qualified to analyze and interpret economic developments, to appraise programs and activities of the Government in the light of the policy declared in Section 2 . . . to formulate and recommend national economic policy."

The Council, whose total staff now numbers thirty-six, has become the institutionalized economic brain trust of the President. Having for twenty years scoffed at Roosevelt's brain trusts and at the wide-eyed, non-payroll-meeting academicians infesting the White House, the Republicans appointed in 1953 as chairman of the Council of Economic Advisers the top theoretician of them all, Arthur F. Burns, the Columbia University economist. With that appointment, the Employment Act of 1946 asserted itself over the noise of political battle as a guiding force in American government.

It is difficult, even for the most skeptical, to overestimate the importance of the Council and the role it plays in advising the President on economic policy. The very operation of the American government increases the usefulness of the Council, which in other countries might have become just another advisory agency in a welter of shifting, now real, now dead, committees and councils, trying to cope with rapidly changing political leaders.

The President is in the White House for four or, more probably, eight consecutive years. The Council, a very small organization, is housed in his immediate physical proximity. The chairman acquires the habit of intimate and continuous communication with the President. He can exercise a steady influence and impart continuity and co-ordination to the President's thinking. If, as has been true for many of the past twelve years, the chairman of the Council is a man of broad and independent vision, conscious of his burden, there is an obviously great cumulative influence on the President through repeated exchanges on all problems of economic life with a man who can speak with wisdom and a sense of direction.

In his last Economic Report, in January, 1953, President Truman, summing up twenty years of New Deal economic policy, reminded the Congress of the historical roots of the Employment Act:

> The lessons of the past had been particularly compelling in the decade and a half which preceded 1946. These had been years of unprecedented contrast, so far as economic abundance was concerned. On the one hand, there was the stark tragedy of the early thirties, and then the seemingly boundless energies of the early forties. The period had been rich in careful social experimentation and legislative reform; the economic role and responsibilities of the Federal Government had increased enormously. Many of the experiments had been temporary in character, to meet the emergencies of the depression or the extraordinary demands of war. But many of them were developed and improved to become permanent additions to our economic and social fabric.[6]

President Truman, in the same Report of 1953, outlined the three chief purposes he saw in the Act. The first was to achieve better economic policy co-ordination:

> In the thirties, and again during World War II, the economic programs of the Government had become increasingly diverse and complex, and any realistic appraisal indicated that they would remain so. The special pressures which were brought to bear upon public economic policy-making had become more powerful, more numerous, and more confusing. . . . But this growth of complexity had not been matched, especially within the permanent institutions of the Government, by the development of adequate means for gauging whether our farm programs, developmental programs, international trade policies, tax policies, credit policies, business regulatory policies, industrial relations, law, and the rest, were consistent with one another and fitted together into a sensible economic policy for the over-all economy. In the thinking of Con-

[6] *The Economic Report of the President,* Washington, January, 1953, p. 8.

gressmen from particular sections and on particular committees, and of leading administrators with specialized responsibilities, the whole too often was lost in preoccupation with the parts.

The second purpose was to prevent depressions:

The minds of most of us in 1946 were still deeply etched with the memory of the winter of 1932–33, when about 15 million American workers, or about 30 per cent of the total civilian labor force, had no jobs; when industrial production was only half what it had been in 1929 and the total output of the economy only about two-thirds; when business was deep in the red; when farm prices and incomes had dropped out of sight; and when banks were collapsing by the hundreds. It has been calculated that the depression cost us some 600 billion dollars of output, measured in 1952 prices, or 3½ times everything we produced in 1929. . . . The Employment Act stands as a pledge on the part of the people voiced through their laws that never again shall any such sacrifice be laid on the altar of "natural economic forces." In the bigger economy we now have, a disaster of anywhere near the same proportions could mean some 20 millions of our workers walking the streets.

The third purpose was described by Truman as follows:

[the] positive resolution of a great people, not simply to avoid pitfalls, but to maintain as a matter of continuing policy a full, bountiful, and growing economy, for themselves, for their children, and as a standard and inspiration toward the freedom and welfare of all peoples—and to do this in full peace no less than in limited war.

President Truman left no doubt of his belief in the value of the Act in providing a central point of reference and in giving coherence to his entire economic program. Similarly, President Eisenhower used his 1957 Economic Report to advance not fewer than forty-one recommendations to Congress and suggestions to the state and local governments. But certainly the effective ultimate significance of the Employment Act cannot be measured by what the Presidents say about it or by the number of recommendations that are made under it. This can be done least of all during the tenure of Presidents who limit themselves to making recommendations and show no inclination to fight for them.

Much still depends upon the personality of the President, and upon the relative weight he is prepared to give to the Council's views. For the possibility of paralyzing conflict between the Council, the Bureau of the Budget, the Treasury, and the personal friends of the President has, of course, not been ruled out. But much also can be said about the steadying influence of institutions upon even the weakest of men and of the insight that can, perhaps reluctantly, be acquired by constant exposure to sound opinion. More educated and dispassionate analyses of United States economic problems have been coming from Washington in recent years, and executive action has been more courageous and better informed.

Though it would be quite wrong to say the possibility of error, or even of inaction, has been eliminated, it is certain that the reflective brooding on the future economic health of the United States induced by the Employment Act has forced the President, since 1946, to speak with a higher sense of responsibility than before, and has facilitated his backing of unpopular legislation, such as the maintenance of high taxes needed for the security of the country or for the realization of desirable social goals.

The tentative gropings and contradictory attempts of the early New Deal to realize policies that would promote the welfare of the community as against that of particular interests have become less frequent. Deviations from objectively determined lines of policy are more quickly noted and standards are vindicated against attempted destruction. On these grounds, the Employment Act has justified itself and has contributed to the strength of the American Presidency and the American economy.

THE NEW MEN

No revolution can be sustained for long without the fighters to man the barricades. The New Deal was notable for its unusual appeal to public-spirited citizens who made Washington their goal and a share in the renovation of the American government their highest ambition. A career in the federal service became something it had seldom been before, a chance to satisfy the craving for doing and to put forth the exertions that traditionally had been reserved for private endeavors.

From the anonymous presidential assistant, whose duty it was to shun the limelight in order to serve the President of the United States, to the heads of the new regulatory agencies battling the still powerful centers of unregulated financial and industrial power, in the glare of an often unfriendly press, and to the rank and file of the humbler civil servants, the story was the same: to serve the government presented one of the highest measures of satisfaction to which any citizen could aspire. As a result, during the twenty years of the New Deal, Washington saw an assemblage of exceptionally able men.

The phenomenon was a striking and almost novel one for the United States. In America, until the Great Depression, the able young man, who in England was channeled by Cambridge and Oxford into the administrative services, or who in France, after the École Politechnique or the École Normale, began a career in government, entered private business. There was the power, the glory, and the money that would in the end give him a meaningful role in the life of his society. Hence, public service was inadequately staffed, for there was not much purpose in devoting one's career to the formulation of decisions that were of no particular consequence. A weakening federal government had exercised after World War I an ever weaker pull even on the most public-minded of citizens.

All this changed after 1932. Not only because there was a great expansion of government activities, nor even because Washington offered a job to the jobless. What really mattered was that what the government was doing had become a matter of central importance in the life of the community. The New Deal was in a position to exert an irresistible fascination on the generation that had reached maturity during the Great Depression. This was true not only for those who had nothing else to do or who would have, in any case, wished to seek public employment, but for many of those who had never thought of public employment and who would have sought a fulfillment of their ambitions through the usual outlets.

For many intellectuals, for the young students and lawyers, the New Deal represented a critical moment in their lives. It enabled some of them to abandon the dreary and unconvinced flirting with Marxism in which they had engaged and to move toward a participation in a democratic experiment rooted in American soil and conditioned by contemporary American realities. Public service became the alternative to the frustrations and pessimism that were determining the activities of sensitive men of high skills. The New Deal offered a chance for positive action in pursuit of new ideals of community action.

As a result, the rise of the new administrative state took place under the auspices of people many of whom had never before been administrators or did not intend to continue as administrators for the rest of their lives. Washington became a prolonged sabbatical for academicians, with their innocent approach to the handling of public affairs. To those members of the merchant, banking, and business classes who did not consider the wealthy and aristocratic Roosevelt of Hyde Park a traitor, it also offered a chance to demonstrate what they could do. And it commanded the services of the thousands of young men who simply wanted to serve.

The convergence on Washington of so many people with

contrasting backgrounds and different purposes, even though united by their devotion to what they thought were the emerging goals of the New Deal, prevented the creation of the much-dreaded "bureaucratic state." The jollity and confusion, the excitement and the experimentation, were too great to allow ossification to set in. Also, in many instances, the world beyond was not forgotten. The high turnover of administrators in Washington remained a characteristic of the period. World War II, with its "dollar-a-year men," had something to do with it. But, even apart from the war, the record is full of examples of civil servants who, having served for a few years, resigned to engage in other activities in the judicial branch, in the universities, in the legal profession, or more recently, in private business.

The consequences of this continuous turmoil have not been all bad, for the constant circulation of the administrative elite can build a useful network of closer links between government and society. There are many advantages—in a highly industrialized society, one in which the decisions of the business community will inevitably have large repercussions no matter how strong the hand of government—in a process that will staff the top managerial ranks of corporations with a good sprinkling of retired public administrators. For if it is true that, with some exceptions from the fields of technology, businessmen can contribute little or nothing to the difficult art of government, good public servants can contribute a great deal to the operation of business firms.

Of course the system will work only if, once a good public servant is lost, another quite as good can replace him. The risks are minimized during a period of high tension, such as that of the New Deal, by continued public interest in what the government is doing. A routine and uninspired administration will find it burdensome to meet the difficulties caused by too rapid turnover. It is not by accident that this has been increasingly true since 1953.

As the New Deal progressed, the number of new federal administrative agencies continued to grow. The TVA, the Housing and Home Finance Agency, the Civil Aeronautics Board, the Securities and Exchange Commission, the National Labor Relations Board, the Federal Deposit Insurance Corporation, the Atomic Energy Commission, the Farm Credit Administration, the Export-Import Bank, the Foreign Operations Administration, the Federal Security Agency—all became part of the new administrative state.

Most of them gained powers of discretionary action, for no effective interpretation and execution of often intricate laws was possible without them. The new agencies acquired substantial quasi-legislative powers. In itself, this was of course not a new development, but its impact was all the more acutely felt in the years after 1933, for the new powers were then being applied to far more important and sensitive areas of human affairs. The new agencies obtained powers of investigation and of execution as well. Finally, the agencies were empowered to settle issues brought forth by aggrieved parties, to hear appeals, and to reach decisions affecting large interests. Here the agencies were acting in a quasi-judicial capacity, completing in the minds of the regulated the horrifying image of a triple-headed monster: legislative, executive, and judicial.

Considering the many possibilities for mischief, corruption, tyranny, and obtuse enforcement of the law, the nearly uniformly high standard of performance of the New Deal administrative agencies must remain a source of wonder. Seldom in history have so complex instrumentalities of government acquitted themselves so well and with such a high sense of public duty and propriety. That this was due to the quality of the men responsible for their operation cannot be doubted.

In 1941, well after the end of the heroic period of the New Deal, James Burnham wrote what has since become a widely known book, *The Managerial Revolution*. Burnham had been struck by the consequences of industrialization, the weaknesses of parliamentary democracy, and the rise of totalitarianism. Many countries, the Soviet Union, Italy, Germany, and the United States, were developing certain common traits. In all of them, the traditional forms of government were being replaced by new forms in which the managerial class occupied a central position. What mattered was the fact that the managers and not the owners were the masters of the economic system, rather than the question of the responsibility or irresponsibility of the managers themselves. Because of this, Burnham felt entitled to lump together as examples of the managerial revolution both Roosevelt's New Deal and Stalin's totalitarian communism and forced industrialization.

Burnham's book will be discussed here only in terms of its validity as a statement on political life in the middle of the twentieth century. In this context, it would seem that the identification of the New Deal with fascism or communism is untenable. There is a fundamental difference between the managers of a Soviet state trust—who could not in 1941 and still cannot in 1959 be held accountable to anyone for their activities, except to a higher and still less accountable top administrator—and the so-called "managers" of the New Deal administrative state, whose every step was controlled by a personal concern for the rights and interests of the individuals affected and by the existing rules and procedures of the constitutional system itself.

Speaking at Harvard University in 1939, John Foster Dulles, then a mere corporation lawyer, rose to the defense of the new administrative agencies. The solution to alleged abuses was obviously not to do away with the administrative process: "There seems to me little present occasion to assume that because administrative agencies have powers which they may abuse, such agencies should in effect be nullified. Before we adopt such a program we should carefully appraise the self-restraint already evidenced by most administrative tribunals and their evident desire to protect the citizens against abuse." [7]

It was absurd to suggest that the New Deal administrative agencies were tyrannical in the exercise of their powers because those powers could be exercised in discretionary fashion. As Jerome Frank—one of the greatest of the New Deal administrators, and chairman of one of its most sensitive agencies, the Securities and Exchange Commission—pointed out, once the people of the United States had decided that certain important functions until then left in the hands of private citizens or corporations were to be exercised by public agencies, it was inevitable that some of the discretion inherent in private action should be transferred to public action. Once public intervention had become part of the accepted reality of the times, it would have been wrong to deprive it of that flexibility which alone could make a success of it.

The care shown in procedural matters and in safeguarding the right of the interested parties was well exemplified by Jerome Frank's own agency, the Securities and Exchange Commission, which traditionally has been anxious to lean over backwards in its efforts to deal fairly with all concerned. Frank himself has written:

> Because the SEC knows that, in each such case, the administrative process itself is on trial before the upper courts, it is excessively judicial when acting quasi-judicially. And thus an administrative agency which was created, partly in order to expedite action, by reducing the time consumed in court because of the "technicalities" involved in court proceedings, has become more time-consuming than the courts, through fear of rebuke by some courts. . . .

[7] Quoted in Jerome Frank, *If Men Were Angels,* New York, 1942, p. 184.

The writer knows of "disciplinary" cases brought by the Commission before itself, in which all five Commissioners were inclined to believe that the respondent was probably guilty, and yet where they found the respondent not guilty on the ground that the evidence was not sufficiently clear. Speaking solely for himself, the writer is frank to say that, if he had been sitting as a federal district judge, in some of those very cases, he would probably have decided that the defendant was guilty. But he feared that, on appeal, some upper court, distrustful of the combination of prosecutory and quasi-judicial functions in the Commission, might hold the evidence insufficient to justify such a finding, although the same court would probably not do so if a similar finding were made by a district judge on even less evidence. And he was unwilling to risk the damage to the reputation and future efficacy of the SEC which would result from a reversal, since, as already noted, a reversal of an order of an administrative agency is often given a significance not attached to a reversal of a trial court's decision.[8]

The instructions issued in 1938 to the SEC staff underlined the care with which witnesses were to be treated, investigations were to be held, interviews were to be conducted, and prudence was to be exercised in order to avoid any possibility of unjustified damage to those whose activities have been questioned.[9] They offer an outstanding example of the *procedural* preoccupations which the men in charge of the New Deal showed whenever it really mattered. The SEC is also a highly important example of the new type of *substantive* concern of the New Deal. As such it warrants separate and more detailed treatment.

WASHINGTON AND WALL STREET

The Great Depression had found in Wall Street its representative symbol, so the New Deal made of it the object of particu-

---

[8] *Ibid.*, pp. 145–46.
[9] Cf. *ibid.*, pp. 265–66, for excerpts.

larly tender care. There were not only specific abuses and mis-
uses of economic power to be corrected. It was quite likely that
on the Wall Street front a basic test of power would have to be
faced by the American government. The Securities and Exchange Commission was conceived, therefore, as one of the
most powerful and careful devices for the vindication of the
purposes of the new state. The SEC is today entrusted with
the enforcement of a long series of legislative enactments that
became effective over a seven-year period from 1933 to 1940,
as the persistence and the continuity of New Deal reforms in
this field never relented.

In signing the last of these major pieces of legislation on
August 23, 1940, Roosevelt said, in words which render incredibly tenuous the argument that, as a result of the advent
of World War II, an interruption or even a repudiation of the
New Deal occurred:

> As the pressure of international affairs increases, we are ready
> for the emergency because of our vigorous fight to put our domes-
> tic affairs on a true democratic basis. We are cleaning house,
> putting our financial machinery in good order. This program is
> essential, not only because it results in necessary reforms, but for
> the much more important reason that it will enable us to absorb
> the shock of any crisis (PPA, 1940, 334).

The SEC has a dominant jurisdiction in four major areas
of the financial life of the United States.

In the first place, the SEC administers the Securities Act
of 1933, requiring the full disclosure to investors of all essential
facts concerning securities publicly offered for sale. Disclosure
is secured by requiring the issuer to file with the Commission
a registration statement and a prospectus containing all significant information, favorable or unfavorable, about the issuer
and the securities offered for sale. These documents are available
for public inspection as soon as they are filed, and a waiting
period of twenty days is usually required before the securities

can be sold. The Commission can refuse to grant registration if it discovers elements of fraud and deceit in the registration statements during these twenty days. The Commission has the right to send out to the registrant so-called deficiency letters whenever the examination of the registration statement discloses omissions or incomplete statements of central facts. This procedure can lead to the withdrawal or the stopping of the registration. On the other hand, if the registration statement is cleared by the Commission, the clearance does not imply approval or disapproval by the Commission of the securities in question. It merely indicates that the issuer has complied with the full-disclosure requirements of the Act, so that the investor himself is in a good position to measure the risks involved in any purchase of the securities in question. The two chief weapons of the Commission are publicity and the right to stop the issue if adequate disclosure of all the facts is not forthcoming.

The second major area is the administration of the Securities Exchange Act of 1934, regulating the operations of the stock exchanges themselves. The Act is designed to insure the integrity and fairness of trading operations on the organized exchanges and on the over-the-counter market. The Act undertakes to eliminate abuses in security trading. It requires that full information concerning securities that are admitted to trading on a stock exchange shall be made available to the public. It also regulates and limits the use of credit in security dealings. (While the authority to issue the specific rules governing such credit is vested in the Federal Reserve Board, the enforcement of the rules themselves is vested in the Commission.)

Next, the SEC administers the Investment Company Act and the Investment Advisers Act of 1940. The Investment Company Act provides for the registration and regulation of all investment trusts. It requires the disclosure of the investment policies of these companies, prohibits them from changing the nature of their business or their investment policies without the approval of their stockholders, regulates the custody of the company's assets, requires management credit checks to be submitted to security holders for their approval, prohibits transactions between the companies and their officers and directors except with the approval of the Commission.

The Investment Advisers Act requires the registration of those who are engaged for compensation in the business of advising others with respect to securities. The Commission is empowered to deny registration or revoke the registration of any investment adviser who, after notice and opportunity for hearing, is found by the Commission to have a record of misconduct in connection with security transactions or to have made false statements in his application for registration. The Act makes it unlawful for investment advisers to engage in practices which constitute fraud or deceit and requires advisers to disclose the nature of their interest in transactions executed for their clients.

Finally, the SEC administers the Public Utilities Holding Company Act of 1935. This alone would more than justify its existence, since the Act has brought about a permanent readjustment of economic power in one of the vital sectors of American economic life. The record of the Commission in this all-important field will be considered in the next chapter.

The scope and detail of these powers are impressive. Their justification is found in the damage done by the financial community to the American economy and to the American public in the years that preceded the Great Depression. It is found in the scandalous practices uncovered by public investigation of the activities of stockbrokers and stock exchanges. It is found in the instances of outright looting on a massive scale of the assets of investment trusts and other companies whose securities were being sold to a public ignorant of the deceit and fraud practiced with notable imagination and daring.

Until 1932, Wall Street leaders had been in the habit of making extravagant claims for themselves. They had attempted to assume powers that could not properly belong to them and they had identified themselves as the mainstay of an ever-improving level of prosperity and economic growth. When these claims were found to be hollow, and when the power was claimed on behalf of the people of the United States by the new agencies of government of the New Deal, the regulations adopted acquired a severity that was proportional to the gravity of the issue.

Here, perhaps more clearly than anywhere else, did the New Deal assert the primacy of politics over economics, the right of the community to regulate private activities undertaken for purposes of gain, in order to see that the public interest as well as the interest of other private citizens would not be damaged. Even from the point of view of classical liberalism, the setting of the rules of important games is a primary function of public power. In the United States, playing with money, other people's money, had become an exceedingly popular game.

The SEC has, therefore, gained the importance due it in a society in which the industrial revolution and its consequences of corporate and financial power have occupied such a large part. The world image of the United States is one of unparalleled economic might, of a country which in the past has been able to manipulate and multiply productive factors so as to produce the greatest aggregate of industrial production the world has ever seen. The public agency which, at a number of crucial points, has succeeded during the past twenty years in regulating, publicizing, and moralizing the financial activities representing the highest flowering of the American productive system is entitled to advance some proud claims for itself. What has the SEC done?

It has forced the New York Stock Exchange to behave, by liquidating the crooks and by imposing strict rules of conduct which have made subsequent efforts at fraud easier to detect and to limit. Short selling and insiders' manipulations are controlled or forbidden. The New York Stock Exchange itself, even though still a private corporation, is no longer run like a private club. Its governors, moving under the constant glare of the SEC, have become sensitive to the demands of public trust inherent in the activities over which they preside. Operations of the members of the Exchange are closely and continuously watched. The Stock Exchange and all those connected with it are now proud of the moral tenor of their daily lives, but no one can as yet forget their pre-New Deal practices, nor the fact that until 1938 they fought attempts at regulation by the SEC and that their current good conduct is the result both of improved habits and of the ever-present big stick of the SEC.

The SEC has, through its enforcement of margin regulations established by the Federal Reserve Board, introduced an element of responsibility and steadiness in stock-market operations. One of the important causes of the 1929 crash was the excessive stock speculation on credit, which made it possible for financially irresponsible individuals, pushed on by stockbrokers, to operate in Wall Street even though often 90 per cent of the money they used was borrowed. Under the rule of the SEC, there have been times when securities could only be purchased for cash, with no borrowing permitted. For the past ten years, on the average, borrowing has been permitted up to 30 per cent of the value of the securities to be purchased. It is easy to maintain that a free society must include the right to go bankrupt on borrowed money. The argument loses much of its validity when it is applied to millions of amateurs and not to a selected few professionals. The difficulties and requirements of mass democracy are not always those of the aristocratic and liberal societies of the nineteenth century.

The SEC has, up to June 30, 1956, inspected 13,000 registration statements concerning the issue of 120 billion dollars of new securities. Of these, about 1,600 (or about 12 per cent) were withdrawn by the issuer or stopped by the Commission because of failure to comply with the full-disclosure requirements of the law. An overwhelming proportion of new issues of securities sold to the public have in this way been subjected to the scrutiny of the SEC. The evidence shows that the SEC has carried out its function of defense of the public interest with skill and with the major purpose in mind of creating a climate of public confidence that would render the capital market of the United States a smoothly functioning operation.

The SEC regulatory procedures have had another, and perhaps unexpected, consequence. They have re-educated the American corporation, the major issuer of new securities, and made it realize that it would be desirable to go even beyond the legal requirements and give to the investor, in plentiful abundance, all kinds of detail about the business whose financial support was to be solicited. Hence, the average prospectus has become a fascinating source of information about the promoters of the industrial venture it describes, their backgrounds and relationships, their interests, the specific outlook of the particular venture, and the general outlook of the industry as a whole. The public's awareness of the nature and of the risks of the private economic process has been much enlarged and the corporations have in yet another way been brought to underline the element of public trust in their activities. (The new mood is now also reflected in many of the annual reports to stockholders.)

Under the Investment Company Act of 1940 the SEC has now registered nearly four hundred investment companies whose total assets have increased in value from 2.5 to 14 billion dollars in the years between 1941 and 1956. It watches daily and from hour to hour the operations of the stock exchanges. It is not an exaggeration to say that the SEC is acting as the conscience and as the watchdog of the American people in all phases of its financial operations. The pervasive influence of the SEC is easy to notice in the financial world. It dominates the thoughts and the actions of Wall Street. It is the one regulatory commission whose presence is continuously felt in the sphere it regulates. Its powers of exposure, of suspension from trading activities and privileges of both brokers and corporations are so drastic and so feared that they have achieved most of the results that could reasonably have been expected.

In recent years, the New York Stock Exchange has developed the theme of "people's capitalism," considered as its peculiar invention or, conceivably, as the fruit of the natural and unaided evolution of the American economic system itself. In the amusing publicity eagerly used to promote the new gospel, an average American housewife—usually carrying a small baby in her arms and surrounded by the top brass of the Exchange—is pictured purchasing one share of General Motors, the income of which will presumably provide for the university education of the baby. The basic characteristics of the new capitalism are that millions of Americans have become the owners of American business and that they have been able to do so in an atmosphere of shining truth, full confidence, open dealings, and complete equality of rights.

It is, of course, quite true that, particularly since the catastrophe of October, 1929, some notable changes have occurred in the operations of the "capitalistic" system and in the behavior of corporations.[10] But in the shower of optimistic words flowing from Wall Street, two things are ignored as a rule. The first is that no one can fully anticipate the ultimate

[10] See Chapter V.

consequences of this multiplication ad infinitum of the numbers of American stockholders. Wall Street does not seem to have taken into account, even supposing it has heard of it, Schumpeter's prophecy in this respect.[11] Regardless of the validity of Schumpeter's main contention, this kind of "people's capitalism" will be vastly different in its meaning, power, and scope from the kind of capitalism whose image is still fixed in the minds of those who write publicity for Wall Street.

The second is that, quite apart from their intrinsic nature, these developments have come about largely because their acceptance has been forced on a bewildered financial and economic community by Roosevelt's New Deal. By a psychological transfer not unknown in historical experience, those who most vociferously opposed reform have now come to like it; its obvious advantages have benefited not only the community at large but also those immediately affected by it, the corporations and the purveyors of financial services. Nothing appears simpler than claiming credit for a new economy to which they have contributed little or nothing at all, by comparison with the contributions of the political community acting through Washington.

What matters, however, is: the control the American people now have exercised in an atmosphere of freedom and of private initiative over the vast flow of their financial life; a new financial morality now accepted by an advanced industrial society; and the praise of the regulated themselves for the regulators. A sweeping transfer of economic power, as far as the general setting up of the conditions and procedures under which private activities are to be carried out, has taken place— from Wall Street to Washington. And what should be remembered throughout the so-called capitalistic West is this: the

---

[11] See Joseph A. Schumpeter, *Capitalism, Socialism, and Democracy,* New York, 1942, especially part II, "Can Capitalism Survive?", on the radical transformation of capitalism.

United States still stands alone in having accomplished this task so completely.

TAXES

The federal taxation of income, either individual or corporate, is a relatively recent development in the United States. In the first ten years of this century, the total tax receipts of the federal government averaged about 250 million dollars a year, and practically the entire amount came from taxes on tobacco and alcohol. Custom receipts provided another 285 million a year. All other federal revenues were 50 million dollars a year. There were no income taxes on individuals and practically none on corporations.

By 1952, federal revenues had multiplied about a hundred times. Custom revenues had increased from 250 million dollars to nearly 9 billion dollars. The income and corporation taxes, which did not exist half a century earlier, yielded 51 billion dollars. This last figure is the real measure of the extent of the fiscal revolution of the New Deal.

To be sure, the constitutional amendment required to permit the federal government to tax incomes antedates the New Deal by twenty years. Approved in 1913, it was hardly noticed in the beginning by taxing authorities. Some use of it was made during World War I chiefly to tax excess wartime profits. By 1923, income taxes on corporations had declined from 3.2 billion to 900 million, even though the net taxable corporate income had remained unchanged at 8.3 billion dollars. Similarly, income taxes paid by individuals steadily declined in the postwar period.

It is not altogether correct to say that before the Great Depression the rich did not pay taxes. It is nearer the truth to say no one paid taxes. In part, the urge for taxation was not there. More significantly, there was a lack of belief in the social role of taxation. We have to wait for the twenty years from 1933 to 1952 to see the federal income tax develop into a major weapon of government action in fighting the Depression, in waging a successful world war, and in maintaining the prosperity of the postwar period. In this respect, the policy of the New Deal is notable for two reasons.

The first is the vast increase of the obligation to give the federal government, once a year, a complete picture of one's own financial affairs, by filing an income tax return. There is dramatic evidence of the democratization of the income tax in the following figures:

NUMBER OF INDIVIDUAL INCOME TAX RETURNS
(*in millions*)

YEAR	TOTAL RETURNS	RETURNS SHOWING TAXABLE INCOME
1921	6.7	3.6
1925	4.2	2.5
1929	4.0	2.5
1933	3.7	1.7
1936	5.4	2.9
1940	14.7	7.5
1941	25.9	17.6
1945	49.9	42.8
1952	56.0	42.8

When, on March 15, 1952, 56 million taxpayers dutifully filed their income tax returns (with some grumbling, it is true, and even, one may assume, some cheating), visible proof was offered of social solidarity and of the shouldering of a serious financial role by the citizens of the United States in the short period of a generation. Practically no one with any income was exempted from the performance of this duty, and a machinery had been perfected which permitted this huge operation to be carried out once a year with remarkable smoothness. Last among Western nations in the adoption of the income tax, the United States under the New Deal had succeeded in universalizing it and in making of it one of the sharp realities of a democratic community.

The second key principle of the taxation policy of the New Deal has not been the popularly assumed one of "soaking the rich," but rather that of forcing everyone, down to the lower reaches of incomes, to contribute his share.

INCOME TAX PAYMENTS (IN PER CENT OF NET INCOME) FOR MARRIED TAXPAYERS WITH NO DEPENDENTS

YEAR	NET INCOME IN THOUSANDS OF DOLLARS						
	2	3	5	8	10	25	100
1921	—	0.7	2.0	4.6	5.9	11.5	31.2
1929	—	—	0.1	0.3	0.5	3.5	14.9
1934	—	0.3	1.6	3.1	4.2	10.0	30.6
1941	2.1	4.6	7.5	10.9	13.1	27.5	52.7
1945	12.3	15.8	19.5	21.6	25.9	41.2	69.4
1952	8.9	13.3	16.9	19.7	21.0	33.8	56.9

The first comment called for by the table is the downward sweep of the income tax. A married taxpayer with a net income of $2,000 has been paying on the average better than 10 per cent in federal income taxes in the last twelve years. This is a substantial amount considering how little $2,000 a year really means in actual purchasing terms, given the complexities of American life. Thus, even those Americans living close to the subsistence level have to contribute an important amount of their earnings to public purposes. Looking at the same problem in a different way, the 56 million individual income tax returns of 1952 declared an adjusted gross income of 216 billion dollars. Of this total less than 20 billion were nontaxable. The balance—better than 90 per cent of the income—was subject to some form of taxation. Even the 2,760,000 taxpayers with an income between $1,000 and $1,500 had to pay 271 million dollars in taxes, equal to about 8 per cent of their total declared income.

The second comment should be that, once World War II fiscal pressures started to decline and some reductions in the income tax rates became possible and were in fact adopted, the cuts were relatively greater in the $25,000 income bracket (a decrease of 18 per cent) than in the income groups between $3,000 and $10,000 a year (which on the average saw their tax load lightened by only 14½ per cent). Once the new middle class had come to life in the twenty years of the New Deal and had been brought within the reach of the taxing power of the federal government, it was kept there. As the greatest beneficiaries of the Roosevelt Revolution, its members had to do their duty toward the welfare of the community. This was more important than the expropriation of the wealth of the rich.

THE FEDERAL SYSTEM

The new system of government of the Roosevelt Revolution has so far been described largely in terms of the vast expansion of federal powers upon which it is based. In the United States, this expansion has a twofold significance. In the first place, it has an intrinsic importance, of course. But, secondly, since the United States is a federal system, any fresh assertion of power by the central government is bound to raise the question of what it will do to the balance of functions between the central and state governments and to the survival of the concept of federalism. After twenty-five years it is still possible to say that the federal system in America is not dead.

One of the views tentatively advanced by the Republicans after their return to power in 1953 was that a redistribution of functions between the federal and state governments was necessary to restore to the American landscape, ravished by the

New Deal, some of its pristine beauties. A Commission on Intergovernmental Relations was appointed jointly by the President and the Congress to look into the matter. Its general inclination was in favor of a revival of state powers. The Commission was ably presided over by a businessman, Meyer Kestnbaum, and a report was given to the President in June 1955.

Because of the Commission's vague longing for the restoration of what he thought was an irretrievable past, one of the members of the Commission, the Democratic Senator from Oregon, Wayne Morse, entered a strong dissent. Senator Morse felt that the report went too far

> . . . in playing down the doctrine of federal sovereignty. There seems to be a growing fear in our country these days that the federal government is something to be feared. Yet when we come to analyze the legislative and administrative record of the federal government throughout its history, and particularly during the last half-century, the conclusion would seem to be inescapable that the federal government has been very responsive to the will and the mandates of the people of the nation. So much so has this been true, that our federal system has stood out among the governments of the world as being that system of government which has served as a vehicle of government by law in promoting the general welfare of people, more than any other government in the world. In my opinion, it is subversive to the cause of freedom to instill distrust and lack of confidence in our system of federal sovereignty.[12]

Senator Morse's fears proved premature, for in effect the Commission had little to suggest that would really alter the new federal-state balance that had gradually asserted itself. Speaking of one of the most important areas of federal intervention in a field that was once exclusively within the jurisdiction of the states, that of public welfare assistance, the Commission had this to say:

[12] The Commission on Intergovernmental Relations, *A Report to the President for Transmittal to the Congress,* Washington, 1955, p. 278.

The extent of the shift in welfare responsibilities can be summarized briefly by pointing out that 25 years ago State and local governments, together with private welfare agencies, bore virtually the entire burden, whereas now the National Government contributes nearly one-half of total public welfare expenditures. This does not, of course, mean that the States and localities are doing less than they were; rather it reflects a great increase in public welfare expenditures by all levels of government, arising chiefly out of governmental acceptance of new responsibilities for the economic security of the individual.[13]

This is an excellent summary of the substance of the matter. The federal government has assumed new, but proper, economic and welfare functions, without thereby weakening federalism. It has done so through the establishment of new techniques of co-operation between federal and state governments redounding to the advantage of all. This is the same phenomenon that has repeatedly taken place in many fields of new government intervention since 1932, one that supports the belief that, once a new area of public responsibility has been defined, many different sources of public and private energies can be brought together to solve the problems at hand. The end result has usually been a job well done, with positive gains all around, if we forget the burden of forcing those obsessed with ancient categorizations and slogans ("creeping socialism," "tyranny of the central government," "destruction of grass-roots democracy") to invent new ones to describe the new perils.

One of the more valuable techniques used in the management of the new relationships between federal and state governments is the grant-in-aid, jointly administered by the federal government and the state and local governments concerned, and of which there are some early examples going back to the second half of the nineteenth century. What was new after 1932 was the scope of the technique and the sensitivity of the

[13] *Ibid.*, pp. 267–68.

areas to which it was applied. Apart from disaster or relief
grants not of a regular nature, grants-in-aid to state and local
governments have increased from an average of 165 million
dollars a year in the three years from 1929 to 1932, to an
average of about 2,500 million dollars a year in the three years
from 1951 to 1953. Regular federal grants represented 1.8 per
cent of total state and local expenditures in the first period
and almost 10 per cent in the second period. Since, on this
showing, 90 per cent of state and local expenditures are even
now expenditure of funds raised directly by the states and the
local governments, it is not reasonable to speak of their
financial domination by the federal government.

It is not enough, however, to measure the phenomenon in
statistical terms. Its key elements are the specific ways in which
the grant-in-aid is used and the fields to which it is applied.

The key areas to which federal grants-in-aid have been
extended since 1933 are those of hospital construction, school
construction in areas particularly affected by exceptional federal
activities, school luncheons, old-age assistance, aid to dependent children and to the blind, aid to the permanently disabled,
and general health services. All these programs require some
matching contribution by the states. In the case of hospital
construction, for instance, from 33 to 60 per cent of the cost
must be contributed by the states; in the case of health services,
33 per cent; in the typical case of old-age assistance and aid
to dependent children, to the blind, and to the disabled, the
state must contribute 20 per cent of the first $25 of monthly
assistance plus half of any balance above that amount.

The "matching idea" is a fruitful one, for it rules out the
assumption that no effort at all has to be made by local agencies
receiving federal assistance. Federal assistance, on the contrary,
will usually call forth, if not always a comparable, certainly a
substantial financial effort on the part of the states. What the
federal government is doing is not to take away from the states

responsibilities of government in large measure still belonging to them, but to give them the guiding standards, the incentive, and the financial means of carrying them out in a way suited to the needs of the times.

For, and this is a no less important consideration, the federal assistance programs are administered by the states themselves. Federal intervention, far from having caused a shriveling of local governments, has caused their expansion and modernization and has forced them to assume powers and responsibilities not only welcome locally but that were interpreted locally as proper and necessary exercises of local power and responsibility.

No readier and more candid admission of these underlying realities comes than from the political leaders of the states themselves. There may be some folkloristic talk about states' rights and the American tradition of local freedom, and an occasional vivid summons to battle against the increments in the power of a remote and inflexible federal government. But where policy is made and administrative decisions are reached, there is substantial agreement that no other system will work and that any return to pre-1933 conditions is out of the question. To believe it is possible to create forty-eight watertight compartments in the United States and an equal number of social-welfare programs is unrealistic.

But not all of federalism is to be found in economic dealing. It is to be found also in the right of the local communities to organize their political life in freedom and without interference from the center. It is to be found in the possibility of experimentation that every state possesses in a wide range of legislative fields. It is to be found in the chance political parties have to recognize themselves on a local scale, and in the undiminished possibility the states have to nurture to maturity and power national political figures. In all of these respects American federalism has been relatively untouched, and the very difficulties that it poses today may surely be taken as evidence both of the continued strength of the system and of the tensions and delays it will entail from time to time.

The South is reacting to a federally imposed school-integration program as no puppet would. No TVA, no federal grant-in-aid, has succeeded in making certain Southern states any less determined to claim their autonomy in matters which they consider, in defiance of the supreme constitutional authority, as within their exclusive domestic jurisdiction.

The truth is: if the new standards established by the New Deal between the federal government and the states in many economic and social areas have by now been accepted by all concerned as in keeping with the historic foundations of American federalism, a different situation prevails in non-economic fields. Here the issues raised by the long-term trends toward fuller democracy, equality of education, elimination of poverty and discrimination—all of them much accentuated since 1932—are often the source of serious conflict, as some states have inevitably lagged behind in making the necessary adjustments.

The federal system has adapted itself remarkably well to the more urgent economic requirements of today. It faces, nevertheless, a long period of difficult crisis as it tries to meet everywhere the human and moral conditions of the new society of the Roosevelt Revolution.

4

Electricity and Freedom

On October 2, 1920, Lenin addressed the third All-Russian Committee of the Russian Young Communist League on the task ahead and the building of a Communist society. "We know that Communist society cannot be built unless we regenerate industry and agriculture," he said. "They must be regenerated on a modern basis, in accordance with the last word of science. You know that this basis is science and that only when the whole country, all branches of industry, have been electrified, only when you have mastered this task will you be able to build for yourselves the Communist society which the older generation cannot build up."

The New Deal shared with Lenin this central concern for electricity, with the difference that it was seeking to achieve an ultimate goal of freedom with the methods of freedom. If the future was not to be surrendered into the hands of the totalitarians and of the technical planners, then the responsible political leaders of a democracy had the duty to accept without hesitation the burdens that modern conditions were thrusting on government. No one realized more than Roosevelt that either democracy would meet the issues facing it within a framework of freedom, or the road would be open to the Leninist taskmasters functioning within a totalitarian system.

The Roosevelt Revolution harbored three fundamental ideas

with regard to power, considered as the unifying core of an industrial society:

The first was this—far more power had to be produced in the future than had been produced in the past. Secondly—power had to be used as an instrument of policy and in coordination with other social and economic goals. Thirdly—the financial web strangling the power industry and threatening both its normal growth and the public welfare had to be swept away.

The first two ideas were to be realized by direct government intervention, seeking an increase in the production of power and, more importantly, the realization of new concepts and techniques of unified management of human and natural resources. The third was to be achieved indirectly through a release of the shackles depriving the economic system of its freedom of movement and through a return to a simplicity of structure that would bring back to it its long-vanished vitality.

Out of the first two was born the Tennessee Valley Authority in 1933. Out of the third, the Public Utilities Holding Companies Act of 1935.

THE TENNESSEE VALLEY AUTHORITY:
HISTORICAL BACKGROUND

In its twentieth Annual Report, the Tennessee Valley Authority traces the historical roots of the ideas upon which it had been founded:

On a day in February, 1907, Gifford Pinchot, chief forester under President Theodore Roosevelt, jogged on horseback on one of his frequent solitary rides through rustic Rock Creek Park in Washington, D.C. Deep in thought, he was struck by a new concept in a manner which he later described as follows:

"The Forest and its relation to streams and inland navigation, to water power and flood control; to the soil and its erosion; to coal and oil and other minerals; these questions would not let [me] be. What had all these to do with Forestry? And what had Forestry to do with them? Here were not isolated and separate problems. My work had brought me into touch with all of them. But what was the basic link between them? Suddenly the idea flashed through my head that there was a unity in this complication—that the relation of one resource to another was not the end of the story. Here were no longer a lot of different, independent, and often antagonistic questions, each on its own separate little island, as we had been in the habit of thinking. In place of them here was one single question with many parts. Seen in this new light, all these separate questions fitted into and made up the one great central problem of the use of the earth for the good of man."

Gifford Pinchot there stated the basic principles of TVA.[1]

Not until 1933 were these principles applied to the Tennessee Valley.

The Tennessee River is one of the great rivers of America. With its tributaries, it flows through an area where some of the heaviest rainfall on the North American continent occurs. It is a wandering river touching many states, running south and then north, and a vicious one that in the past has inflicted deep damage to the lands along its course. The Tennessee had also long been known as a river with an unusual economic potential. At many of the rapids encountered by its waters in their 650-mile run to the Ohio and the Mississippi rivers, some very large hydroelectric power sites were to be found.

During World War I, as part of its emergency program for the production of explosives, the federal government decided to build at Muscle Shoals in Alabama, on the Tennessee River, a dam, a powerhouse, and explosive plants. The war ended before work could be completed and not until 1925 was the dam, known as Wilson Dam, finished. After the war, there was strong pressure for the disposal of these properties. In July, 1921, Henry Ford proposed to buy the two nitrate plants and to lease the Wilson Dam for one hundred years once it had

[1] *Tennessee Valley Authority, 1953 Report,* Washington, pp. 51–52.

been completed at public cost. But Ford wanted to pay only five million dollars for new property which had cost eighty-eight million dollars, and his control of the Wilson Dam for a century would severely hamper any subsequent integrated development of the Tennessee River. The offer was rejected.

The man directly responsible for the defeat of Ford's proposal was Senator George W. Norris of Nebraska. Norris was then, and was to remain for the rest of his life, the chief exponent and defender of the ideas of Gifford Pinchot and of the principle that it was the responsibility of the American government to lead the way in a unified program of resource development, wherever the welfare of the people was deeply affected. The Tennessee Valley was one of the poorest in the United States. It had some of the greatest potentialities for fruitful growth. Private interests lacked the vision and the means to do the required job.

For twelve years Senator Norris battled in Congress against the indifference and the hostility of his own colleagues, of public opinion, and of the presidents of the United States. He suggested the government should operate the nitrate plants to carry out experiments in the production of better and cheaper fertilizers, build additional dams in the watershed for flood-control purposes, and sell, preferably to public bodies, power not needed by the government. The fifth bill introduced by Senator Norris was at last passed by Congress in May, 1928. President Coolidge killed it with a pocket veto, the ideal type of veto for a silent president. The same bill was re-introduced by Norris in May, 1930, and by 1931 it emerged from the Congress. More voluble than his predecessor, President Hoover vetoed the bill on March 3, 1931, with a message warning against "degeneration." [2]

A meeting of minds between Norris and the White House did not occur until after March 4, 1933, when Roosevelt started

[2] Cf. Introduction.

on his first term of office. As we have seen, Roosevelt had committed himself fully to a "new deal" for the Tennessee Valley. After his election, the urgency of action was more than ever apparent: important government property was going to waste, unusual possibilities for large-scale growth were left untapped, while human poverty and despair were growing. In the conditions in which the country found itself at that time, it was unthinkable to accept inaction. Federal action in the Tennessee River would touch and give life "to all forms of human concerns." On April 10, 1933, the President recommended the creation of the Tennessee Valley Authority:

> I, therefore, suggest to the Congress legislation to create a Tennessee Valley Authority—a corporation clothed with the power of Government but possessed of the flexibility and initiative of a private enterprise. It should be charged with the broadest duty of planning for the proper use, conservation and development of the natural resources of the Tennessee River drainage basin and its adjoining territory for the general social and economic welfare of the Nation. This Authority should also be clothed with the necessary power to carry these plans into effect. Its duty should be the rehabilitation of the Muscle Shoals development and the co-ordination of it with the wider plan (PPA, 1933, 122).

On May 18, 1933, the President signed the bill that Congress had promptly passed. On that day Senator Norris could rightly say that the creation of the Tennessee Valley Authority "marked an epoch in the history of our national life . . . was emblematic of the dawn of that day when every rippling stream that flows down the mountainside and winds its way through meadows to the sea, should be harnessed and made to work for the welfare and comfort of man."

THE TVA ACT

The preamble of the Act justifies the intent of Congress as follows: "to improve the navigability and to provide for the flood control of the Tennessee River; to provide for reforestation and the proper use of marginal land of the Tennessee Valley; to provide for the agricultural and industrial development of said Valley; to provide for the national defense."

The appeal to navigability and flood control was included in order to create a sound constitutional basis for the experiment, navigability and flood control being among the clearest of federal powers. But the preamble stated in no uncertain terms what was to be the broad intent of the law.

The instrument chosen by the Congress to direct the Tennessee Valley Authority was the autonomous public corporation with full powers vested in a board of directors composed of three members to be appointed by the President with the consent of the Senate, for nine-year terms. One of the three members would be designated by the President as chairman. The three members were to be persons professing "a belief in the feasibility and wisdom" of the purposes of the law, that is persons convinced of the propriety and necessity of the goals set out for the Tennessee Valley Authority and ready to do battle on their behalf. The board of directors was free to appoint TVA employees and officers on the basis of its own rules, without regard to the provision of civil service laws regulating other federal employees. No political test was to be tolerated; all appointments and promotions were to be on the basis of merit and efficiency.

The Authority was granted the power to construct dams on the Tennessee and its tributaries, to provide a nine-foot navigable channel in the river and to control floods, both in the Tennessee and in the Mississippi river basins. The Authority was to have the power to buy or build power plants and structures and transmission lines and to link them together in order to create a unified system.

The directors were authorized to arrange with farmers and their organizations for large-scale experimentation of new fertilizers, to manufacture fertilizers at the Muscle Shoals plants in order to improve their quality and cheapen their costs, and to establish and operate laboratories and plants for the same purposes. The board was also authorized to donate or sell fertilizers, through county demonstration agents, agricultural colleges, or otherwise, for educational purposes.

The Authority was to be administered outside of Washington. Its principal office was to be established in the immediate vicinity of Muscle Shoals in Alabama.

The board was to operate its dams and reservoirs so as to promote navigation and prevent floods. Once these purposes were served, the board could generate electrical energy in order not to waste water power. The energy could be carried over transmission lines and sold to meet the production and maintenance costs of the projects of the Authority. In the sale of electricity, preference was to be given to states, county, municipalities, and co-operatives organized not for profit but for the purpose of supplying electricity to its own citizens or members. The board was to construct transmission lines to farms and rural villages, to promote and encourage the use of power, to make studies and experiments in co-operation with state and local agencies of government in the application of electrical power to the fuller development of the resources of the region. It was authorized to include in any contract for the sale of power such terms and conditions, including resale rate schedules, as might be considered necessary for carrying out the purposes of the law.

To compensate the states and other local agencies of government for the loss of taxes that might have been paid to them by private utilities, the Tennessee Valley Authority was required to pay to them a percentage, fixed at 5 per cent after 1948, of its total gross proceeds from the sale of power (excluding power used by the TVA itself or sold by it to the United States government).

The board of directors, after investigation, was to allocate the cost of all present or future dams and related facilities, among flood control, navigation, fertilizer, national defense, and power programs, in order to arrive at a clear view of the respective costs of each of them. Power projects were to be self-supporting and self-liquidating and power was to be sold at rates capable of producing gross revenues in excess of production costs.

In conclusion, these were to be the final goals of TVA, as stated in Section 23 of the Act:

1. The maximum amount of flood control; 2. The maximum development of said Tennessee River for navigation purposes; 3. The maximum generation of electrical power consistent with flood control and navigability; 4. The proper use of marginal lands; 5. The proper method of reforestation of all lands in said drainage basin suitable for reforestation; and 6. The economic and social well-being of the people living in said river basin.

In this carefully drawn piece of legislation, Congress left no doubt as to what TVA's tasks were to be. The land was to be protected from the ravages of water, and the waters were to be kept under strict control all along the way. Resources were to be developed and navigation made possible throughout the length of the river. Multipurpose dams were to be built, capable of checking flood waters, making navigation possible, and producing power. Power, not in itself the major purpose of the Act, was to be produced in the greatest possible amount and to be sold at the lowest possible price compatible with the interests of the TVA and of the government. Experiments were to be carried out in reforestation, fertilizer development, land management. The facilities of government at all levels were to be used for the mutual benefit of all. The administrators were to enjoy unusual freedom but they were held strictly accountable. The entire operation was to be a grass-roots experiment in democracy, carried out amid the people and the lands and the rivers directly concerned.

WHAT THE TVA HAS ACCOMPLISHED

The Authority's initial years, from 1933 to 1939, were difficult ones. Some of the states were suspicious of the intervention
of a federal agency which might conceivably threaten their own
survival. The private producers of power, speaking through
their financial mouthpieces, the holding companies then being
attacked by the New Deal on several other fronts, tried to kill
the TVA by challenging its constitutionality. In 1936 the TVA
won a limited victory when the Supreme Court ruled favorably
on the constitutionality of the TVA's operation of the Wilson
Dam.[3] Since the broader powers and plans of the TVA were
passed over in silence by the Court, the future still looked uncertain. Most of the private utilities companies of the valley
joined together in a suit against the TVA challenging its very
existence. Not until 1938 did a lower federal district court in
Tennessee validate TVA's power to produce and sell electricity
available to it in the performance of its functions as defined
by the Congress. When the Supreme Court confirmed this decision in January, 1939, the legal battle was over.[4] With the
subsequent purchase of existing private power facilities in its
area, the TVA came into its own. The public purposes fixed by
Congress in 1933 could begin to be translated into reality.

The TVA operates in the watershed of the Tennessee River,
a 40,000-square-mile area which includes parts of seven states,
but TVA electricity is sold in an area of 80,000 square miles,
inhabited by five million people. Some large cities are within
the TVA jurisdiction: Knoxville, Chattanooga, and Memphis.
From Knoxville, where the Tennessee River is formed by the
junction of the Wolston and French Broad rivers, to Paducah,
where the Tennessee flows into the Ohio River, the distance is

[3] *Ashwander* v. *TVA*, 297 U.S. 288.
[4] *Tennessee Electric Power Company* v. *TVA*, 306 U.S. 118.

650 miles and the river falls from 815 to 300 feet above sea level.

Over the entire Tennessee River system, thirty dams have been built, to control the annual average of fifty-two inches of rain that fall in that part of the country. Over-all, this is by far the largest undertaking of engineering and dam construction ever carried out by any enterprise in the history of the United States. As a result, the once destructive floods of the Tennessee River have been checked. Direct flood damages thus avoided average, at a very conservative estimate, 11 million dollars a year. The costs properly chargeable to flood control are 2.5 million dollars a year, including depreciation.

A 630-mile navigation channel with a main depth of 11 feet has been built. In 1933 the river carried 33 million ton-miles of traffic. In 1956 the traffic was estimated at 2,000 million ton-miles, or sixty times more. Costs are quite low, so that private shippers are now saving 17 million dollars a year, while the maintenance of the channel, including depreciation, comes to about 4 million dollars.

To control the course of water before it reaches the river bed, 300,000 acres have been reforested and about one million acres of land have been acquired by TVA for reservoir operations. About 720,000 acres are still in TVA's hands, and are used for recreation, fish and wildlife conservation, forestry, and other purposes.

In the operation of its fertilizer and chemical plants, the TVA has carried out experiments in soil conservation to farm techniques. At the peak of this activity, in 1946–1947, 28,000 farms, averaging 100 acres each, were carrying out, under TVA auspices, test-demonstrations intended to alter gradually the traditional agricultural unbalance of the South. Fundamentally the hope was to move away from soil-consuming crops such as cotton to soil-nourishing crops such as alfalfa.

By 1949, in the Alabama counties within the TVA area,

16 per cent of the hay crop was alfalfa, as compared with less than 1 per cent in 1934. In the non-TVA Alabama counties, the increase over the same period of time was from 1 per cent to 3 per cent. The flight from the land which could be seen in the steady decline in the number of middle-sized farms, has abated in the 125 TVA counties, since for the first time the average farmer has realized the possibility of successful operation by using improved techniques.

The one connecting thread of all these developments has been the production of electricity. In 1933, the average family in the Tennessee Valley consumed 17 per cent less power than the average family in the United States. In 1955, the average TVA family consumed twice as much power as the national family average, with the added advantage that, in spite of a consumption twice as great, the TVA consumer spent 10 per cent less than the average United States consumer. The average cost of electricity for residential use in the TVA area was 1.16 cents per kilowatt-hour in 1955, compared to 2.62 cents for the United States as a whole. In the Valley, 90 per cent of the farms were electrified by 1953 and 93 per cent by 1955, as against 3 per cent in 1933. This is, one should add, an accomplishment nearly duplicated throughout the American countryside by another New Deal agency, the Rural Electrification Administration, with striking consequences on the way of life of the farmers.

In the twenty years from 1933 to 1953, private and industrial consumption of electricity in the valley increased twelve times, from 1.5 to 18 billion kwh. By 1957, the total was 28 billion kwh, or an increase of more than eighteen times over the consumption of 1933. But, in addition, the TVA was able to sell to the federal government, mostly for its atomic energy program at Oak Ridge, another 31.5 billion kwh. In 1957, the total electrical output of 60 billion kwh was therefore forty times greater than the output of 1933.

These results were achieved by the biggest integrated power system in the world, with an installed capacity of 10 billion kilowatts at the end of 1956, of which four billion were in hydroelectric plants and six billion in steam plants. For, in a radical transformation of its initial operations, to a large extent induced by the needs of the Atomic Energy Commission, the TVA is now producing more electricity from coal than from water.

THE METHODS OF TVA

These material achievements are in themselves astonishing. More important are the methods by which they have been brought about. Because of them TVA acquires its meaning for the democratic world. For if we were only anxious to be impressed by spectacular material achievements, the doings of the Soviet Union would have an equal claim to our attention (as, indeed, they may, for other reasons).

The Tennessee Valley Authority has first of all successfully applied the unified approach to the strengthening of the human and material resources of a region. Until 1933, the traditional pattern had been to have the Department of Agriculture take care of farmers' problems, the Corps of Engineers control floods and improve navigation, and the Department of the Interior deal with reclamation and power on public lands. The novelty of the TVA consisted in bringing together under the roof of one single federal agency activities which were widely scattered when they were undertaken at all, and which because of the scattering could usually be carried out only in limited fashion, in a way that was both wasteful and likely to create conflicts and misunderstandings among the various agencies involved. On its twentieth anniversary, the Authority rightly described its work as a "departure from the traditional organization of the federal government":

For the first time, a single agency was given responsibility for a unified approach to the development and wise use of natural resources in a specific region. The eternal cycle of the raindrops was to be harnessed—in the forests, on the cultivated land, and in the streams. Laboratories created for munitions were to convert the minerals of the earth for restoring strength to the soil.

None of these activities was new to the Federal Government, nor was TVA endowed with any powers new to government. The uniqueness of TVA lay in the range of functions combined for administration in one agency in one area—a river valley.[5]

One of the best examples of the unified approach was the building of multipurpose dams that could at the same time check floods, facilitate navigation through locks, and produce power. In the same way, control of waters outside of the river channel was realized through reforestation, improvement of farmers' techniques and proper use of TVA-produced fertilizers —that is, with a variety of means hitherto not available to any one government agency. TVA's experimental chemical work was related to the needs of the farmers, and the problems of the eroded lands of Tennessee was met with a variety of weapons. These included the widest co-operation with educational units and with local, county, state, and other federal agencies. The unified approach meant an integrated approach capable of using all available resources and of making the TVA a clearing-house for the region.

In the second place, the TVA did not proceed according to any master plan, even though the multiplicity of its tasks and the complexity of its programs led naturally to the assumption that a "plan" there must be. The TVA was always at pains to deny the existence of such a plan. "The reason the TVA plan is not available is that there is no such document," the former Chairman of the Authority, David E. Lilienthal, likes to point out.[6] There have been instead many plans changing

---

[5] *Tennessee Valley Authority, 1953 Report*, p. 1.
[6] *TVA, Democracy on the March*, New York, 2nd ed., 1953, p. 186.

all the time and there have been persistent and difficult exchanges of ideas with many people. There has been a hard drive to build dams as fast as conditions permitted, as there has been a patient, slow educational drive to show the farmers better methods, to help in the establishment of rural co-operatives, and to bring the states and other local agencies of government to a fuller appreciation of what their powers and duties were. There were the years of waiting while the constitutional processes of the country ground their way forward. There was confidence that by bringing the many aspects of the Valley problems under the co-ordinated scrutiny of the Authority, ways could be found to fulfill, over a period of time, the mission entrusted by the Congress to the TVA. No one quite knew how many years would be needed. There were no five-year plans. TVA managers accepted conditions as they were and human nature as it was, as proper limiting and guiding factors.

Bearing all this in mind, it would seem that some of the implications contained in Friedrich Hayek's reference to the TVA do not apply to it. Having recognized "the urgent need for amelioration" of economic conditions in the Danube Basin, Hayek continues:

. . . But this is not the same thing as to wish to see economic life in this region directed according to a single master-plan, to foster the development of the different industries according to a schedule laid down beforehand in a way which makes the success of local initiative dependent on being approved by the central authority and being incorporated in its plan. One cannot, for example, create a kind of Tennessee Valley Authority for the Danube Basin without thereby determining beforehand for many years to come the relative rate of progress of the different races inhabiting this area or without subordinating all their individual aspirations and wishes to this task.[7]

Perhaps Hayek is saying there is no possibility of transplanting TVA techniques to the strange world of the Danube, where

[7] *The Road to Serfdom,* Chicago, 1944, pp. 225–26.

democratic aspirations and methods would wither away and where the harsh policies he envisages would have to be enforced. This may be a justifiedly pessimistic view on the chances of exporting to foreign lands the ideas or institutions of America, in spite of the evidence that the TVA has provided at least partially useful inspiration to many countries and that, as a concept, it has extraordinary flexibility and applicability, much more so than, let us say, that of the Supreme Court with its powers of judicial review. But, surely, the TVA has never determined beforehand, even less for many years, the fixed rate of progress of the many communities within its jurisdiction, and has never subordinated individual hopes and wishes to the achievement of its tasks.

The third major characteristic of TVA methods has been its democratic nature. The TVA has backed from the beginning what Lilienthal calls "democracy at the grass-roots," as in the test-demonstration farm program. "We did not want a method of restoring soil whereby the farmer would be ordered. He would learn by doing on his own place; his neighbors would learn by watching him and by doing what would 'work out' on their own farms." [8]

This has been the normal procedure: the farmers themselves selected the demonstration farms. Each farm would then be submitted to a general review of its problems, with the farmer himself, his neighbors, the county agent, and TVA technicians participating. Once a program of rehabilitation was adopted, the TVA would provide phosphate fertilizer at a nominal cost. As needed, the program would be modified to meet new conditions. The effort continued as a joint individual and community one, with the TVA very much in the background except for its contribution of improved fertilizers.

More than fifty thousand farmers have participated in the experiment, while tens of thousands more, in the Valley and

[8] *Op. cit.,* p. 81.

beyond, were influenced by their activities. As a consequence, root crops have increased, the brown hills of Tennessee are greener, and cattle, the total absence of which had struck Harcourt Morgan many years before, have appeared. With the TVA a better cycle of nature has been restored.

It will be said that nothing similar would have been achieved had it not been for human traits that are rather more common in the United States than elsewhere. There were fifty thousand farmers ready to become guinea pigs, to admit that all was not well with their farms and that they could learn by listening to the advice of others and by trying new techniques, ready to bear the burden of keeping records and accounts and of discussing them with their neighbors and other distant visitors who would be tramping up and down their fields. These fifty thousand farmers must have felt that their self-imposed burdens were more than made up by the hope of a more tolerable life for themselves. But without community spirit, without a sense of allegiance to the larger political body, the experiment would not have succeeded. Nor would it have succeeded without the judicious use of the one decisive weapon the TVA had at its disposal: fertilizers better than any private manufacturer had been able, or willing, to concoct up to that time.

It would be wrong to suggest that good and responsive human material like the people of the hills of Tennessee cannot be found elsewhere and similar results obtained, once a feeling of responsibility and participation is awakened. The TVA was lucky, perhaps, with its pupils. The decisive factors were TVA itself and the devotion it inspired.

Democracy, in the concrete world in which it must seek its realization, is made up essentially of the network and relationships of mutual obligation and ties that give substance to community life. It is because it was eminently able to translate the verbalized appeals and the generalities of the politicians into a stronger connecting tissue reinforcing the body politic that the TVA has been successful as a democratic experiment.

If it is also to be maintained that the spirit of democracy lies in the ability of each community and region to meet its problems unaided or at least with primary reliance on its own abilities and strengths, then the TVA has made its next great methodological contribution by being the first important federal agency to work on an effectively decentralized basis.

The debate between centralization and decentralization is an old one. All large aggregates of human activities, be they government or private organizations, when overwhelmed by the awkwardness and complexities of their operations, tend to retreat to decentralization as offering the key to salvation.

Too often decentralization has meant merely that the offices of a federal agency will be shifted from Washington to the Maryland or Virginia countryside or those of an industrial corporation will be moved from New York to the semirustic glades of Westchester County. The congestion that makes life in Washington or New York unbearable is relieved by the bodily transfer of certain activities to the midst of the so-called rural amenities of the countryside. Traffic problems in Washington or New York may be slightly improved; the activities of the machine remain as centralized as before. Or decentralization has meant branch offices will be opened throughout the land. The citizens subject to the jurisdiction, for instance, of the Internal Revenue Service will pay homage to the agency in any one of the many cities in which it has district offices. But the scattered offices are mainly links in a transmission belt, even though in certain instances (the SEC) for example, the regional offices have acquired some autonomy. The third significance of "decentralization" has often been that the government agent managing an enterprise far away from Washington will establish his operating offices in the field. Decentralization will remain a mere illusion if policy continues to be fixed at the center.

With all due allowance for the fact that in wide areas there is an incompatibility in principle between "decentralization" and "central government policy," it still is true that decentralization has seldom been meaningfully tried where it was possible and logical to do so. The TVA represents, on the other hand, a notable experiment in administrative decentralization because (1) there is no Washington office where policy is made; (2) all power is vested with the officers on the spot and; (3) power is exercised only in consultation with the public and private agencies and groups directly concerned.

These three pillars of regional decentralization are described by David Lilienthal as follows:

> A federal autonomous agency with authority to make its administrative decisions within the region;—responsibility to deal with resources, as a unified whole, clearly fixed in the regional agency not divided among several centralized federal departments or agencies with their headquarters in Washington;—a policy fixed by law that the federal regional agency work cooperatively with and through local and state agencies.[9]

Integration and decentralization are both present in the TVA picture. As Senator Hill of Alabama has said, "We sought . . . to give one agency responsibility for federal leadership in the development of all the resources of the river valley, to locate its management in the region, close to the problem and out of Washington." [10]

The result has been an exciting combination of power and democracy—power to do all that was necessary to achieve the goals of the Act, and democracy realized through procedures and policies born of a close contact with the people affected. The hopes of seeing a national agency working entirely and responsibly in the field have been fulfilled in an atmosphere of

---

[9] *Op. cit.,* p. 151.
[10] Quoted in Gordon R. Clapp, *The TVA, An Approach to the Development of a Region,* Chicago, 1955, p. 27.

efficiency and *esprit de corps* due to the sense of direct participation in a historic experiment.

"PUBLIC" AND "PRIVATE"

The meaning of decentralization can be measured further by looking at yet another TVA phenomenon, a federal agency which with the greatest persistence has done its best to resist the temptations of empire-building, so as not to forget its original and central goal: water controls on the land and along the rivers.

The geographical boundaries of TVA were fixed at an early stage. After a few years, they became settled, and the TVA has not tried to extend them. The TVA has grown in significance and power since it was founded in 1933, yet it has grown within a territory that has been substantially unchanged for the past twenty years.

Within these well-defined limits, the TVA has done its best to abide by one fundamental policy: While it would exercise to the fullest possible extent the main grant of power it had received, that of controlling and utilizing the course of waters, it would seek to encourage the growth of the activities of state and local agencies and in every other field over which it had acquired some control. The TVA is the one key example of a public corporation which has done that.

All too often in those Western countries which have turned over certain economic powers to public corporations, the assumption has been that public and private activities were incompatible. It has also been assumed that the existence of a public corporation established by the central government meant of necessity the withering away of local government, and further, by the same warrant, that the public corporation would inevitably extend the sphere of its operations. The adoption of any self-denying policy that will make room for expanding local or private activities and will in the end limit the power of the public corporation, is seldom seen in Europe; indeed, the opposite is true. Many of the accepted slogans and fears current in this area of public policy, of the laws of bureaucratic growth ("Parkinson's Law"), are largely based on European experience and trends.

It is important, therefore, to underline the fact that, in a series of significant examples, the policies of the TVA have moved in a different direction.

When the TVA started its reforestation program in 1934, it contributed 100 per cent of the seedlings planted that year in the Tennessee basin. By 1956, the TVA was contributing only 45 per cent of the total seedlings planted, while the remaining 55 per cent was being planted by the seven states of the Tennessee Valley. This was the result of a twenty-year program by the TVA to induce the states to assume tasks which were theirs in the beginning. Throughout this period, the Tennessee Valley Authority contributed the technology, the ideas, the men, the money needed to get the states to begin doing something that properly belonged to them. The ultimate goal is to shift the full burden to the states.

The TVA's fertilizer program is a larger example of the same policy. The TVA has been a most inventive and stimulating factor in an industry vital to the welfare of the exhausted American land of the Middle South. The American farmer, blessed until recently by virgin and fertile soil, was slow in realizing the necessity of supporting its productivity. The fearful depletion wrought by thoughtless agricultural techniques was not seen in all its implications until quite late.

The introduction of artificial nourishment of the soil was, therefore, a turning point in the agricultural life of America. Private industry, along with the farmers, had been uninterested in the problem and unaware of its chances; accordingly, most of the fertilizers offered to farmers before TVA entered the picture were low-potency and sluggish compounds. The TVA from the first used its Muscle Shoals plants to experiment on a large scale in the production of new concentrated chemical agents. Concentrated super-phosphate was one. Another was calcium meta-phosphate; yet another was ammonium nitrate, first produced by the TVA and now the most widely used nitrate fertilizer in the United States.

In all these instances, the story has been the same—one that a political scientist is bound to find very exciting. Under the stimulus of TVA leadership, total United States fertilizer output multiplied to an extraordinary degree (a tenfold increase for super-phosphate between 1938 and 1955, a sixtyfold increase for ammonium nitrate between 1943 and 1956). But the key point was that the percentage of total output represented by TVA production declined steadily: from 43 per cent in 1938 to 2.5 per cent in 1955 in the case of super-phosphates, from 70 per cent in 1943 to 12 per cent in 1956 in the case of ammonium nitrate.

Speaking of super-phosphate, Gordon Clapp, the last TVA Chairman appointed by a Democratic administration, writes: "Private manufacturers have picked it up as a good product. Consequently TVA will soon withdraw from the production of concentrated super-phosphate." Speaking of calcium meta-phosphate, Mr. Clapp writes that TVA "plans to continue [its] production . . . until a few industrial groups actually begin producing it in considerable quantities. When that happens, TVA will push another process and product, of higher concentration into trial and use." Speaking of ammonium nitrate: "Again as in the case of concentrated super-phosphate, the Board plans to shift its ammonia supplies to the production of new fertilizers, as production of ammonium nitrate by private industry increases." [11]

And so the story unfolds, in other fields as well, from home

[11] Clapp, *op. cit.,* pp. 149–52.

freezers to tractors, with the TVA acting as the path-breaker and experimenter, as the stimulator and inventor, arousing private interest in new economic processes and then withdrawing from the scene and turning its attention elsewhere.

The classical liberal position concerning the state has been this: it is the state's primary function to create the conditions which will make it possible for private interests to come to life and give free rein to their unlimited daring and inventiveness. The traditional "framework theory" relied on a number of basic tools, chief among them law, order, and justice. TVA's political significance is its addition of some new tools to the framework theory: electric power and industrial experimentation. Using them to revive the flagging imagination of private enterprisers, the TVA has often succeeded in making real rather than potential the fulfillment of private man's capabilities.

As a consequence, the growth of industry has been faster in the Valley than in other parts of the United States. Farmers have been helped through subsidies as has been the custom elsewhere, but also through a strengthening of their own determination and of their chances of achieving a rational and productive plan for their land. Local agencies of government have been made aware of their duties. In many instances, TVA maps have made towns and counties conscious for the first time of the land upon which they could lay legitimate tax claims. Given the alternatives of claiming credit for itself or of giving credit to the people in the local communities, the TVA has always chosen the latter course.

The TVA has gone a long way in showing that, with the right kind of initial legislation and with subsequent managerial policies that aim at the effective strengthening of democratic processes, not all invasions of hitherto sacred private grounds contradict the requirements of freedom and of individual responsibility in a democratic society. Indeed, it has shown that they can be the necessary condition of their existence.

POWER: POLICIES, PROFITS, AND TAXES

At the heart of TVA we find a power policy of a special kind. That policy can best be summarized in the words of Lilienthal, who was chiefly responsible for its adoption and its later strenuous application:

> To effectuate the law's policy of a wide and extensive use of electricity it was necessary for the TVA Board, at the very outset, to break sharply with the ways of fixing electricity rates that with few exceptions had been followed in the electricity industry. The rates announced in September of 1933 were considered low, extraordinarily low, judged by then prevailing ideas. Those rates to the ultimate user were based on the principle that people wanted to use electricity not in a niggardly way but generously and for many new uses. To reach that goal of wide use, rates had to be drastically cut, cut not after the use had grown, but as a way of making it grow. This, we were convinced, would be financially sound, for people would then use so much more electricity that the income of the distributors would rise proportionately. What had proved to be a good business principle for Henry Ford in the pricing of his first automobiles, what was good business in the mass production field generally, would be good business in electricity supply.[12]

The establishment of a power policy was to be the first major concern of the board of directors of the TVA. Its main lines were fixed as early as 1933.[13] Following this statement

---

[12] Lilienthal, *op. cit.*, pp. 22–23.

[13] Because of their historic interest, the main points of the power policy announced by the TVA at that time are reproduced here. The formulation of a power policy was the first step in carrying out the power program required by the Act. The announcement was made on August 25, 1933:

1. The business of generating and distributing electric power is a public business.

2. Private and public interests in the business of power are of different kind and quality and should not be confused.

3. The interest of the public in the widest possible use of power is superior to any private interest. Where the private interest and this public interest conflict, the public interest must prevail.

of principle, TVA announced electricity rates that were low and frankly promotional. They were about one-half of the

4. Where there is a conflict between public interest and private interest in power which can be reconciled without injury to the public interest, such reconciliation should be made.

5. The right of a community to own and operate its own electric plant is undeniable. This is one of the measures which the people may properly take to protect themselves against unreasonable rates. Such a course of action may take the form of acquiring the existing plant or setting up a competing plant, as circumstances may dictate.

6. The fact that action by the Authority may have an adverse economic effect upon a privately owned utility should be a matter for the serious consideration of the Board in framing and executing its power program. But it is not the determining factor. The most important considerations are the furthering of the public interest in making power available at the lowest rate consistent with sound financial policy, and the accomplishment of the social objectives which low-cost power makes possible. The Authority cannot decline to take action solely upon the ground that to do so would injure a privately owned utility.

7. To provide a workable and economic basis of operations, the Authority plans initially to serve certain definite regions and to develop its program in those areas before going outside.

8. To make the area a workable one and a fair measure of public ownership, it should include several cities of substantial size (such as Chattanooga and Knoxville) and, ultimately, at least one city of more than a quarter million, within transmission distance, such as Birmingham, Memphis, Atlanta, or Louisville.

While it is the Authority's present intention to develop its power program in the above-described territory before considering going outside, the Authority may go outside the area if there are substantial changes in general conditions, facts, or governmental policy, which would necessarily require a change in this policy, of regional development, or if the privately owned utilities in the area do not cooperate in the working of the program.

9. Every effort will be made by the Authority to avoid the construction of duplicate physical facilities, or wasteful competitive practices.

Accordingly, where existing lines of privately owned utilities are required to accomplish the Authority's objectives, as outlined above, a genuine effort will be made to purchase such facilities from the private utilities on an equitable basis.

10. Accounting should show detail of costs, and permit a comparison of operations with privately owned plants, to supply a "yard-stick" and an incentive to both private and public managers.

11. The accounts and records of the Authority as they pertain to power will always be open to inspection by the public.

Tennessee Valley Authority, 1934 Report, pp. 22–24.

residential rates then prevalent in the United States. Even to-day, TVA's basic rates are still 30 per cent lower than the average private residential rates.

The TVA has limited itself to the production and transmission of power. As the policy statement of 1933 indicated, the TVA believed in the right of local agencies to distribute power to the consumer. Having limited final sales to the federal government and to large industrial users, the TVA encouraged the growth of municipal and co-operative distributors, who now number about 150. These distributors, each linked to the TVA by a contract specifying resale terms of the power purchased from the TVA, have in turn invested (by 1955) 380 million dollars in local distributing plants. By 1955, the TVA itself had made a net investment assignable to power of about 1,130 million dollars. Thus the TVA and the distributors together had by then invested about 1,500 million dollars in their power plant.

A large issue in the debates surrounding TVA since its beginning has been that of the efficiency and profitability of the system. Having challenged the private power companies and having succeeded in increasing power consumption in the Valley to a level 100 per cent greater than the national average, the TVA was inviting attack from private interests, eager to show that the successes of TVA were due only to the special circumstances and privileges surrounding it. The questions thus raised have to be taken up, for they are certainly serious ones.

Most of the money that TVA has used in the building of its power plants has come from congressional appropriations. The Congress appropriated money that became available to the Treasury either as a result of tax revenues or of borrowing. Contrary to current opinion, if we leave aside borrowing required from 1941 to 1946 for war purposes, about 95 per cent of the money came from taxation and only 5 per cent from borrowing during the years the TVA was building its dams and power plants.

It seems legitimate, then, in the absence of any significant borrowing, to speak of the investment made by TVA in its power plant as an equity investment made by the people of the United States in order to realize certain public ends—an equity investment that, from a financial point of view, does not differ from a similar one made by private investors in the shares of a corporation. The difference lies in the purposes of the two investments. The purpose of the private investor is private gain. The purpose of the TVA is the strengthening of the general welfare of the country.

Let us consider, then, the 1,130 million dollars of TVA's power investment as the net equity investment of the people of the United States. As in all instances of equity investments, the returns to be expected from it are variable and uncertain. (In the case of electricity the uncertainty is somewhat less than in most fields.) By taking a typical fiscal year, 1954–1955, we find out what the returns were:

TVA POWER OPERATION
FOR THE FISCAL YEAR 1955
(*all figures in millions of dollars*)

Total power revenues		188
Production expense	91	
Transmission expense	8	
Other operating expenses	7	
Local tax equivalents paid	4	
Depreciation and amortization	30	
Total	140	140
Net Income		48
Average 1954–55 investment assignable to power		1,130
Per cent return on investment		4.25

These figures, as well, of course, as the similar figures for all preceding and succeeding years, have been challenged by the private public utilities, aware of the burning consequences of the application of TVA's yardstick, on three grounds: (1) The investment in the power plant is understated, as a result of the allocation of exaggerated charges to navigation and flood control; (2) the TVA is not paying interest on the money it has received from the federal government; and (3) the TVA does not pay any federal income taxes.

If these three points were properly taken into account, say the private utilities, the TVA power operations would reveal a steady and widening deficit. As it is, the people of the entire United States are paying the costs of a project of limited benefit to a limited section of the country.

These contentions appear void of real substance.

As to the first ground, it should be noted that total net TVA investments for navigation and flood control are only about 300 million dollars, a modest figure in view of the great benefits that have been secured. Conservative estimates by TVA compute at 60 million dollars by 1955 (and at 132 millions by 1957) the value of the direct flood damages averted in the Valley as a result of its control system. As for navigation, private shippers are currently saving between 15 and 20 million dollars a year in transportation charges, while it costs the TVA and the Corps of Engineers only 4 million dollars a year to maintain the system. Considering these unusual benefits, the 1,130-million-dollar investment in power is, if anything, an overstatement rather than an understatement, for a higher proportion of the total TVA investment could quite legitimately have been allocated to flood control and navigation.

With regard to the second argument, it is not clear why the TVA should pay "interest" on the money it has received from the federal government. TVA's "capital" is equity money obtained through the exercise of the taxing power vested in the federal government by the Constitution and invested for constitutional purposes according to laws duly enacted by the Congress and declared valid by the Supreme Court. On "equity" investments, it is not "interest" payments that are due, but "profits" that are expected. In an enterprise such as the TVA, the primary concern of the government is that all assets be well maintained, operations be efficiently carried out, and the purposes of the law be fulfilled. If, in addition, a net profit is shown, the community shall have every reason to consider its servant exceptionally bright. Is the TVA profitable? This query leads to the tax question.

This, the third argument, poses the biggest question of all, for the fact that the TVA does not pay federal income taxes sets it apart from the private utilities which do pay federal income taxes.

The figures given earlier showed a 1954–1955 net return on TVA's power investment of 4.25 per cent without any payment of federal taxes. This net return would increase to 4.5 per cent if we consolidate the capital and income accounts of the TVA and of the 148 TVA distributors and thus make possible a fair comparison with the private utilities (which are in the main both producers and distributors of energy).

All private public utilities in the United States in the year ending December 31, 1954, earned 4.8 per cent on their plant, after payment of federal taxes, which on the average were the equivalent of 44 per cent of net income before taxes.

To meet the income tax preoccupations of the private utilities (and one can admit that it might be useful for certain purposes to estimate what, if anything, would be left after payment of income taxes), all one has to do is charge against the net TVA consolidated income a sum equal to 44 per cent of it. The result is that, after payment of taxes equal to those paid by private utilities, the TVA consolidated system shows a net profit of 2.52 per cent on its invested capital. It is not clear, from the public point of view, what the advantages would be (beyond adding to the general confusion and satisfying a mildly justifiable curiosity) of having TVA's real 4.5 per cent net return on the money invested entered entirely in the "profit" column, or 2 per cent of it entered in the "tax" column and 2.5 per cent in the "profit" column. The substance is the same and cannot be changed.

The substance is that the TVA investment is a profitable one and that, over the years, the American people will recover their money twice over (this has already started to happen with the accelerated payments to the Treasury that TVA is making out of its power revenues and which added up on June 30, 1957, to 240 million dollars).

This is not yet the entire story. For the 1955 TVA return of 4.5 per cent (or, shall we say, of 2 per cent plus 2.5 per cent) was obtained by selling power at an average of 0.64 cents per kilowatt-hour, while the 4.8 per cent return of private utilities resulted from sales averaging 1.76 cents—a rate nearly three times that of TVA's.

A comparison of relative efficiencies seems unavoidable at this point. It reveals an extraordinary level of efficiency in public power operations, as shown in the table on page 187.

As the TVA writes:

> Total operating expense in the Tennessee Valley thus is about half that for the private utility industry as a whole. How explain this wide difference? TVA is, of course, in an area having economical hydro resources. Because of the rapid growth of power demand in the area, TVA's generating plants, including the steam plants, are mostly large and modern. But more important than these, TVA's operations are on a mass production basis, made possible by low rates, stemming from TVA's primary concern in bringing about the widest and most abundant use of electricity consistent with a modest return on the investment.[14]

[14] Tennessee Valley Authority, *Facts About TVA Operations*, 1955, p. 8.

COST OF PRODUCING AND MARKETING ELECTRIC POWER
(*Mills per Kilowatt-Hour of Energy Sold*)

	TVA AREA 1952–1953	PRIVATELY OWNED UTILITIES IN U.S. 1952	TVA AREA COSTS (*Approximate Percentage of Privately Owned Utilities*)
Production Expense	2.3	4.8	50
Transmission and Distribution Expense	0.9	1.8	50
Customer Accounts and Collection Expense	0.2	0.6	40
Sales Promotion Expense	0.1	0.3	30
Administration and General Expense	0.5	1.1	40
Depreciation Expense	1.4	1.5	90
Total	5.4	10.1	54

The evidence then shows the TVA to be the most efficient power enterpriser in the United States; thanks to its policies, consumption of electricity has increased to a level far beyond that of the United States as a whole. No matter how the accounts are drawn up and even if we submit the TVA to a federal "tax" charge, the TVA still shows a profit. It is this combination of profitable operations with the achievement of important economic and social goals made possible by massive doses of cheap electricity that has made the TVA unique.

Few can deny the TVA has fulfilled its function of establishing a power yardstick that has influenced the rest of the United States, a standard by which the performance of the industry is to be judged. The record shows that, in the areas immediately adjacent to the TVA area, private utilities have improved services and lowered prices, out of fear of a possible expansion of TVA's activities, to a far greater degree than in the areas more removed from the immediate influence of TVA. Looking at a rate map of the United States, one sees that the cost of power increases with the increase in the distance of the producer from TVA, a phenomenon which justifies Roosevelt's dream of establishing TVAs in the far corners of the United States.

This dream has not been fulfilled and one can well ask, a quarter of a century later, the reason why it failed. The most satisfactory explanation comes from David Lilienthal, who sees the TVA as a great experiment in democratic government whose duplication has so far been prevented by the interests of centralization.

> The real reason . . . is the great bi-partisan power of the Washington bureaucracy. Bureaus of the Departments of Interior and Agriculture, and the Army Corps of Engineers, have so used their political power as to make more TVAs impossible, and thereby have preserved their "vested interest" in the jurisdiction and prerogatives of their bureaus. For they have seen that if other regional agencies, embodying the TVA idea, were created, many of their functions that are now centered in Washington would be unified and coordinated regionally, and in large measure would be delegated or turned back to the states and localities, as has happened in the Tennessee Valley since 1933.
>
> The TVA came into being after an uphill battle extending over many years prior to 1933. But with this sole exception these Washington agencies have been able to defeat every proposal for unified valley development. . . . And, as a consequence, lack of coordination, expensive rivalries, "improvident use" of resources, and floods of ever-increasing magnitude continue to be the story in such a major river basin as that of the Missouri, comprising one-sixth of the land area of the country.[15]

TVA is thus an unparalleled triumph, an experiment both profitable and moving, one whose influence has reached throughout the world, attesting to the vitality of a modernized democratic faith. It is also evidence, however, of the difficulties experienced in making of it a precedent to support widening action under comparable conditions.

[15] Lilienthal, *op. cit.*, pp. xiv–xv.

One can still say, however, looking at the range of the accomplishments of TVA, that it has fulfilled the aspirations of a generation caught in the dilemma of freedom and of totalitarianism; it stands as a monument to freedom. When everything is said about TVA, what matters most is its quality and the tension of the labor and devotion that went into it. This explains the extraordinary appeal of TVA for the rest of the world. Peoples everywhere see in TVA one of the bright victories of man in the twentieth century over the forces of unregulated nature and over the greed and poverty that are still too much a part of industrial societies.

THE HOLDING COMPANIES ACT OF 1935

One of the most rewarding financial games of the 1920's had been the building up of complex holding company empires, through which skillful financial operators, and very few of them, acquired control over large segments of the nation's economic life.

The key to the operation was to gain control over operating companies enjoying a franchised monopoly in the production and distribution of electricity and gas. If these were regulated activities, they were the beneficiaries as well of steady and secure profits. In order to take over the operating companies, the holding companies issued new securities, easily sold in the speculative markets preceding the crash of 1929. To justify excessive issues of securities, the holding companies began to write up the bookkeeping values of the physical assets of the underlying operating companies, a practice which in turn had to cause an increase in the rates charged to the public. By the early thirties, as we have seen, holding systems had acquired a dominant position throughout the United States.

In the subsequent defense of their activities, the holding companies suggested that their intent was to help and not to hinder the development of the industry, to do for it what had already been done in other industrial fields in answer to the pressures of modernization and integration, and that without the Great Depression the purchasers of their securities would have enjoyed greater financial security, because of the diversification of the assets controlled by any one holding company.

None of these contentions had much foundation. In the fierce competition against each other, the holding company systems readily undertook the haphazard acquisition of scattered plants and in effect rather prevented the gradual, regional, economically justified integration of operating companies that would naturally have come about. William Douglas, now a Justice of the Supreme Court and earlier a New Deal chairman of the Securities and Exchange Commission, points out: "operating units owned by rival holding companies cut across territories in the fashion of a crazy quilt, with the result that the power requirements of many areas were not planned or served in an efficient manner." [16]

The financial collapse of the holding company pyramids in the course of the Depression created one of the worst problems confronting the New Deal, both of a financial nature, and of monopoly and power. Roosevelt spoke of his uneasy feeling at this show of overconcentrated economic power (PPA, 1935, 138–39) and of the dangers for democracy resulting from the

---

[16] *Democracy and Finance,* New Haven, 1940, p. 145. Douglas continues: "For example, an area in a Middle Western state, ideally suited to the operation of a single system or at the most two systems, is actually served by half a dozen operating companies controlled by as many holding companies. Waste results; power costs are unnecessarily high; returns to investors are affected: and the stability and efficiency of each of the operating units are unnecessarily diminished. Let me give one simple illustration. One of these companies recently built a new generating plant to provide for a load of less than 10,000 kilowatts. It was located somewhat less than twenty-five miles from a large efficient plant of a neighboring company which had ample capacity to supply this load. In all probability, if these companies were integrated, duplication would not have been needed" (pp. 145–46).

fact that ownership of about 4 per cent of the securities controlled the other 96 per cent. "There my friends," Roosevelt said at a Jackson Day dinner at the height of the struggle with the holding companies, "is a case of a 96-inch dog being wagged by a 4-inch tail. If you work it out in feet and inches it is an amazing dog" (PPA, 1938, 43–44).

The issue was the restoration of the freedom of economic movement to the industry and a redistribution of power to do away permanently with the dangers of fund juggling. These were the goals written into the Public Utilities Holding Companies Act of 1935.

According to the Securities and Exchange Commission, which was charged with the administration of the Act, three main areas of regulation are provided by the law:

> The first area embraces those provisions of the Act which require the physical integration of the public utility and related properties of a holding company system and the simplification of intercorporate relationships and financial structures of the system. The latter includes the removal of unnecessary holding company complexities, the correction of inequitable distribution of voting power among security holders, and the strengthening of the financial position of the system.
>
> The second area of regulation covers financing operations of holding companies and their subsidiaries, acquisitions and dispositions of properties and securities by such companies, their accounting practices, and intrasystem servicing arrangements and other intercompany transactions in holding company systems.
>
> The third area encompasses a number of sections of the Act which are designed to insure that newly created holding company or affiliate relationships shall meet certain standards prescribed by the statute, and other provisions of the Act which require a limited degree of surveillance over exempt holding company systems.[17]

The SEC, from the beginning, regarded as the most im-

[17] Securities and Exchange Commission, *18th Annual Report,* Washington, 1952, p. 81.

portant the first area with its provisions requiring it, in effect, to force the liquidation of holding company systems. Section 11 of the Act was its core, for it included the so-called death sentence (called by Roosevelt "health sentence") clause.

In essence, Section 11 called for the liquidation of all holding company systems whose continued existence could not be justified on economic grounds. Only those holding companies would be allowed to survive which had physically interconnected assets and which under natural conditions could be operated efficiently as a single system confined to a single area not so large as to impair the advantages of localized management and effective operation. Douglas writes:

> The philosophy is that while our technological advances have created economic principalities in many spheres of national activity, the size and power of these principalities must correspond with the economic or social facts. No man or group of men should be permitted to expand this financial and economic control beyond limits justified by those facts.[18]

The message of this economic philosophy was—there was room in the United States for General Motors but not for Samuel Insull.

In spite of the severity of the financial crisis confronting them and of the obvious hostility of public opinion, of politicians, and of investors, the holding companies put up a stubborn resistance between 1935, the date of the passage of the Act, and 1938, the year in which the Supreme Court sanctioned the constitutional validity of the Act.[19] During those three years, most of the companies refused to register with the SEC as required by law, and engaged in a most intensive propaganda campaign in the country and in the Congress. Once the constitutional battle was lost, surrender was total and co-operation

---

[18] *Op. cit.*, pp. 148–49.
[19] *Electric Bond and Share Company, et al.* v. *Security and Exchange Commission*, 303 U.S. 419 (1938).

complete. The financial world realized that an era had come to an end and that the power of government had asserted itself.

The history of the enforcement of the Holding Company Act between 1938 and 1956 (to take the most recent available data), is a remarkable example of orderly processes of government quickly producing decisive results. In these eighteen years, 2,314 holding company systems and subsidiary companies have come under the jurisdiction of the SEC. From June 30, 1938, to June 30, 1956, 2,012 of these companies have been released from the active jurisdiction of the Act or have ceased to exist as individual corporate entities. Included in this number are 916 companies, with assets aggregating approximately 15 billion dollars, which have been released by their respective parent holding companies and are no longer subject to the Act as components of registered systems. As of June 30, 1956, twenty-three public utilities holding company systems, controlling net assets of about 10 billion dollars, were still subject to the regulatory provisions of the Act.

By June 30, 1952, the SEC could say that as against the percentages of twenty years before:

> . . . electric utility plants owned by registered holding company systems constituted approximately 30 per cent of the aggregate dollar amount of plant owned by all private utility companies. Manufactured and natural gas plant (including gas transmission properties) owned by registered systems represented 28 per cent of the total for the nation. When the Section 11 reorganization program is completed, these percentages will decline to 23 per cent and 18 per cent, respectively.[20]

Finally, as the 1952 SEC Report proudly, and rightly so, points out:

> . . . in what is probably the only instance of its kind in the history of the nation, an entire major industry has been almost completely reorganized in the short space of 12 years and this has

[20] SEC, *18th Annual Report,* 1952, p. 3.

been accomplished with a staff which has declined steadily from 175 in 1940 to the present force of 35 employees engaged in this work in the fiscal year 1952. When the work under Section 11 is completed in another couple of years there will be no further expense to the taxpayer on this score.[21]

How should these statistics be evaluated in economic and political terms?

One should first of all point to the political and moral advantages resulting from the elimination of diseased institutions from the body politic. The elimination of the holding companies is a net advantage. This elimination, furthermore, is not imaginary or only apparent. Gone are the men, the legal complexes, the machinery, the relationships, everything that went into the making of those systems. There has been no retreat to prepared positions, no rebuilding behind a novel façade of what the law was destroying. New stockholders, by the hundreds of thousands, have been found as purchasers of the operating companies whose forced sale the mother companies had to accept. This remains one of the primary examples of fostering a solidly founded "people's capitalism," of the kind of which Wall Street is today so proud. There is no doubt the great financial empires have been physically broken up and dispersed and have not been reconstituted.

The next most remarkable factor is the immensity of the task accomplished. Assets with a value of 15 billion dollars have been taken away from the dead hand of the holding systems and reorganized into effective economic and producing entities. The figure of 15 billion dollars is arrived at on the basis of book values at the time of divestment. Since the peak years of enforcement of the Act were from 1942 to 1950, the total reflects values much below any current appraisal. Certainly the 15 billion dollars of divested property cannot be compared to the 10 billion representing the value of holding companies still under the jurisdiction of the SEC. The dollars that go into the

[21] *Ibid.,* p. 2.

making of the two figures are different dollars. It is probably fair to say the 15 billion dollars are the equivalent of 25 billion 1957 dollars.

This last figure can best give us an idea of the size of the task undertaken by a government agency which, as it approached the end of its mission, was run by a mere handful of employees. At the end of 1956, the total assets of the American automobile industry were 12 billion dollars. The total assets of the seventeen largest oil corporations, representing probably 75 per cent of the industry, were 30 billion dollars. No matter what the standards of comparison, the job must probably be described as the biggest reorganization task of a fundamental branch of economic life carried out by a modern state.

In the third place, it is quite likely it was only as a result of this program of simultaneous financial dismantling and economic integration that the public utility industry recovered the confidence in itself and the support of the investor that enabled it to face successfully the very large wartime and postwar demands for energy. The installed capacity of electric utilities in the United States increased by 200 per cent between 1939 and 1956. This expansion could hardly have been contemplated and carried out in the demoralized and critical financial conditions in which the industry found itself in the thirties. Only an industry brought down to earth, having seen its structure simplified and remolded to meet the actual requirements of its operations, having been rid of its excess Wall Street baggage, could face the constructive tasks of the last twenty years. The only conclusion possible on the basis of the evidence is that the intervention of the federal government, far from harassing private industry, and far from discouraging private investors, created the conditions that permitted the public utilities to flourish and expand and attract capital investments beyond any level attained before. This is another instance of creative government regulation multiplying private endeavor.

The Public Utilities Holding Companies Act of 1935 was also a move for decentralization and freedom. Having defined the problem as one of artificial concentration, not based on any economic necessity, the New Deal sought the answer in the restoration of an authentic framework of local or regional management free from irrelevant outside influences. The choice facing a modern industrial community has usually been defined in terms of the following alternative: either tolerate bad and monopolistic controls or accept nationalization of the industry. The New Deal refused to accept this as a tenable choice and preferred to choose another way out of the impasse—the restoration of a genuinely free and efficient system of private property.

Lastly, this was a self-liquidating enterprise. The continued enforcement of a drastic industrial reorganization did not bring with it a permanent extension of the bureaucratic machine. It is hard to realize that financial operations involving tens of billions of dollars were handled by a staff that as of 1952 numbered 35 government employees. Parkinson's Law was inoperative here, as it was in the case of the TVA.

Repeatedly, then, the New Deal was responsible for policies that, whether new or old, meant an increase in the role and activities of private citizens and organizations. The majesty and power of government were able to assert themselves by virtue of the validity of the principles expounded and applied. The weight of the bureaucratic machine itself was not needed.

The New Deal built in the Tennessee Valley a monument to democracy in action. In the Act of 1935, it destroyed an intricate web of artificial restrictions that were threatening freedom. With a two-pronged attack, one positive and the other negative, it came to grips with two of the major aspects of the responsibility of government in our industrial civilization. In doing so, it used principles and practices that have a right to be included among the "inventions" of twentieth-century democratic government.

5

The Supreme Court
and the Constitution

There is no need to labor the point of the uniqueness of the Supreme Court of the United States. Since the inception of the American republic, it has been an institution essential to the operation of the American system. With the passage of time, it has developed powers which, given the complexity of the issues that come before the Court, find no parallel anywhere else. And this has been particularly true of the years since 1932.

Consider the Court's activities with reference to the federal government. The Court stands ready to review the actions of administrative agencies and the manner in which they impinge upon individual freedoms and rights. The Court may review the exercise of Presidential powers in their civil and military, domestic and foreign, aspects. The Court may review the legislative activity of Congress as well as its important non-legislative work. The Court may allow decisions of lower federal and state courts to stand or it may invalidate them. But the Court acts beyond the vast area of the federal system. It has to keep a proper balance between the federal system and the governments of the member states, and in the long run, accept responsibility for the maintenance of federalism in the United States.

These vast responsibilities reach the Supreme Court through the narrow opening of individual cases. For the Court does not issue sweeping and generalized rulings on matters of constitutional law brought to its bench, in the absence of a specific lawsuit, by the government or other public bodies. The Court has never accepted any such generic jurisdiction, and has made known from the beginning that it would limit itself to settling specific cases in which a judicial dispute has arisen as to what the law of the land is. This is a procedure making for delay, and years may elapse before a clear-cut test of the constitutional validity of important legislation reaches the Court. It is also possible for the Supreme Court to refuse to consider basic constitutional issues because of lack of sufficient clarity or of sufficient urgency in the case brought before it. The Court may at times want to feel it has its back against the wall before it undertakes to act. When the Court acts, however, its decision is intended to apply to all similarly situated cases. The tradition of special interest to us here is the refusal by the Supreme Court to enforce a statute in a concrete instance of a case affecting federal legislation. This has the effect of invalidating the statute.

It is possible, however, for an important question never to reach the Supreme Court at all. The influence of the Supreme Court on government and law may be intermittent and partial. There is nothing the Supreme Court can do about it, for it will never reach out and of itself seize problems it may well consider—in the privacy of its chambers—vital to the nation. The Court sits back and waits; the initiative belongs to the aggrieved party. Sometimes, however, the activities of government are such that there is no clearly aggrieved party or, at least, no one who feels aggrieved to the point of fighting an issue up to the Supreme Court.

When all this is said and understood, this fact remains: The role of the Supreme Court has been a fundamental one in the history of the United States. The American system requires, as an absolutely necessary condition for its operation, the existence of the Supreme Court and the exercise on its part of

certain powers. More specifically still, it requires the exercise
by the Supreme Court of its ultimate power of review whereby
executive and legislative acts can be invalidated. Let us be
clear as to why this is so.

There is first of all the task of the maintenance of the
federal system. American federalism is, as we have seen, not
a paper federalism, in which the central government can at any
time it wishes to do so destroy the substance of the powers of
the member states. Any federal system in which real power has,
at all times, to be duly apportioned between central and state
governments requires a final judicial arbiter capable of determining, in instances of conflict, to which government belongs
the power under dispute. This is by no means an easy task, nor
has the Supreme Court acquitted itself easily of it. There have
been times when power to act was simultaneously denied to the
federal and state governments. There have been times when the
delegated powers of the federal government have been interpreted
in an exceedingly narrow way, thus imperiling the federal
system itself. The point is that a supreme judicial agency must
exist in an authentically federal system. It may not do its job
well and government will suffer, but without it there would be
no federalism at all.

The second historic and logical reason for the existence of
the Supreme Court, with its power of judicial review, is the
United States' written constitution. Not only must the federal
system be maintained, but the Constitution must be kept alive
as the supreme law of the land. Now it should be obvious that
the Constitution is not the clear-cut and simple document that
will permit the Supreme Court, as some of its members have
from time to time appeared to believe, to place the constitutional and the statutory provisions in parallel columns to decide
whether they can be reconciled or not by a simple process of
verbal comparison. There are words and concepts in the Constitution of immensely difficult construction, such as those of the

general welfare, of due process of law, or even of equality before the law. No immutably fixed meaning can be attached to
ideas whose content and scope is bound to change with changing conditions.

Some of these elusive concepts have either baffled generations of lawyers and justices or have at times led them to what
today would be considered ill-founded conclusions. When, for
instance, in the half-century between 1890 and 1936, the words
"interstate commerce" were interpreted in a static way which
excluded flow and movement and consequences from the pur-
view of the Court, or when the words "due process of law" as
contained in the Fourteenth Amendment were given the substantive meaning of defense of property rights and were used
by the Court for the wholesale condemnation of federal and
state legislation, the Court created more difficulties than it
solved. Many students of government at the time, and after
1932 an overwhelming majority of the American people,
thought of those decisions as an improper exercise of the power
of judicial review, given the premises upon which the authority
of the Court rested. A constitutional democracy, however, has
no built-in guarantee that it can avoid periods of stress and
crisis.

Even then no one in a position of authority or influence
suggested that the power itself be taken away from the Court,
for that power is inherent in its jurisdiction (although Congress
can play with the precise definition of that jurisdiction). The
hope of constitutional democracy must be that in the long run
the interplay of the Constitution, of the operation of its institutions, and of the general will of the community will all
merge in one single stream. These expectations have proved to
be well founded, for the words "interstate commerce," "due
process of law," and "equal protection of the laws" are now
being interpreted by the Court in ways appearing to correspond,
on balance, to the long-range requirements of the American

community—the requirements of effective and flexible government, of community life, of individual and group freedom, of common-sense distribution of political power among the agencies entitled to its exercise. And, withal, the Supreme Court has maintained its right of judicial review, of saying what the Constitution allows and what the Constitution does not allow. This turns out to be, in the middle of the twentieth century, a vital power in the defense of human rights.

The Constitution may be obscure, the Constitution may be ambivalent, the Constitution may appear today under a light different from yesterday's, the Constitution may permit an altogether amazing expansion of the powers of government beyond anything contemplated by the Founding Fathers, for indeed they could not contemplate the consequences of the industrial revolution which had then not even gotten under way. But when all these qualifications and doubts have been raised and once we have become, happily, aware of the fact that a written Constitution can be a flexible and changing instrument even without the benefit of amendments, we reach an area of clarity, where there is a minimum of fog and of uncertainty—an area where, in spite of the natural reluctance one must show to speak of absolute and unqualified principles, such principles are in effect found: the Bill of Rights.

The thickest fog may surround constitutional debates on the economic and social consequences of the Constitution, yet the limpid quality of the first article of the Bill of Rights cannot be obscured.

> Congress shall make no law respecting an establishment of religion, or prohibiting the free exercise thereof; or abridging the freedom of speech, or of the press; or the right of the people peaceably to assemble, and to petition the government for a redress of grievances.

The prohibition addressed to Congress is as absolute as any prohibition can be. True, at times the sensibilities of the

Court may be dull and its reactions slow. The duty of the Court is nonetheless clear, its mandate imperative. Here is one field in which the Court, with the assistance of the Fifth and Fourteenth Amendments, can sweep aside attempts to interfere with the exercise of the fundamental freedoms of democracy. This is the final test of the essentiality of the Supreme Court power of judicial review of executive and legislative actions, be they state or federal in origin.

The Bill of Rights cannot be circumvented or avoided for very long if constitutionalism is to survive. It is an awkward body of rules to dispose of. One may have to wait a while, but in the end one comes up against the series of flat and uncompromising articles which are the bulwark of American freedom. It would be unwise to make the Supreme Court the sole custodian of this bulwark, and a fair reading of American history will show that other agencies of government high and low have shown due regard for the Bill of Rights and contributed much to its vitality. But this is not the question. The question is whether, in as complicated a system as the American one, and with so many temptations available to authorities to tamper with the freedoms of the citizens, a power should not be vested somewhere to determine what the law is and what the Constitution permits.

Once all mistakes are duly reckoned and all lapses noted and all evidences of timidity lamented, the Supreme Court seems to have accepted this responsibility, considering itself the special guardian of the Bill of Rights, and performing its duty well, or as well as can be expected of a human agency subject to the tensions of our civilization.

Critics usually assume impossible standards of perfection and of performance. They assume an even and peaceful tenor of political life, the same, for instance, in Switzerland and in the United States. They refuse to see that the United States has been struggling with some of the most difficult domestic and international problems ever to face a great country, some of them not of its own making and several of them the result of a generous (even if not wholly altruistic) reaction to the difficulties of other peoples.

Viewed against the realities of modern life, the record of the Supreme Court as the supreme dispenser of the law in the maintenance of freedom is a good one.

The Supreme Court, then, must be seen as a body central to the operation of the constitutional system and to the survival of the Bill of Rights. The record of the twenty years which come under the special scrutiny of these pages shows indeed that in both fields the Court has played roles of the utmost significance.

To place in focus and to give its full flavor and meaning to the Roosevelt Revolution, the story will be told at some length, and in some instances even carried beyond 1952 for the sake of completeness. This chapter is, therefore, built around the "constitutional revolution" of 1937, out of which have come the constitutional concepts and issues of the present. The next chapter will deal with the views on freedom and equality entertained by the Court. The upheaval discussed in the first was caused in the main by the New Deal; some of the main ideas with which we are concerned in the second find their initial formulation in the climate of the years from 1937 to 1950.

THE STRUGGLE OVER DUE PROCESS

The half-century which preceded the Great Depression and the New Deal was a time of unparalleled expansion for the American economy. The nation which had survived the Civil War and had succeeded in linking East and West, North and South, through an intricate railway network, was capitalizing on its successfully retained unity and vigorous strength through an economic and industrial drive of extraordinarily sustained intensity.

The decisive expression of freedom in those decades was the freedom of economic man in a free enterprise system to be released from the restraints of public power at any level. It was strongly felt that the American dream of full development of the continent would never be realized if the spirit of adventure of the citizens was to be thwarted by puny politicians and bureaucrats.

It is now possible to view those days with more detachment and sympathy than in 1932. Much that is marvelous and awe-inspiring was accomplished. The forces which gave America its industrial might were probably the only ones in a position to do so. Sometimes a high cost in terms of human happiness and natural beauty was paid but this is not the main issue, for fantastically high prices have been paid by all nations that have become industrial powers, from the United States to the United Kingdom and to the Soviet Union. The inescapable, if unwelcome, reality is that the creation of an industrial society entails the loss of some earlier values, and the acceptance of many sacrifices. This is likely to happen regardless of who is in the driver's seat.

What is of immediate interest to us is the attitude of the highest constitutional body to the issues posed by a growing industrial society. It seems certain that, during this long and critical period, roughly from 1890 to 1936, a period including both a phase of ascendancy and one of deep crisis, the Supreme Court—moving away sharply from earlier nineteenth-century positions built upon the strong foundations of Chief Justice John Marshall—reinterpreted the meaning of the Constitution in a way to weaken the power of government. To do this, the Court had to deal first of all with the power of the national government, a power resting on what seemed to be the unshakable basis provided by the opinions of the Marshall Court. And, secondly, with those of the forty-eight states, with their reserved and with their inherent police powers, which had been loudly restated in 1876 in the first of the Granger cases, when the Supreme Court, speaking through Chief Justice White, admitted the right of the states through the exercise of their police power to regulate economic activities endowed with a public interest.

What the Supreme Court did in the fifty years before the New Deal was to set embarrassing limits to the efforts of all these governments, by telling the federal government on the one hand that its delegated powers were limited by the reserved powers of the states and that no broad interpretation of such clauses as the "general welfare" or "interstate commerce" was possible and, on the other hand, by telling the states that their exercise of police powers was rigorously limited by the due process clause of the Fourteenth Amendment. To show its dead earnestness, the Supreme Court, between 1890 and 1937, declared invalid 228 state statutes on the basis of the due process clause.

The issue can be summed up in this way: Was it proper for the Supreme Court to identify itself to such a large extent with one view of economic freedom and of economic policy, and to nullify, therefore, so many of the intermittent, tentative, and scattered efforts that legislative bodies were making to keep economic life within changing and better defined boundaries of public policy? At the root of the problem was the readiness of the Court—in the absence of a clearly unavoidable constitutional mandate—to substitute its political and legislative judgment for the judgment of other and politically responsible bodies.

Was a clear constitutional mandate absent? Was it not true that the Court had to administer due process and that its destructive moves against the states on that basis were therefore constitutionally grounded and beyond reproach?

The due process clause of the Fourteenth Amendment reads: "nor shall any State deprive any person of life, liberty, or property, without due process of law." Since decisive documentary evidence is missing, the simplest and most logical interpretation of the clause is this: it was meant to extend to the states the prohibition already existing for the federal government in the Bill of Rights adopted in 1791 and reading, in practically identical words: "No person shall be . . . deprived of life, liberty, or property, without due process of law." These words appear in the Fifth Amendment to guarantee the essentials of a fair trial according to the traditions of common-law justice.

For nearly half a century, beginning with an 1890 railway case,[1] the Supreme Court chose to give to the Fourteenth Amendment's due process clause a substantive rather than a procedural meaning, and to read into it a warning addressed to the states not to interfere with the free and unregulated operation of the economic system, not to limit profits, not to control rates and tariffs, not to try to enforce certain types of restrictive contractual obligations. Any of these things, the Court thought, would inflict on the citizen a loss of property without due process of law, no matter how careful or procedurally correct the regulations might have been.

That public regulation may inflict a loss of profits and a loss of freedom of economic movement cannot be denied, even though a short-term shrinking of private gains imposed by regulation may often in the long run broaden the security of the commonwealth and expand private gains. Even assuming the immediate loss of some of the benefits to be derived from property, neither the Fifth nor the Fourteenth Amendments contain any guarantees against such loss. What they do is to guarantee property against that loss without due process. And what the Court did was to assume that regulation, properly provided by responsible public agencies through the adoption of rational procedures, could not satisfy the requirements of due process.

[1] *Chicago, Milwaukee, and St. Paul R.R. Co.*, v. *Minnesota*, 134 U.S. 418 (1890).

We have examined in the Introduction some of the early highlights of this trend, as a background to the Great Depression, and its continuation well beyond the times when it might have been said such a rapidly growing country as the United States could afford to pay the price of unregulated economic life. The trend persisted beyond 1929, beyond 1932, and through the first four years of the New Deal.

By the end of 1936, the list of important decisions of the Supreme Court which had barred federal legislation in economic matters as exceeding the limited spheres of its delegated jurisdiction had become a lengthy one.[2] And the due process clause of both the Fifth and Fourteenth Amendments had been used over and over again to upset federal or state legislative attempts to regulate economic relationships in industries which the Court felt were not affected with a public interest.[3]

Of the use made of these magic words—"due process"—a bitter critic of the Supreme Court writes:

> Well over a thousand of the Supreme Court's full-dress decisions have revolved around the little due process clause. These decisions have rarely dealt with Negroes, or with people of any color, accused of crime. They have dealt instead with corporations or, less often, with real (not corporate) "persons" who claimed through their lawyers that some duly enacted and fairly administered state law, taxing them or regulating their business activities, "deprived" them of property "without due process of law." In sum, the Fourteenth Amendment's due process clause has become the last, and quite often successful, resort of men or companies who stand to lose money through the normal working of some

[2] For example: *United States* v. *E. C. Knight Co.*, 156 U.S. 1 (1895); *Hammer* v. *Dagenhart*, 247 U.S. 251 (1918); *United Mine Workers* v. *Coronado Coal Co.*, 259 U.S. 344 (1922); *Schechter Poultry Corporation* v. *United States*, 295 U.S. 495 (1935); *Railroad Retirement Board* v. *Alton Railroad Co.*, 295 U.S. 330 (1935); *United States* v. *Butler*, 297 U.S. 1 (1936); *Carter* v. *Carter Coal Co.*, 298 U.S. 238 (1936).

[3] *Lochner* v. *New York*, 198 U.S. 45 (1905); *Adair* v. *United States*, 208 U.S. 161 (1908); *Coppage* v. *Kansas*, 236 U.S. 1 (1915); *Adkins* v. *Children's Hospital*, 261 U.S. 525 (1923); *Morehead* v. *New York ex rel. Tipaldo*, 298 U.S. 587 (1936).

state law, properly passed by a properly elected legislature, properly signed by a properly elected governor, and properly put into effect by properly chosen state officials, including judges—some law that perhaps clamps down on sweat-shops, or taxes big fortunes handed on at death, or orders a monopoly like an electric company not to charge so much.[4]

As the New Deal gathered strength, the writing off of the constitutional powers of government by the Supreme Court in defense of views on economic freedom which by 1933 had, under the most charitable interpretation, failed to achieve the benefits that had been so confidently expected, became a dangerous exercise. Yet it continued, and between the beginning of 1935 and the middle of 1936 the New Deal was rebuked many times while the Court did not forget to do the same with any state daring to act independently.

Addressing himself to the efforts of the federal government to bring some order out of the economic chaos afflicting the basic industries of the country, such as coal mining, Justice Sutherland sums up with vigor the philosophy of the Court majority:

> Much stress is put upon the evils which come from the struggle between employers and employees over the matter of wages, working conditions, the right of collective bargaining, etc., and the resulting strikes, curtailment and irregularity of production and effect on prices; and it is insisted that interstate commerce is greatly affected thereby. [But] the conclusive answer is that the evils are all local evils over which the Federal Government has no legislative control. The relation of employer and employee is a local relation. . . . The wages are paid for the doing of local work. Working conditions are obviously local conditions. The employees are not engaged in or about commerce, but exclusively in producing a commodity. And the controversies and evils, which it is the object of the act to regulate and minimize, are local con-

---

[4] Fred Rodell, *Nine Men, A Political History of the Supreme Court from 1790 to 1955,* New York, 1955, pp. 147–48.

troversies and evils affecting local work undertaken to accomplish that local result. Such effect as they may have upon commerce, however extensive it may be, is secondary and indirect. An increase in the greatness of the effect adds to its importance. It does not alter its character.[5]

In a case dealing with agricultural controls, Justice Roberts is unmoved by the helplessness of local and state governments to deal with a crisis national in scope:

> From the accepted doctrine that the United States is a government of delegated powers, it follows that those not expressly granted, or reasonably granted, or reasonably to be implied from such as are conferred, are reserved to the States or to the people. To forestall any suggestion to the contrary, the Tenth Amendment was adopted. The same proposition otherwise stated, is that powers not granted are prohibited. None to regulate agricultural production is given, and therefore legislation by Congress for that purpose is forbidden.[6]

In the same opinion, Justice Roberts appeared happily convinced the duty of the Court was so clear and obvious no alternatives concerning questions of substance and of policy ever presented themselves:

> There should be no misunderstanding as to the function of this court in such a case. It is sometimes said that the court assumes a power to overrule or control the action of the people's representatives. This is a misconception. The Constitution is the supreme law of the land ordained and established by the people. All legislation must conform to the principles it lays down. When an act of Congress is appropriately challenged in the courts as not conforming to the constitutional mandate the judicial branch of the Government has only one duty,—to lay the article of the Constitution which is invoked beside the statute which is challenged and to decide whether the latter squares with the former. All the court does, or can do, is to announce its considered judgment upon the question. The only power it has, if such it may be called, is the power of judgment. This court neither approves nor condemns any

[5] *Carter* v. *Carter Coal Co.,* 298 U.S. 238 (1936).
[6] *United States* v. *Butler,* 297 U.S. 1 (1936).

legislative policy. Its delicate and difficult office is to ascertain and declare whether the legislation is in accordance with, or in contravention of, the provisions of the Constitution: and, having done that, its duty ends.

It was as simple as that.

These majority opinions were not of course going unchallenged. By a notable tradition of the Supreme Court, majority and minority views are both made public. In all fundamental constitutional matters in which a conflict has arisen, the minority has not been silent and has expressed its views with the firm determination of exposing the fallacies of the majority views. In this century, some of the most famous members of the Court—such as Holmes, Brandeis, Cardozo, Stone—have for many years publicly led the opposition to their conservative colleagues. This open debate, leading sometimes to contradictions and subtle shadings of constitutional interpretation, has been criticized as weakening the authority and majesty of the law. No one, however, who is aware of the nature of American constitutionalism and of the spirit of the common law can lament a procedure which shows constitutional law as a living and adaptable body of thought.

Essentially, the position of the minority was: one, the Constitution of the United States had made far-reaching grants of power to the federal government in the interest of the general welfare; two, while broad constitutional limits existed to the exercise of those powers, the wisdom of legislation within those limits had to be decided by the people and their elected assemblies and not by the judges; three, federalism meant a variety of experimentation with all the governments of the complex structure sharing in it; and finally, the growing interdependence of the modern industrial community was a reality too harsh to be set aside by narrow legal interpretations.

In the years of crisis, Justice Stone was one of the more eloquent spokesmen of the minority. Holmes had resigned from the Court in 1932, and Brandeis was often willing to let the younger Stone carry the burden of dissent. In 1936, in the Butler case, Stone spoke with vigor against the provincial thinking of the majority in nullifying the Agricultural Adjustment Act:

> A tortured construction of the Constitution is not to be justified by recourse to extreme examples of reckless Congressional spending. . . . Such suppositions are addressed to the mind accustomed to believe that it is the business of courts to sit in judgment on the wisdom of legislative action. Courts are not the only agency of government that must be assumed to have capacity to govern. Congress and the courts both unhappily may falter or be mistaken in the performance of their constitutional duty. But interpretation of our great charter of government which proceeds on any assumption that the responsibility for the preservation of our institutions is the exclusive concern of any one of the three branches of government, or that it alone can save them from destruction is far more likely, in the long run, "to obliterate the constituent members" of "an indestructible union of indestructible members" than the frank recognition that language, even of a constitution, may mean what it says: that the power to tax and spend includes the power to relieve a nationwide economic maladjustment by conditional gifts of money.

If the views of the Court's majority were followed, the federal government could not rescue the nation from its predicament but would be bound to leave the initiative to the states— that is, to governments unable or unwilling to develop the necessary policies. Stone pointed out that "the power of Courts to declare a statute unconstitutional is subject to two guiding principles which ought never to be absent from judicial consciousness." The first was that the Court must only be concerned with the constitutional right of the legislative body to pass the legislation under review. The Court should never look into the wisdom of the legislation. The second is that while executive and legislative actions are subject to the final constitutional review that the courts provide, there is no review of a decision of the Supreme Court: "the only check upon our own exercise of power is our own sense of self-restraint. For the removal of unwise laws from the statute books appeal lies not to the courts but to the ballot and to the processes of democratic government."

The minority views triumphed with dramatic suddenness in 1937. Long-established doctrines were overruled and new ones were developed which, without expressly overruling earlier decisions of the Court, in effect did so. Fresh powers were read into the Constitution, and the experimental approach which had been characteristic of the federal government for four years suddenly found itself welcomed on the bench of the Supreme Court.

In its approach to a series of historic cases that began in the spring of 1937—an approach which has continued ever since without change in any essential trait—the Supreme Court proceeded once again to interpret the Constitution of the United States in the spirit of those who had drafted it.

THE CONSTITUTIONAL REVOLUTION

This change has rightly been called a "Constitutional Revolution." [7] As a witness who was himself later to become a member of the Supreme Court said:

> . . . the spectacle of the Court that day frankly and completely reversing itself and striking down its opinion but a few months old was a moment never to be forgotten.[8]

The case in question was that of *West Coast Hotel Company* v. *Parrish*. The Chief Justice was speaking for the Court and he was now attacking the earlier reasoning of the Court which had

---

[7] Edward S. Corwin, *Constitutional Revolution, Ltd.*, Claremont, 1941.

[8] Robert H. Jackson, *The Struggle for Judicial Supremacy*, New York, 1941, pp. 207–8; quoted in Bernard Schwartz, *The Supreme Court*, New York, 1957, p. 20.

denied the right of New York State to regulate the minimum wages of women and children. For, as Hughes eloquently said:

> What can be closer to the public interest than the health of women and their protection from unscrupulous and overreaching employers? And if the protection of women is a legitimate end of the exercise of state power, how can it be said that the requirement of the payment of a minimum wage fairly fixed in order to meet the very necessities of existence is not an admissible means to that end? . . . The legislature had the right to consider that its minimum wage requirements would be an important aid in carrying out its policy of protection. The adoption of similar requirements by many States evidences a deep-seated conviction both as to the presence of the evil and as to the means adopted to check it. Legislative response to that conviction cannot be regarded as arbitrary or capricious and that is all we have to decide. Even if the wisdom of the policy be regarded as debatable and its effects uncertain, still the legislature is entitled to its judgment.
>
> There is an additional and compelling consideration which recent economic experience has brought into a strong light. The exploitation of a class of workers who are in an unequal position with respect to bargaining power and are thus relatively defenceless against the denial of a living wage is not only detrimental to their health and well-being but casts a direct burden for their support upon the community. . . . We may take judicial notice of the unparalleled demands for relief which arose during the recent period of depression and still continue to an alarming extent despite the degree of economic recovery which has been achieved. It is unnecessary to cite official statistics to establish what is of common knowledge through the length and breadth of the land.[9]

Then came the validation of the National Labor Relations Act in the Jones and Laughlin case.[10] Here the earlier and narrow interpretation of interstate commerce was abandoned. Chief Justice Hughes, again speaking for the Court, refused to

---

[9] *West Coast Hotel* v. *Parrish,* 300 U.S. 379 (1937).
[10] *National Labor Relations Board* v. *Jones and Laughlin Steel Corporation,* 301 U.S. 1 (1937).

belittle the consequence of industrial strife involving steel corporations, among the largest and most powerful of an industrial society. To refuse to recognize the validity of the National Labor Relations Act would mean

> . . . to shut our eyes to the plainest facts of our national life and to deal with the question of direct and indirect effects in an intellectual vacuum. . . . When industries organize themselves on a national scale, making their relation to interstate commerce the dominant factor in their activities, how can it be maintained that their industrial labor relations constitute a forbidden field into which Congress may not enter when it is necessary to protect interstate commerce from the paralyzing consequences of industrial war? We have often said that interstate commerce itself is a practical conception. It is equally true that interference with that commerce must be appraised by a judgment that does not ignore actual experience.
>
> Experience has abundantly demonstrated that the recognition of the right of employees to self-organization and to have representatives of their own choosing for the purpose of collective bargaining is often an essential condition of industrial peace. Refusal to confer and negotiate has been one of the most prolific causes of strife. . . . The steel industry is one of the great basic industries of the United States, with ramifying activities affecting interstate commerce at every point. The government aptly refers to the steel strike of 1919–1920 with its far-reaching consequences. The fact that there appears to have been no major disturbance in that industry in the more recent period did not dispose of the possibilities of future and like dangers to interstate commerce which Congress was entitled to foresee and to exercise its protective power to forestall.

Next, two of the leading spokesmen of the erstwhile minority, Justices Stone and Cardozo, were given a chance to lead the new majority in the three historic Social Security cases which settled the controversies over the federal power to tax and spend for the general welfare and "settled [it] in favor of the existence of that power in the Federal Government." [11]

[11] Robert H. Jackson, *The Supreme Court in the American System of Government,* Cambridge, 1955, p. 67.

In the first of them, Stone redefined the concept of federalism:

> The United States and the State of Alabama are not alien governments. They coexist within the same territory. Unemployment within it is their common concern. Together the two statutes now before us embody a cooperative legislative effort by state and national governments, for carrying out a public purpose common to both, which neither could fully achieve without the cooperation of the other. The Constitution does not prohibit such cooperation.[12]

In the second, Cardozo pulled the "general welfare" out of hiding:

> Of the many available figures a few only will be mentioned. During the years 1929 to 1936, when the country was passing through a cyclical depression, the number of the unemployed mounted to unprecedented heights. Often the average was more than 10 million; at times a peak was attained of 16 million or more. Disaster to the breadwinner meant disaster to dependents. Accordingly the roll of the unemployed, itself formidable enough, was only a partial roll of the destitute or needy. The fact developed quickly that the states were unable to give the requisite relief. The problem had become national in area and dimensions. There was need of help from the nation if the people were not to starve. It is too late today for the argument to be heard with tolerance that in a crisis so extreme the use of the moneys of the nation to relieve the unemployed and their dependents is a use for any purpose narrower than the promotion of the general welfare.[13]

Finally, in the case which sustained the old-age benefit clauses of the Social Security Act, Cardozo went to the heart of the economic evidence in favor of federal intervention:

> Congress did not improvise a judgment when it found that the award of old-age benefits would be conducive to the general welfare. The President's Committee on Economic Security made an investigation and report, aided by a research staff of Government officers and employees, and by an Advisory Council and

---

[12] *Carmichael* v. *Southern Coal and Coke Co.,* 301 U.S. 495 (1937).
[13] *Steward Machine Co.* v. *Davis,* 301 U.S. 548 (1937).

seven other advisory groups. Extensive hearings followed before the House Committee on Ways and Means and the Senate Committee on Finance. A great mass of evidence was brought together supporting the policy which finds expression in the act. . . . We summarize in the margin the results of other studies by state and national commissions. They point the same way. The problem is plainly national in area and dimensions.[14]

Three years later, in 1941, the Fair Labor Standards Act was found valid.[15] There was no minority any longer at that time, and Stone could speak for a unanimous Court. The powers delegated to the federal government cannot be limited in their exercise by the powers that the Constitution reserves to the states. The Tenth Amendment does not deprive the national government of authority to resort to all means for the exercise of powers which are appropriate and plainly adapted to the permitted end.

> The power of Congress over interstate commerce "is complete in itself, may be exercised to its utmost extent, and acknowledges no limitations other than are prescribed in the Constitution." That power can neither be enlarged nor diminished by the exercise or non-exercise of state power. Congress, following its own conception of public policy concerning the restrictions which may appropriately be imposed on interstate commerce, is free to exclude from the commerce articles whose use in the states for which they are destined it may conceive to be injurious to the public health, morals or welfare, even though the state has not sought to regulate their use.

Speaking for the Court, Stone proceeded to overrule *Hammer* v. *Dagenhart,* vindicating the minority views of Justice Holmes in that case.[16]

---

[14] *Helvering* v. *Gerhardt,* 304 U.S. 405 (1938).
[15] *United States* v. *Darby,* 312 U.S. 100 (1941).
[16] "But if there is any matter upon which civilized countries have agreed—far more unanimously than they have with regard to intoxicants and some other matters over which this country is now emotionally aroused—it is the evil of premature and excessive child labor. I should have thought that if we were to introduce our own moral conceptions

At long last the Court had come around to another of Holmes's celebrated views, expressed in 1905—a statute should not be held invalid "unless it can be said that a rational and fair man necessarily would admit that the statute proposed would infringe fundamental principles as they have been understood by the traditions of our people and our law." [17]

The traditions of American constitutionalism were not traditions of anarchy and of refusal to admit the necessity of government. Keeping all the vital procedural safeguards alive to guarantee a government of law, the Supreme Court had recognized the responsibilities of government.

This was correctly interpreted by one of the more distinguished members of the Court as a return to John Marshall's position of a century before. In his *Declaration of Legal Faith,* Justice Rutledge said in 1947:

> Just as in recent years the permissible scope for congressional commerce action has broadened, returning to Marshall's conception, the prohibitive effect of the clause has been progressively narrowed. The trend has been toward sustaining state regulation formerly regarded as inconsistent with Congress' unexercised power of commerce . . . the scope of judicial intervention has been narrowed by the more recent trends, affecting both the affirmative and the prohibitive workings of the clause. Greater leeway and deference are given for legislative judgments, national and state, formally expressed. Larger emphasis is put on scrutiny of particular

where in my opinion they do not belong, this was preeminently a case for upholding the exercise of all its powers by the United States. But I had thought that the propriety of the exercise of a power admitted to exist in some cases was for the consideration of Congress alone and that this Court always had disavowed the right to intrude its judgment upon questions of policy or morals. It is not for this Court to pronounce when prohibition is necessary to regulation if it ever may be necessary— to say that it is permissible as against strong drink but not as against the product of ruined lives. The act does not meddle with anything belonging to the States. They may regulate their internal affairs and their domestic commerce as they like. But when they seek to send their products across the state line they are no longer within their rights." *Hammer* v. *Dagenhart,* 247, U.S. 251 (1918).

[17] *Lochner* v. *New York,* 198 U.S. 45 (1905).

facts and concrete consequences, with an eye on their practical bearing for creating the evils the commerce clause was designed to outlaw. Correspondingly, less stress . . . is placed upon large generalizations and dogmatism inherited from levels of debate time has lowered. More and more controlling considerations of policy implicit in thinking, judgment, and decision are brought into the open.[18]

In the field of state powers, the constitutional revolution, for the first time, gave the states the freedom of movement that should have been theirs (and can still be theirs in spite of the great expansion of federal powers). Between 1938 and 1946, as a rule, the due process clause of the Fourteenth Amendment was used to sanction state action, the very opposite of the condition that had prevailed during the previous fifty years. As the late Justice Jackson wrote:

> For more than half a century the Supreme Court found in the Fourteenth Amendment authority for striking down various social experiments by the states. The history of judicial nullification of state social and economic legislation is too well known to justify repetition here. It came to its culmination when the Court wound up the October 1935 term by declaring that there was no power in either state or nation to enact a minimum wage law, a position repudiated within a few months by the conventions of both political parties and retracted by the Court itself with some haste. That retraction probably brought an end to the use of the Fourteenth Amendment to prevent experiments by the states with economic and social and labor legislation.[19]

As the Court itself made clear in 1955, "The day is gone when this Court uses the Due Process Clause of the Fourteenth Amendment to strike down state laws, regulatory of business and industrial conditions, because they may be unwise, im-

---

[18] Quoted in Robert L. Stern, "The Problems of Yesteryear—Commerce and Due Process," *Vanderbilt Law Review*, 1951, p. 446, reprinted in Robert G. McCloskey, ed., *Essays in Constitutional Law*, New York, 1957, pp. 150–80.

[19] Jackson, *The Supreme Court*, p. 68.

provident, or out of harmony with a particular school of thought." [20]

The Court is the guardian of the Constitution but not of any particular economic doctrine, nor does it guarantee the wisdom of legislators. As Justice Black said in 1949, this has meant a return to earlier constitutional doctrines declaring the states have the power to legislate against what are found to be injurious practices in their internal commercial and business affairs, so long as their laws do not run afoul of some specific federal constitutional prohibition, or of some valid federal law.[21]

The question fascinated observers of the American scene have tried to answer ever since 1937 has, of course, been this: Why did the Supreme Court reverse itself so drastically? Why did the Supreme Court apparently find it so simple, after 1936, to justify both the bold intervention and the expansion of federal and state governments in novel directions? Why indeed, when during the worst period of the national emergency the Court had firmly refused to alter its constitutional thinking?

President Roosevelt was never in doubt for an answer. The change had been due to political pressure exercised on the Supreme Court, culminating with his plan for judicial reform. There is a great measure of validity in this answer.

One should rule out, as in reality not clarifying anything, the generic explanation that the times were ripe for a re-evaluation of the Court's positions. The times had been ripe for that fresh look at the Constitution for a long time, probably since the beginning of the century. A degree of almost desperate urgency had existed since 1930 and yet the Court had remained unmoved.

There can hardly be any doubt, on the other hand, that for

---

[20] *Williamson* v. *Lee Optical Co.,* 348 U.S. 483 (1955).
[21] *Lincoln Union* v. *Northwestern Co.,* 335 U.S. 525 (1949).

a period of nearly two years preceding the decisions of the spring of 1937 political pressures had been building up. In the end, even the Supreme Court could not ignore them.

One may begin by recalling the "horse-and-buggy" press conference of President Roosevelt on May 31, 1935, which was an effective analysis of the inadequacy of the Supreme Court's doctrines on the great economic problems of the day.[22] Next, the overwhelming electoral victory of the New Deal in 1936 proved that the country was supporting the reform legislation of the government. The attempts to stem the tide of federal controls could not appear even to the Supreme Court to be based on too solid foundations after the decisive outcome of the elections.

There was the added evidence which must have impressed with particular forcefulness judges who, like Hughes and Roberts, either were politically sensitive or occupied a middle-of-the-road position, of the damaging quality of some of the labor disturbances which were then sweeping across the country. The Detroit labor strikes showed up the helplessness of state governments and the urgency of a national approach to the maintenance of labor peace.

Finally, in his message to Congress of January, 1937, Roosevelt left no doubt about his views on the proper relationship of the three branches of government. And on February 5, 1937, the President announced his Court reform plan.

The chronological evidence discloses that it was on March 29, 1937, that the Supreme Court took the first step on the road to revolution, and thus supports the conclusion that outside political pressures convinced the Court to change its mind. The conclusion remains true in spite of the fact that the chronology of events was actually more complicated than had usually been supposed.[23] All the while, the Court was a deeply

[22] Cf. Chapter I.

[23] Usually Justice Roberts is described as the "switch man," for, having voted on June 1, 1936, to invalidate a New York State minimum-wage

divided tribunal; the conservative core was losing ground before the sustained attacks of the minority and the changing climate of the country.

Justice Stone played a decisive role in this transformation.[24] He, together with Cardozo and Brandeis, brought to the debates within the Supreme Court a sense of awareness of the transformation of the outside world and of the need for going back to the origins of American constitutional life. His arguments were not falling on insensitive ears, for the Chief Justice, Charles Evans Hughes, was beginning to be equally conscious of the political necessities of the times and of the standards imposed by Roosevelt. He knew the survival of the Supreme Court was perhaps linked to the performance of the task which both the Constitution and the general welfare of the community required. Finally, Justice Roberts, even though reluctant to take the lead, remained open to persuasion and gradually became convinced of the need for change. In Corwin's summary, "Justice Stone's relentless insistence on argument, the Chief Justice's political skill, and Justice Roberts' eagerness for the light—these were the chief intra-curial factors in bringing about the Court's reversal of position on the New Deal." [25]

The Court had not changed. Sitting on the bench in 1937

law in the Morehead case, he supported on March 29, 1937, a similar Washington State law in the West Coast Hotel case. Roosevelt's reform plans had been announced on February 5, 1937. Evidence recently disclosed shows that in the course of the internal Court proceedings, the decisive argument in the West Coast Hotel case had taken place from December 16 to 19, 1936, and that Roberts had then voted to sustain the Washington statute. This vote then had taken place forty-eight days before Roosevelt's attack against the Court. However, the elections of 1936 were already several weeks old by December 19. For a clarification of Roberts' position, see the articles by Felix Frankfurter, "Mr. Justice Roberts," and by Erwin N. Griswold, "Owen J. Roberts as a Judge," *University of Pennsylvania Law Review,* December, 1955.

[24] See the biography by Alpheus T. Mason, *Harlan Fiske Stone: Pillar of the Law,* New York, 1956.

[25] Corwin, *op. cit.,* p. 76.

were the same nine Justices who had been sitting there since 1932, when Cardozo had succeeded Oliver Wendell Holmes. And yet a radical transformation had taken place. Within the broad framework of the Constitution, government was free in its efforts to cope with the problems of the modern world. The Roosevelt Revolution had been extended to the Supreme Court.

THE COURT TODAY

A review of the Court's position since 1937 should look at the key areas of the maintenance of federalism, and of controls over legislative review and administrative activities.

The Supreme Court's shift on federalism in the course of the last twenty years can be described, as Edward Corwin has done, as one away from a competitive conception which had prevailed throughout the century preceding the New Deal, toward a co-operative conception of the federal relationship, under which "the states and the national government are mutually complementary parts of a single governmental mechanism all of whose powers are intended to realize, according to their applicability to the problem at hand, the purposes of good government." [26] This conception refuses to view federalism as based on a series of watertight compartments among which no communication is possible. The solidarity, the joint endeavors, upon which the New Deal was predicated, have been accepted by the Court as of the essence of modern federalism. Federalism means both the fragmentation of the impact of governmental power and the acceptance of serious responsibilities by the local communities. It does not mean paralysis, just as national policy does not rule out grass-roots democracy.

As a reviewer of legislation, the Supreme Court has carried

[26] *Ibid.*, p. 99.

out during the last generation one of the great retreats in constitutional history—a retreat caused by the recognition of the complexities of modern life and by the awareness that long-cherished theories have become both inapplicable in the twentieth century and incompatible with effective government under the Constitution of the United States.

If, in substance, this retreat means acceptance, whenever possible, of the wisdom of legislative bodies, or, at least, of their right to legislate unwisely within the Constitution, it does not mean that the Supreme Court is now viewing the government of the United States as a mere variant of the parliamentary system. The government of the United States is still a constitutional one in which the long-range general purposes of the community as embodied in a written document must prevail over the temporary wills of majorities as expressed by legislative bodies.

This is, indeed, the concept that has helped to fix the current boundaries of judicial review by the Supreme Court. The Supreme Court is no longer anxious to suspect too readily the violation by Congress of the constitutional purposes of the community, and hence to rush to nullify legislative action. It will stand back and wait. It will assume that, under normal circumstances, out of conflicting legislative decisions some good over a longer period of time is bound to come. It will stand ready to perform its duty of interpreter of the constitutional will of the community as a last resort. To use the weapon of judicial review sparingly does not mean to give it up. The Supreme Court is saying that a great country, working hard in the midst of unprecedented complexities to face its destiny, cannot be halted and kept in check at every step on the assumption that its legislators are incompetent men who do not know what they are doing.

The task of the old Supreme Court was easier than the task of the new one. What is simpler than declaring a legislative measure unconstitutional? One can set up any number of constitutional tests and have only the embarrassment of the choice. But a policy of self-restraint, which at the same time does not entail abdication in practice of the power of judicial review, and even less its renunciation in principle, is much more difficult to administer. The Court may believe a number of legislative measures to be unwise and improper and yet say that the community is entitled to its own mistakes. The precise identification of the right moment at which the Court's intervention becomes essential and can no longer be postponed if the constitutional system is to be saved, is a difficult matter requiring much brooding and reflection and much delicate weighing. The decision may then take place in the midst of a public opinion climate no longer accustomed to the exercise of judicial review.[27]

This is a risk that may have to be taken. It is worth taking, if, in spite of the shift of legislative responsibility to the elected bodies which should assume it in the first place (and should do so knowing what they will do will probably stand and have to be tested in practice), the ultimate power of the Court remains unimpaired.

In the modern state, administrative action is no less important than legislative action. And if judicial review of legislation has been held in abeyance, judicial review of administrative acts has moved forward. In recent years, the Court, following a congressional mandate, has taken a fresh look at its role as controller of administrative agencies. Until not long ago, its new policy of restraint vis-à-vis legislative actions had been

[27] See, for some warnings against the danger of obsolescence of the power of judicial review of legislative action: Eugene Rostow, "The Democratic Character of Judicial Review," *Harvard Law Review,* December, 1952; Arthur E. Sutherland, "The Supreme Court and the General Will," *American Academy of Arts and Sciences, Proceedings,* Vol. 82, 1952–1953, p. 169; Robert G. McCloskey, "The Modern Court and Economic Legislation," *Essays in Constitutional Law,* pp. 149–50; Schwartz, *The Supreme Court,* p. 198.

extended to the administrative field. In 1942, Justice Frank-furter had said, "We certainly have neither technical competence nor legal authority to pronounce upon the wisdom of the course taken by the Commission." [28] And in 1944, Justice Rutledge suggested:

> . . . where the question is one of specific application of a broad statutory term in a proceeding in which the agency administering the statute must determine it initially, the reviewing court's function is limited. . . . The Board's determination that specified persons are "employees" under this Act is to be accepted if it has "warrant in the record" and a reasonable basis in law.[29]

In the same year, Justice Douglas, who himself had as-cended to the bench following his very successful management of one of the more important administrative agencies created by the New Deal, the Securities and Exchange Commission, ad-mitted the essentiality of administrative action:

> In terms of hard-headed practicalities Congress frequently could not perform its functions if it were required to make an appraisal of the myriad of facts applicable to varying situations, area by area throughout the land, and then to determine in each case what should be done. Congress does not abdicate its functions when it describes what job must be done, who must do it, and what is the scope of his authority. In our complex economy that indeed is frequently the only way in which the legislative process can go forward.[30]

In 1946, two years after this opinion was delivered, Congress passed the Federal Administration Procedure Act. Section 10 of the Act is the most important, for it establishes the basis for judicial review of administrative agency actions and requires the reviewing courts to consider the whole record in order to discover whether substantial evidence supports administrative

---

[28] *Board of Trade* v. *United States*, 314 U.S. 534 (1942).

[29] *National Labor Relations Board* v. *Hearst Publications*, 322 U.S. 111 (1944).

[30] *Bowles* v. *Willingham*, 321 U.S. 503 (1944).

decisions. Passage of the Act was due to congressional dissatis-
faction with the restricted scope of review developed by the
Supreme Court. And since 1946, "the Supreme Court has
molded its jurisprudence to accord with the congressional intent
expressed in the statute; the Court's desire to leave the field
to the administrative expert has yielded in the face of the legislative desire that the judge exercise positive responsibility
here." [31]

The new trend was well established by 1951:

> Whether or not it was ever permissible for courts to determine
> the substantiality of evidence supporting a Labor Board decision
> merely on the basis of evidence which in and of itself justified it,
> without taking into account contradictory evidence or evidence
> from which conflicting inferences could be drawn, the new legisla-
> tion definitely precludes such a theory of review and bars its
> practice. The substantiality must take into account whatever in
> the record fairly detracts from its weight. This is clearly the signifi-
> cance of the requirement . . . that courts consider the whole
> record.[32]

Justice Douglas himself, the former administrator, has given
impressive expression to the new point of view in the concluding
sentences of one of his recent books:

> The judiciary is in a high sense the guardian of the conscience
> of the people as well as of the law of the land. It is much further
> removed from the political arena than the administrative agencies
> or the legislative. It sits aloof and detached from the community,
> not subject to the political stresses and storms of the other branches.
> It is made up of men who have tenure and other protections against
> the political forces of the day. Its decisions are more apt to reflect
> tradition and first principles than political expediency.
> Judicial review gives time for the sober second thought. It in-
> terrupts the administrative process, to be sure, and makes it more
> time-consuming. But there are few decisions that must move pell-

---

[31] Schwartz, *op. cit.*, p. 133.
[32] *Universal Camera Corporation* v. *National Labor Relations Board*,
340 U.S. 474 (1951).

mell into action. The cooling period is good for most hotly-contested issues. And where basic fundamental rights of the citizen are at stake, the contemplative pause, necessitated by judicial review, may be critical. The confidence of the citizen in modern government is increased by more, rather than less, judicial review of the administrative process. It assures that basic unfairness will be corrected. And the administrator who knows he must ultimately account to a judicial body for his actions will tend to be a more responsible public official.[33]

The conclusion must be that, whether left in abeyance in the field of legislation or actively used in that of administration, the vast powers of the Supreme Court are there. They rest on the "logical implication" of the system, as Justice Jackson has said. Speaking in 1946 to a legal gathering at the French Ministry of Justice in Paris, Jackson pointed out:

> Opinion, of course, will differ as to the advantages and disadvantages of this constitutional and judicial system. The United States on the whole has been a prosperous country, with varied resources, making a favorable background for any experiment in government. Its inhabitants have not faced the strains that beset some less-favored nations. Even so, our history has not been free of sanguinary internal conflicts. It would not be realistic to contend that judicial power always has been used wisely. The Court has been sharply attacked by Presidents Jefferson, Jackson, Lincoln, and both Roosevelts. Yet no substantial sentiment exists for any curtailment of the Court's composition, none in its constitutional prerogatives. The real strength of the position of the Court is probably in its indispensability to government under a written Constitution. It is difficult to see how the provisions of a 150-year-old written document can have much vitality if there is not some permanent institution to translate them into current commands and to see to their contemporary application.[34]

Since this is a book about the Roosevelt Revolution, the question is bound to arise once more: What, in the sum total, has been the relationship of the Court to it? Some of the

[33] *We the Judges,* Garden City, N.Y., 1956, p. 445.
[34] Jackson, *The Supreme Court,* p. 26.

strongly specific relationships of the constitutional revolution of 1937 to the political revolution of the New Deal have already been discussed. Of course the over-all role of the Court has been more complex, as have the influences at work on it. As will be seen in the next chapter, important trends preceded the New Deal; and some weak opinions have been written as a result of President Truman's appointment of Fred Vinson as Chief Justice of the Court, while important values of freedom have been emphatically restated under the leadership of the new members, including the new Chief Justice, Earl Warren, appointed by President Eisenhower. In brief, the Supreme Court cannot be reduced to fit any rigid pattern and cannot be tied to the chariot of any particular party or political movement.

What one can say, however, is that, within the contemporary scene of New Deal America, the Supreme Court has performed a function that is on balance coherent and compatible with the reorientation of public policy and of social values that has come about during the last generation. The Court has played a role in the amazing modernization of institutions, in the strengthening of the role of government, and in the defense of the rights of a free society, which has been of central importance in the gradually evolving course of contemporary American civilization.

There have been times in the history of nations when, in the face of revolutionary stresses, one or the other instrumentalities of government has had to be left behind as no longer suited to the new circumstances. The striking phenomenon in modern America has been that, without any change in the substance of a document written in the eighteenth century, all of the parts of the systems have been able to adapt themselves to the new conditions and, without doing violence to the historical foundations of the commonwealth, have succeeded in fulfilling the role expected of them.

The Supreme Court, from its exposed position, could have

played a "counterrevolutionary" role. It did not. It chose—even if under pressure—to become part of the seamless web of change, the dominant reality of life in the United States since 1932, and has thus added greatly to the solidarity of the communal effort, and to the efficacy of what was being done. One cannot say that the Supreme Court has merely followed the Roosevelt Revolution. One can say it has understood the purpose and the program of the revolution, has sought hard to become a part of it in a manner to keep faith with its purpose, and, drawing deep upon a vast reservoir of historic precedents, it has succeeded in giving new luster and vigor to the spirit of American constitutionalism.

6

The Meaning of Freedom
and Equality

HUMAN AND CIVIL RIGHTS

The constitutional revolution of 1937 and the subsequent evolution affected for the most part the social and economic doctrines of the Court. Their outlines represent a clearly marked watershed in the history of the country.

The evolution of the Court's position on other fundamental matters falling within its jurisdiction offers, on the other hand, a more complicated picture, with many shadings, fitful advances, and changes of direction. It is a story that must be told, a fascinating account of the ways in which the United States has come to grips with issues, old and new, of freedom and equality that other Western countries have usually sidestepped (what are the juridical problems posed by communism to a constitutional system?), or more often have not had to face (how does one deal with the very difficult questions raised by a proud and ever stronger racial minority?).

It is a recital, furthermore, that, in brief compass, can best be told by reference to the views expressed by that catalytic agent and mirror of the conscience of the country, the Supreme Court. Let us begin, in spite of the difficulties that lie in wait, with certain generalizations and chronological classifications.

During the last thirty years, the Supreme Court has shown a greater concern for the problems of human freedom and for

230

the fate of minorities and racial groups than ever before in its history. One can venture to say that, as the Supreme Court was gradually surrendering its claims to check government intervention in economic and social life, it widened the scope of its concern in the field of civil liberties. As the Court was induced to accept the necessity of sweeping social controls, it sought compensation in a stronger defense of individual human freedom and dignity.

During the period of particularly acute domestic political tension extending from the eve of communist aggression in Korea to the Twentieth Congress of the Communist party of the Soviet Union, the Supreme Court strongly felt the anxieties and confusion of government, public opinion, and private groups. Since then, however, owing both to changes in the composition of the Court and to a re-evaluation of the nature of the problem posed by communism, the Court has, on balance, once more shifted to the earlier position of support of the absolute value of the freedoms of Western constitutionalism.

The Court's increasing readiness to use the Constitution for the protection of individual liberty, mostly against restrictive action by the states, became visible during the middle 1920's. Those were the years, as we have seen, when the Supreme Court was using the Fourteenth Amendment and its due process clause to limit economic and social legislation of the states on the ground that it represented a violation of property and contractual rights guaranteed to individuals by the Amendment. Gradually the Court came to realize that the uses of the Fourteenth Amendment might not be restricted to keeping in check the social and economic experiments of the states. Conceivably, the constitutional mandate against deprivation by the states of an individual's right to liberty without due process of law could be construed as requiring, first, observance by the states of the procedural obligations of a free trial and, secondly, respect of the substantive rights of freedom guaranteed by the First Amendment.

Thirty years later, it can be said that the Fourteenth Amendment, no longer employed as it was hundreds of times between 1890 and 1936 to stop state social and economic action, has become one of the most powerful instruments for the protection of personal freedoms. As Justice Cardozo pointed out as long ago as 1937,[1] constitutional restraints valid against the federal government have been found to be implicit in the concept of ordered liberty, and, through the Fourteenth Amendment, have become valid against the states.

The rights that have found shelter under the wings of a due process clause used until then mainly in the interest of the business community, include freedom of speech, of the press, of religion and assembly, and the right to counsel.

In 1931, Chief Justice Hughes defended freedom of the press threatened by the state of Minnesota: "It is no longer open to doubt that the liberty of the press, and of speech, is within the liberty safeguarded by the due process clause of the Fourteenth Amendment from invasion by state action. It was found impossible to conclude that this essential personal liberty of the citizen was left unprotected by the general guaranty of fundamental rights of person and property." Hughes quoted with approval Blackstone who declared liberty of the press to be essential to the nature of a free state, with the core of this liberty the protection of the press from suppression before publication.[2]

In another press freedom case, decided in 1936, the Court intervened to protect the Louisiana press harassed by Huey Long. Justice Sutherland, an extreme conservative, spoke for a unanimous court:

---

[1] *Palko* v. *Connecticut,* 302 U.S. 319 (1937).
[2] *Near* v. *Minnesota,* 283 U.S. 697 (1931).

. . . freedom of speech and of the press are rights of the same fundamental character. . . . The word "liberty" . . . embraces not only the right of a person to be free from physical restraint, but the right to be free in the enjoyment of all his faculties as well. . . . A free press stands as one of the great interpreters between the government and the people. To allow it to be fettered is to fetter ourselves.[3]

As Chief Justice Hughes said in 1937, the state of Oregon could not sentence a Communist party organizer to jail under its Criminal Syndical Act, in violation of the fundamental rights safeguarded by the due process clause of the Fourteenth Amendment.

The right of peaceable assembly is a right cognate to those of free speech and free press and is equally fundamental. . . . The First Amendment of the Federal Constitution expressly guarantees that right against abridgment by Congress. But explicit mention there does not argue exclusion elsewhere. For the right is one that cannot be denied without violating those fundamental principles of liberty and justice which lie at the base of all civil and political institutions.[4]

Removed from the dry and egoistical world of economic relationships, the Fourteenth Amendment gradually developed into a weapon with which to fight the large or petty tyrannies that will prevail unless constant vigilance is exercised. But, even more significantly, the Supreme Court began to outline a new doctrine giving to the rights of personal freedom a privileged or "preferred" status. The rights guaranteed by the First Amendment, the Court now said, are not ordinary rights: they are prior rights that make possible the exercise of other rights. Therefore, any attempt by government action to restrict or to qualify them, must be scrutinized with a care and an adherence to absolute values not always necessary in other instances.

[3] *Grosjean* v. *American Press Co.*, 297 U.S. 233 (1936).
[4] *De Jonge* v. *Oregon*, 299 U.S. 353 (1937).

The "preferred" doctrine was first put forward tentatively, often in dissenting opinions. It later became the doctrine of the Court itself, particularly from 1943 to 1950. It suffered a subsequent temporary decline, only to be revived once more. It is a doctrine of historic significance, keeping alive under the most difficult conditions of our century the substance of freedom in America.

Justice Cardozo was in effect its originator when he said in 1937 for the Court:

> We reach a different plane of social and moral values when we pass from the privileges and immunities that have been taken over from the earlier articles of the federal bill of rights and brought within the Fourteenth Amendment by a process of absorption. These in their origin were effective against the federal government alone. If the Fourteenth Amendment has absorbed them, the process of absorption has had its source in the belief that neither liberty nor justice would exist if they were sacrificed. This is true, for illustration, of freedom of thought and speech. Of that freedom one may say that it is the matrix, the indispensable condition, of nearly every other form of freedom. With rare aberrations a pervasive recognition of that truth can be traced in our history, political and legal. So it has come about that the domain of liberty, withdrawn by the Fourteenth Amendment from encroachment by the states, has been enlarged by latter-day judgments to include liberty of the mind as well as liberty of action.[5]

Justice Stone is usually credited with the initial formulation of the preferred status doctrine,[6] to be found in 1938 in his indirect and rather cryptic remarks in a footnote to his opinion for the Court:

> It is unnecessary to consider now whether legislation which restricts those political processes which can ordinarily be expected to bring about repeal of undesirable legislation, is to be subjected to more exacting judicial inquiry under the general prohibitions of

---

[5] *Palko* v. *Connecticut*, 302 U.S. 319 (1937).
[6] Alpheus T. Mason, *Security Through Freedom*, pp. 126ff., and *Harlan Fiske Stone*, pp. 512–17.

the Fourteenth Amendment than are most other types of legislation. . . . Nor need we enquire whether similar considerations enter into the review of statutes directed at particular religious . . . or national . . . or racial minorities . . . whether prejudice . . . may be a special condition, which tends seriously to curtail the operation of those political processes ordinarily to be relied upon to protect minorities, and which may call for a correspondingly more searching judicial inquiry.[7]

In more direct and emphatic language, Justice Black's 1941 dissenting opinion declared:

I view the guaranties of the First Amendment as the foundation upon which our governmental structure rests and without which it could not continue to endure as conceived and planned. Freedom to speak and write about public questions is as important to the life of our government as is the heart to the human body. In fact, this privilege is the heart of our government. If that heart be weakened, the result is debilitation; if it be stilled, the result is death.[8]

The following year Chief Justice Stone, forced into a dissenting position, openly referred to the preferred position of First Amendment rights:

The First Amendment is not confined to safeguarding freedom of speech and freedom of religion against discriminatory attempts to wipe them out. On the contrary, the Constitution, by virtue of the First and the Fourteenth Amendments, has put those freedoms in a preferred position. Their commands are not restricted to cases where the protected privilege is sought out for attack. They extend at least to every form of taxation which, because it is

[7] *United States* v. *Carolene Products Co.,* 304 U.S. 144 (1938). "Though a footnote hardly seems to be an appropriate way of announcing a new constitutional doctrine, the Stone footnote has in fact been the foundation upon which some members of the high Court have attempted to construct the doctrine that the judicial function in reviewing statutes restricting a First Amendment freedom differs sharply from the Court's normal duty in sitting in judgment on legislation." Schwartz, *The Supreme Court,* p. 234.

[8] *Milk Wagon Drivers' Union* v. *Meadowmoor Co.,* 312 U.S. 287 (1941).

a condition of the exercise of the privilege, is capable of being used to control or suppress it.[9]

The point has now been reached at which the minority becomes the majority. With Rutledge a member of the Court, Justice Douglas could in 1943 speak for the Court and overrule the just-decided Opelika case. Douglas maintained that a tax laid specifically on the exercise of First Amendment freedoms is unconstitutional. The municipal license tax imposed by the ordinance that had come under the scrutiny of the Supreme Court was just that.

> An itinerant evangelist, however misguided or intolerant he may be, does not become a mere book agent by selling the Bible or religious tracts to help defray his expenses or to sustain him. Freedom of speech, freedom of the press, freedom of religion are available to all, not merely to those who can pay their own way. . . . Freedom of the press, freedom of speech, freedom of religion are in a preferred position.[10]

With the one conspicuous and tragic exception of the acceptance by the Supreme Court of the military point of view in the wartime case of the American citizens of Japanese descent,[11] a majority of the Supreme Court was now ready, through

---

[9] *Jones* v. *Opelika,* 316 U.S. 584 (1942).

[10] *Murdock* v. *Pennsylvania,* 319 U.S. 105 (1943).

[11] The two key decisions by the Supreme Court sanctioning the World War II evacuation of 70,000 American-Japanese from their Pacific Coast homes to the interior of the United States are *Hirabayashi* v. *United States,* 320 U.S. 81 (1943), and *Korematsu* v. *United States,* 323 U.S. 214 (1944). The Korematsu decision was written by Justice Black. Roberts, Jackson, and Murphy wrote separate dissents. The dissents were vehement. Justice Murphy said that "there was no adequate proof that the Federal Bureau of Investigation and the military and naval intelligence services did not have the espionage and sabotage situation well in hand over this period." Justice Jackson said that his duties as a judge did not require him to make a military judgment. But he did not think that the courts could "be asked to execute a military expedient that has no place in law under the Constitution." Justice Frankfurter, in a separate concurring opinion siding with the majority, shifted responsibility elsewhere: "To find that the Constitution does not forbid the military measures now complained of, does not carry with it approval of that which Congress and the Executive did. That is their business, not ours." On the whole

the final phase of the war and the postwar period, to support the preferred-status doctrine.

No one grew more eloquent in its defense than Justice Murphy. He was in principle ready to support personal freedom, the rights of minorities, regardless of the conditions that might in certain instances justify public restraint. He had come to the bench from the heavy political battles of the early period of the New Deal. As Governor of Michigan, he had taken a hand in the settling of some of the major labor disputes of the times. As Attorney General in the second Roosevelt administration he had established within the Department of Justice a Civil Liberties Unit, saying that "where there is social unrest . . . we want to be more anxious and vigorous in protecting the civil liberty of protesting and insecure people." In justifying the establishment of the new office, he had pointed out that:

> In a democracy, an important function of the law enforcement branch of government is the *aggressive protection* of fundamental rights inherent in a free people. In America these guarantees are contained in express provisions of the Constitution and in acts of Congress. It is the purpose of the Department of Justice to *pursue a program of vigilant action in the prosecution* of infringement of these.[12]

Once on the bench, Murphy decided to maintain an uncompromising position where freedom was involved. Sometimes he spoke for the minority. From 1943 to 1949, he spoke for the majority of the Court, as when he wrote:

> The utter disregard for the dignity and the well-being of colored citizens shown by this record is so pronounced as to demand the invocation of constitutional condemnation. To decide the case and to analyze the statute solely upon the basis of legal niceties, while remaining mute and placid as to the obvious and oppressive

problem, see the careful and critical study by Jacobus Ten Broek, Edward N. Barnhart, and Floyd W. Matson, *Prejudice, War, and the Constitution*, Berkeley, 1954.

[12] John P. Roche, "The Utopian Pilgrimage of Mr. Justice Murphy." *Vanderbilt Law Review*, February, 1957, p. 375.

deprivation of constitutional guarantees, is to make the judicial function something less than it should be. . . . Racism is far too virulent today to permit the slightest refusal, in the light of a Constitution that abhors it, to expose and condemn it wherever it appears in the course of a statutory interpretation.[13]

Justice Rutledge was not far behind in his 1945 defense of freedom of speech, press, and assembly. These are indispensable democratic freedoms that have been given a preferred place in our scheme of government:

> That priority gives these liberties a sanctity and a sanction not permitting dubious intrusions. . . . For these reasons any attempt to restrict those liberties must be justified by clear public interest, threatened not doubtfully or remotely, but by clear and present danger. The rational connection between the remedy provided and the evil to be curbed, which in other contexts might support legislation against attack on due process grounds will not suffice. These rights rest on firmer foundation. Accordingly, whatever occasion would restrain orderly discussion and persuasion, at appropriate time and place, must have clear support in public danger, actual or impending. Only the gravest abuses, endangering paramount interests, give occasion for permissible limitation. It is therefore in our tradition to allow the widest room for discussion, the narrowest range for its restriction.[14]

Even Reed was caught by the libertarian fever that was sweeping through the Court. In 1946, defending a newspaper publisher against a Florida charge of contempt of court, Reed pointed out:

> . . . we must weigh the impact of the words against the protection given by the principles of the First Amendment, as adopted by the Fourteenth, to public comment on pending court cases. We conclude that the danger under this record to fair judicial administration has not the clearness and immediacy necessary to close the door of permissible public comment. When the door is closed, it closes all doors behind it.[15]

[13] *Steele* v. *Louisville and Nashville R.R. Co.*, 323 U.S. 192 (1944).
[14] *Thomas* v. *Collins*, 323 U.S. 516 (1945).
[15] *Pennekamp* v. *Florida*, 328 U.S. 331 (1946).

This was the crucial point the Supreme Court never tired of restating: When the door is closed against free speech and a free press, all doors are closed with a finality beyond retreat. The injustice of suppressing thought and speech is a final one. Citizens can agitate for the redress of grievances contained in a legislative measure, but a citizen who is stopped from expressing his thoughts suffers a supreme injustice which cannot be remedied. These are the freedoms that condition everything else, and they must be protected at all cost.

COMMUNISM AND AFTER

In 1949, Murphy and Rutledge died. The mood of the Court changed, as it began to reflect both the temper of the new men who became members of the Court and the increased anxieties of the times.

A policy of prudence, personified by the new Chief Justice, Fred M. Vinson, controlled the proceedings of the Court. Vinson was above all a good administrator and a shrewd politician who felt that, since the Supreme Court had wisely adopted a doctrine of restraint in dealing with the legislative activities of the federal and state governments, the same doctrine should also be applied to the administrative, judicial, and police actions of government, since the same presumption of validity in their favor could be said to exist. This was a pragmatic position less concerned with principles than with the necessities of survival. The "clear and present danger" doctrine, guaranteeing a practically untrammeled freedom of speech, should be interpreted, the Chief Justice appeared to say, in the light of far deeper and subtler dangers that threatened Western democracy in mid-century. A Court was not a political organism and it should yield, as a rule and unless a clear violation of rights could be shown, to the political decisions of the politically responsible bodies.

In these views, the Chief Justice was supported, on balance, by the outstanding theoretical mind on the Court, Felix Frankfurter, who even before 1949 had never shown much sympathy for the libertarian preferred-status doctrine of the Bill of Rights developed by the Court's majority. It would be the height of absurdity to describe Frankfurter as the enemy of freedom, for he very clearly is not. His entire life, as a teacher at Harvard University and as one of the most influential of Roosevelt's advisers, is testimony to his concern for freedom. His greatest day, he has said, was reached when the Supreme Court no longer believed that protection of strikers and pickets meant interference with the rights of property. But Frankfurter feels that the issues coming before the Supreme Court are made complex by procedural aspects not to be dismissed by mere appeals to absolute concepts, even to absolute concepts of freedom. To do a workmanlike job, the Court must use the same technique of constitutional interpretation in all cases coming before it.

Frankfurter is keenly aware of the unrepresentative character of the Court. Therefore, the Court's powers are to be used with humility. If such caution may from time to time produce decisions that will appear anti-libertarian at first reading, its long-run results are better than those of an aggressive policy. As one commentator explains,

> These apparently antilibertarian doctrines and results, however, can be at least partially explained on the basis of a libertarian theory—the theory that the primary responsibility of a liberal justice is to restrain the exercise of judicial power. This theory sees the Court not as a crusader or advocate but as one of the instruments of political and social accommodation and adjustment in a complicated governmental system.[16]

No Justice of the Supreme Court may permit personal

[16] C. H. Pritchett, *Civil Liberties and the Vinson Court,* Chicago, 1954, p. 201. See the entire Chapter 11, "Libertarian Restraint: Justice Frankfurter."

preferences to determine the way his decision is made. Speaking for himself in explanation of his refusal to hold unconstitutional the compulsory flag statute in public schools, Frankfurter said:

> One who belongs to the most vilified and persecuted minority in history is not likely to be insensible to the freedoms guaranteed by our Constitution. Were my purely personal attitude relevant I should wholeheartedly associate myself with the general libertarian views in the Court's opinion, representing as they do the thought and action of a lifetime.

By 1953, Justice Reed, speaking for the Court, could say: "It is a *non sequitur* to say that First Amendment rights may not be regulated because they hold a preferred position in the hierarchy of the constitutional guarantees. . . . This Court has never so held and indeed has definitely indicated the contrary." [17]

This is a statement of doubtful accuracy, in view of the record we have just examined, but one by then reflecting the more cautious views of the majority of the Court, including Justice Jackson, who already in 1949 in a dissenting opinion had said, "We cannot give some constitutional rights a preferred position without relegating others to a deferred position; we can establish no firsts without thereby establishing seconds." [18]

By now, the old libertarian majority was once again reduced to a minority rallying around Justices Black and Douglas, who resumed their vigorous dissents in the face of what seemed to them a retreat of the Court as a result of outside pressures for conformity.

Douglas found untenable Reed's position in the Poulos case, for the command of the First Amendment is

> . . . that there shall be *no* law which abridges those civil rights. The matter is beyond the power of the legislature to regulate, con-

---

[17] *Poulos* v. *New Hampshire*, 345 U.S. 395 (1953).
[18] *Brinegar* v. *United States*, 338 U.S. 160 (1949).

trol, or condition. The case is therefore quite different from a legislative program in the field of business, labor, housing, and the like where regulation is permissible and the claim of unconstitutionality usually can be determined only by the manner or degree of application of the statute to an aggrieved person.

Black was scornful of the majority decision in the Dennis case:

> Public opinion being what it now is, few will protest the conviction of these Communist petitioners. There is hope, however, that in calmer times, when present pressures, passions and fear subside, this or some later Court will restore the First Amendment liberties to the high preferred place where they belong in our free society.[19]

Addressing himself to a majority opinion written by Chief Justice Vinson sanctioning the practice of withholding the names of informers and the content of their evidence, Douglas said, in a case involving conscientious objectors:

> The use of statements by informers who need not confront the person under investigation or accusation has such an infamous history that it should be rooted out from our procedure. A hearing at which these faceless people are allowed to present their whispered rumors and yet escape the test and torture of cross-examination is not a hearing in the Anglo-American sense. We should be done with the practice—whether the life of a man is at stake, or his reputation, or any matter touching upon his status or his rights.[20]

Finally, dissenting in 1952 in a New York teachers' loyalty case in which the Court had validated a New York State loyalty act, Douglas eloquently defended academic freedom as an essential part of the freedom protected by the First Amendment:

> What happened under this law is typical of what happens in a police state. Teachers are under constant surveillance; their pasts

[19] *Dennis* v. *United States,* 341 U.S. 494 (1951).
[20] *United States* v. *Nugent,* 346 U.S. 1 (1953).

are combed for signs of disloyalty; their utterances are watched for clues to dangerous thoughts. A pall is cast over the classrooms. There can be no real academic freedom in that environment. Where suspicion fills the air and holds scholars in line for fear of their jobs, there can be no exercise of free intellect. Supineness and dogmatism take the place of inquiry. A "party line"—as dangerous as the "party line" of the Communists—lays hold. It is the "party line" of the orthodox views, of the conventional thought, of the accepted approach. A problem can no longer be pursued with impunity to its edges. Fear stalks the classroom. The teacher is no longer a stimulant to adventurous thinking; he becomes instead a pipe line for safe and sound information. A deadening dogma takes the place of free inquiry. Instruction tends to become sterile; pursuit of knowledge is discouraged; discussion often leaves off where it should begin.

This, I think, is what happens when a censor looks over a teacher's shoulder. This system of spying and surveillance with its accompanying reports and trials cannot go hand in hand with academic freedom. It produces standardized thought, not the pursuit of truth. Yet it was the pursuit of truth which the First Amendment was designed to protect. A system which directly or inevitably has that effect is alien to our system and should be struck down. Its survival is a real threat to our way of life. We need be bold and adventuresome in our thinking to survive. A school system producing students trained as robots threatens to rob a generation of the versatility that has been perhaps our greatest distinction. The Framers knew the danger of dogmatism; they also knew the strength that comes when the mind is free, when ideas may be pursued wherever they lead. We forget these teachings of the First Amendment when we sustain this law.[21]

No one could fail to see the principles around which the minority had rallied in its unyielding and eloquent protection of First Amendment freedoms. These were the same principles so well sustained by the Court in the 1940's. In the more difficult climate of the early 1950's, the fresh question was being raised whether the strong language of the minority was not damaging to the interests it sought to protect. The Supreme

[21] *Adler* v. *Board of Education*, 342 U.S. 485 (1952).

Court does not wear a prophetic mantle enabling it to dispense justice with a certitude and a sweep beyond challenge and doubt. A reflective student of the Supreme Court's work (as Justice Frankfurter has called him), Paul Freund, called attention to what appeared to him the striking contrast between the Court's empirical approach to the economic market and the Court's more rigid handling of the market of ideas:

> A free market in ideas and a free national market in goods are basic processes in our constitutional system. Each must nevertheless submit to qualifications in collision with other public interests. If the Court has on the whole been more successful in finding serviceable accommodations under the Commerce Clause between a national free market and the claims of local welfare then under the First Amendment between liberty of the mind and the claims of public order, one reason may be the more empiric, particularistic approach that has generally characterized the performance of the former role.[22]

This may conceivably be true—no mere rhetoric and generalized language can replace the careful and discriminating analysis which one must expect to find in every decision of the highest Court of the land—including those dealing with the free market of ideas. The fact remains that in its anxiety to recognize the difficulties of government and the legislative rights of parliamentary assemblies, the Vinson Court had embarked on a retreat whose end could not be foreseen. One must therefore sympathize with Justices Black and Douglas for thinking the retreat was going to jeopardize the well-established views of the Court in support of the fundamental principles of the republic and that, in its efforts to back the executive and the legislative in the defense of the United States against the dangers of totalitarianism, the Court was helping to weaken the best defense of all, the spirit of freedom.

[22] Paul A. Freund, "The Supreme Court, 1951 Term," *Harvard Law Review,* November 1952, p. 97.

*

No one will underestimate the difficulties the Supreme Court was facing in the early fifties. Eleven years after its enactment, the Smith Act had reached the Court. In addition, three major items of legislation passed by Congress during the Truman administration—the Taft-Hartley Act of 1947, the Internal Security Act of 1950, the Immigration and Nationality Act of 1952—were pressing their bewildering and complicated claims on the attention of the Court.[23] Finally, the complex loyalty programs concerning government employees were presenting no less baffling issues. The sum total of these pressures represented an ordeal for the Supreme Court seldom matched in intensity. The clamor of public opinion was loud, the influence of the Court on the administration in the awkward—and in America unfortunately long—period of transition from the

---

[23] The Smith Act of 1940 provided for the punishment of anyone who knowingly or willfully advocated "the duty, necessity, desirability, or propriety of overthrowing or destroying the Government of the United States or the government of any State . . . by force or violence," or who published or distributed any written or printed matter advocating or teaching the overthrowing of any government in the United States by force or violence, or who organized or attempted to organize any society or group teaching and advocating the overthrow of government by force or violence or became a member of it. Section 9(h) of the Taft-Hartley Act of 1947 on labor-management relations, required officers of any labor union using the machinery of the National Labor Relations Board to file an annual affidavit stating: "I am not a member of the Communist party or affiliated with such party. I do not believe in, and I am not a member of nor do I support any organization that believes in or teaches the overthrow of the United States Government by force or by any illegal or unconstitutional methods." The Internal Security Act of 1950, popularly known as the McCarran Act and also designated in part as the Subversive Activities Control Act, required the registration of all "Communist-action" and "Communist-front" organizations and provided penalties for any organization refusing to do so. The Immigration and Nationality Act of 1952 introduced stringent controls affecting aliens or nationalized citizens. A useful collection of legal, public and judicial materials relating to communism is found in *Digest of the Public Record of Communism in the United States,* published by the Fund for the Republic, New York, 1955. For a discussion of the nonlegal aspect of the communist problem, see Chapter VI.

Truman to the Eisenhower presidency, was not clear, and the strength of some of the new justices appointed by President Truman was not notable. All this has to be taken into account to understand the attitude of the Court's majority, as well as the dismayed anger of the dissenting minority.

The official Court record is not easy to disentangle. In some areas, the Court courageously maintained a firm position, as in dealing with conscientious objectors. In 1953, the Court held where Federal Bureau of Investigation reports are used, the conscientious objector is entitled to a fair résumé of adverse evidence.[24] In the same year, the Court held a draft board's conclusion that a conscientious objector is lying must be supported by at least some evidence, not merely the board's belief. In 1955, the Court went so far as to say that a conscientious objector is entitled not as a matter of grace but as a matter of right to a summary of F.B.I. reports.[25] And again in 1955, the Court held Jehovah's Witnesses to be conscientious objectors in spite of the contention they do not oppose all wars but would fight in a religious one.[26]

In 1953, the Court appeared ready to limit congressional investigations. Speaking through Justice Frankfurter (who acknowledged the power of Congress to conduct inquiries by quoting from Woodrow Wilson's *Congressional Government,* "The informing function of Congress should be preferred even to its legislative function"), the Court said that the right to call for testimony must be found in the language of the congressional authorization. In this instance, the authorization of the committee was limited to an inquiry into lobbying. Therefore, witnesses could not be asked questions that did not relate to it, and Rumely, the witness in question, could not be forced

[24] *United States* v. *Nugent,* 346, U.S. 1 (1953).
[25] *Simmons* v. *United States,* 348 U.S. 397 (1955).
[26] *Sicurella* v. *United States,* 348 U.S. 385 (1955). See Robert Cushman, *Civil Liberties in the United States,* Ithaca, 1956, pp. 94ff.

to disclose to the House committee the names of all those who had purchased books from him.[27]

On the question of loyalty oaths the Court was clearly vacillating. Confronted by a jungle-like flowering of measures intended to secure the loyalty of all government employees at all levels, the Court was of a divided mind. Its task was not made simpler by the different approach of each state and municipality to the problem. In 1951, the Supreme Court upheld a Los Angeles municipal ordinance requiring a loyalty oath and an affidavit on communist activities on the part of all municipal employees.[28]

Similarly, in 1952, the Court upheld a New York State statute, the Feinberg Law, requiring the removal of all public schoolteachers advocating the overthrow of the government

---

[27] *United States* v. *Rumely,* 345 U.S. 41 (1953). The warning language of the Court did not have any immediate visible consequence on the scope and methods of congressional inquiries. Justice Douglas, who concurred with Frankfurter in the Rumely case, felt that the danger was greater than the Court had admitted, and that a more forceful marking of the boundaries of congressional power should have been made. In his concurring opinion he wrote: "If the present inquiry were sanctioned, the press would be subjected to harassment that in practical effect might be as serious as censorship. . . . The finger of government leveled against the press is ominous. Once the government can demand of a publisher the names of the purchasers of his publications, the free press as we know it disappears. Then the spectre of a government agent will look over the shoulder of everyone who reads. The purchase of a book or pamphlet today may result in a subpoena tomorrow. Fear of criticism goes with every person into the bookstall. The subtle, imponderable pressures of the orthodox lay hold. . . . But that will be minor in comparison with the menace of the shadow which government will cast over literature which does not follow the dominant party line. . . . Through the harassment of hearings, investigations, reports, and subpoenas government will hold a club over speech and over the press. Congress could not do this by law. The power of investigation is also limited. Inquiry into personal and private affairs is precluded. . . . And so is any matter in respect to which no valid legislation could be had. Since Congress could not by law require of respondent what the House demanded, it may not take the first step in an inquiry ending in a fine or imprisonment."

[28] *Garner* v. *Board of Public Works,* 341 U.S. 716 (1951).

by unlawful means or belonging to organizations that do. Justice Minton, speaking for the Court, did not find the freedom of speech and assembly of those affected to be impaired.[29]

In the same year, however, the Court declared invalid, on appeal from some faculty members of an Oklahoma state college, an Oklahoma statute prescribing a loyalty oath for all state employees.[30] The Court agreed the oath offended due process of law and membership could be innocent. In a concurring opinion, Justice Frankfurter noted the Oklahoma statute penalized "a teacher for exercising a right of association peculiarly characteristic of our people." He quoted with approval the testimony given by Robert M. Hutchins, the former president of the University of Chicago, before a House investigating Committee:

> A university, then, is a kind of continuing Socratic conversation on the highest level for the very best people you can think of . . . about the most important questions, and the thing that you must do to the uttermost possible limits is to guarantee those men the freedom to think and to express themselves.

In a 1953 case in which, according to Justice Black, the Court had added "the right to bail to the list of other Bill of Rights guarantees that have recently been weakened to expand governmental powers at the expense of individual freedom," the Supreme Court sustained the Attorney General's denial of bail to certain alien Communists held in custody by the government pending determination of their deportability. The Court felt that the Constitution does not require bail in all

---

[29] *Adler* v. *Board of Education*, 342 U.S. 485 (1952).

[30] *Wieman* v. *Updegraff*, 344 U.S. 193 (1952). The text of the loyalty oath was in part as follows: ". . . That I am not affiliated directly or indirectly . . . with any foreign political agency . . . or group whatever which has been officially determined by the United States Attorney General or other authorized agency of the United States to be a communist front or subversive organization; . . . that within the five years immediately preceding the taking of this oath . . . I have not been a member of [the groups identified above]."

cases, but merely guarantees bail shall not be excessive in those cases where it is proper to require it.[31]

In another deportation case, decided in 1956 by one of those tantalizing 5 to 4 majorities which often in the past have been the prelude to a change in the position of the Court, Justice Reed refused to accept an alien's plea that his deportation be stayed because it had been obtained through secret information not revealed to him.[32] The Court maintained that the government's refusal to disclose information was valid, for the Immigration and Nationality Act of 1952 prevented disclosure when it would be prejudicial to the public interest or safety. This decision evoked sharp dissents. Chief Justice Warren did not believe that the discretion granted the Attorney General is unfettered. The hearing the alien had received was not "an administrative hearing in the American use of the term. It is no hearing . . . to me this is not due process." Justice Frankfurter argued discretion does not mean "to invest subordinates with such arbitrary authority over the lives of men." And Douglas, stressing the fundamentals of fair play, wrote:

> Fairness, implicit in our notions of due process, requires that any "hearing" be full and open with an opportunity to know the charge and the accusers, to reply to the charge, and to meet the accusers.

Running through all these cases as a thread is the communist issue. This was the one fundamental problem facing the Supreme Court then, persuading it at times to express itself in favor of legislative or executive policies dealing with communism, regardless of their consequences and of the Court's own misgivings.

The views of the Court on the nature of communism, of the threat it poses to a free and constitutionally organized society and of the extent to which that society is entitled to resort

[31] *Carlson* v. *Landon,* 342 U.S. 524 (1952).
[32] *Jay* v. *Boyd,* 351 U.S. 345 (1956).

to defensive measures in order to survive, have, inevitably, undergone certain changes over the years. No one, not even a Supreme Court justice, could deal with communism in a temper unaffected by the changes communism has brought to the world, and express the same views about it in 1937 (when little was known about it), in 1943 (when the Soviet Union was an ally), or in 1951 (when the United States was fighting on the battlefields against the widening threat of the last years of Stalin's rule).

Justice Roberts could, in 1937, take a relatively casual attitude toward communism. Herndon, a Communist party organizer, had been convicted, in the midst of the Depression, for soliciting new members for the party and for distributing materials. When arrested, he had on his person a number of communist pamphlets which underlined the use of violence in the attainment of communist goals. The Court found that to put him in jail for holding his meetings was to limit unreasonably freedom of speech and of assembly in violation of the Fourteenth Amendment:

> The appellant induced others to become members of the Communist Party. Did he thus incite to insurrection by reason of the fact that they agreed to abide by the tenets of the party, some of them lawful, others, as may be assumed, unlawful, in the absence of proof that he brought the unlawful aims to their notice, that he approved them, or that the fantastic program they envisaged was conceived by anyone as more than an ultimate ideal? . . . The only objectives appellant is proved to have urged are those having to do with unemployment and emergency relief which are void of criminality. His membership in the Communist Party . . . wholly fails to establish an attempt to incite others to insurrection. Indeed . . . he had but a single copy of the booklet the State claims to be objectionable. . . . In these circumstances, to make membership in the party and solicitation of members for that party a criminal offense . . . is an unwarranted invasion of the right of freedom of speech.[33]

[33] *Herndon* v. *Lowry,* 301 U.S. 242 (1937).

In 1943, the crusading liberal Justice Murphy led the Supreme Court in a reversal of a lower court decision to revoke the citizenship of a naturalized citizen.[34] Murphy quoted Holmes to this effect: "Surely it cannot show lack of attachment to the principles of the Constitution that . . . one thinks it can be improved," and added that sincerity "should not be judged by conformity to prevailing thought." After reviewing the position of the appellant, on various political questions, Murphy maintained it is possible to advocate such changes and still be attached to the Constitution:

> Apart from his membership in the League and the Party, the record is barren of any conduct or statement . . . which indicates in the slightest that he believed in and advocated the use of force and violence, instead of peaceful persuasion, as a means of attaining political ends.

Having reviewed excerpts of "bombastic writing," Murphy concluded although not in agreement with them, he could no more accept the government's contention that Schneiderman or the Communist party advocated the use of force and violence:

> So uncertain a chain of proof does not add up to the requisite "clear, unequivocal, and convincing" evidence for setting aside a naturalization decree. Were the law otherwise, valuable rights would rest upon a slender reed, and the security of the status of our naturalized citizens might depend in considerable degree upon the political temper of majority thought and the stresses of the times. Those are consequences foreign to the best traditions of this nation and the characteristics of our institutions.

By 1950, the mood had changed. The Court, through Chief Justice Vinson, backed the constitutionality of Section 9(h) of the Taft-Hartley Act:

> . . . the Board does not contend that political strikes, the substantive evil at which Section 9(h) is aimed, are the present or impending products of advocacy of the doctrines of Communism

---

[34] *Schneiderman* v. *United States,* 320 U.S. 118 (1943).

by force. On the contrary, it points out that such strikes are called by persons who, so Congress has found, have the will and power to do so *without* advocacy or persuasion that seeks acceptance in the competition of the market. . . . Section 9(h) is designed to protect the public not against what Communists and others identified therein advocate or believe, but against what Congress has concluded they have done and are likely to do again.[35]

In a 1951 comment on this decision, which he supported with some reservations, Justice Frankfurter revealed the delicacy of the balancing act to which the Court had resorted in order to make up its mind:

> Our decision in *American Communications Association v. Douds* recognized that the exercise of political rights protected by the First Amendment was necessarily discouraged by the requirement of the Taft-Hartley Act that officers of unions employing the services of the National Labor Relations Board sign affidavits that they are not Communists. But we held that the statute was not for this reason presumptively invalid. The problem, we said, was "one of weighing the probable effects of the statute upon the free exercise of the right of speech and assembly against the congressional determination that political strikes are evils of conduct which cause substantial harm to interstate commerce and that Communists and others identified by Section 9(h) pose continuing threats to that public interest when in positions of union leadership." . `. . On balance, we decided that the legislative judgment was a permissible one.[36]

The most difficult case of all, as well as the most famous, was of course the Dennis case. Here the Supreme Court had to decide the constitutionality of the Smith Act.[37] The case involved the conviction of eleven top Communist party leaders. The Court upheld their conviction for conspiracy under the Smith Act. Seven of the justices agreed that the standard to

---

[35] *American Communications Association* v. *Douds,* 339 U.S. 382 (1950).

[36] Frankfurter's concurring opinion, *Dennis* v. *United States,* 341 U.S. 494 (1951).

[37] *Dennis* v. *United States,* 341 U.S. 494 (1951).

be used was the one provided by the "clear and present danger" doctrine of Justice Holmes, reinterpreted in the light of new dangers facing democracy. The case caused much soul-searching among the justices; even though six concurred with the opinion of Vinson, both Frankfurter and Jackson felt compelled to write separate concurring opinions to outline their views with greater precision. Each of the two dissenting justices, Black and Douglas, also wrote separate opinions.

The Chief Justice, in justifying the application of the "clear and present danger" test to activities of Communist leaders which were neither clear nor such as to pose a present threat of revolution, said:

> Obviously, the words cannot mean that before the Government may act, it must wait until the *putsch* is about to be executed, the plans have been laid and the signal is awaited. If Government is aware that a group aiming at its overthrow is attempting to indoctrinate its members and to commit them to a course whereby they will strike when the leaders feel the circumstances permit, action by the Government is required. The argument that there is no need for Government to concern itself, for Government is strong, it possesses ample powers to put down a rebellion, it may defeat the revolution with ease, needs no answer. For that is not the question. Certainly an attempt to overthrow the Government by force, even though doomed from the outset because of inadequate numbers or power of the revolutionists, is a sufficient evil for Congress to prevent. The damage which such attempts create both physically and politically to a nation makes it impossible to measure the validity in terms of the probability of success, or the immediacy of a successful attempt. . . . Chief Judge Learned Hand, writing for the majority below, interpreted the phrase as follows: "In each case [courts] must ask whether the gravity of the 'evil', discounted by its improbability, justifies such invasion of free speech as is necessary to avoid the danger." . . . We adopt this statement of the rule.

In spite of the Chief Justice's careful justification, it was obvious the clear and present danger doctrine had been rewritten to

mean something altogether different from the intent of its originator. The Supreme Court was accepting the political judgment
of the government as binding, because it agreed on the reality
of the dangers threatening the maintenance of freedom in the
United States.

Better than the opinion of the Court, the concurring opinion
of Justice Frankfurter reveals the quandaries of the justices.
In a long statement which is a fascinating, informative, and
extraordinary performance, Frankfurter pleads for a reading
of the language of the First Amendment "not as barren words
found in a dictionary but as symbols of historic experience."
He reviews in detail the way in which the Court has in the past
resolved the "conflicts between speech and competing interests." This is the heart of the matter: Abstract rights have to
be reconciled with legitimate competing and concrete interests
of the society in which they are asserted. In the choice between
rights and interests, full responsibility cannot be given to the
Courts:

> Courts are not representative bodies. They are not designed to
> be a good reflex of a democratic society. Their judgment is best
> informed, and therefore most dependable, within narrow limits.
> Their essential quality is detachment, founded on independence.
> History teaches that the independence of the judiciary is jeopard-
> ized when courts become embroiled in the passions of the day and
> assume primary responsibility in choosing between competing po-
> litical, economic and social pressures.
>
> Primary responsibility for adjusting the interests which com-
> pete in the situation before us of necessity belongs to the Congress.

This rule applies to free-speech cases as well as to other
cases. Questions of proximity and degree force themselves on
the Court. Speaking of the tendency to use a dogmatic approach
instead of critical analysis in the interpretation of the clear and
present danger doctrine, Frankfurter writes:

> It were far better that the phrase be abandoned than that it be
> sounded once more to hide from the believers in an absolute right

THE MEANING OF FREEDOM AND EQUALITY

of free speech the plain fact that the interest in speech, profoundly important as it is, is no more conclusive in judicial review than other attributes of democracy or than a determination of the people's representatives that a measure is necessary to assure the safety of government itself.

Nor can it be said that every type of speech occupies the same position in the scale of values:

> There is no substantial public interest in permitting certain kinds of utterances: "the lewd and obscene, the profane, the libelous, and the insulting or 'fighting' words—those which by their very utterance inflict injury or tend to incite an immediate breach of the peace." (*Chaplinsky v. New Hampshire.*) We have frequently indicated that the interest in protecting speech depends on the circumstances of the occasion. . . . It is pertinent to the decision before us to consider where on the scale of values we have in the past placed the type of speech now claiming constitutional immunity. The defendants have been convicted of conspiring to organize a party of persons who advocate the overthrow of the Government by force and violence. The jury has found that the object of the conspiracy is advocacy as a "rule or principle of action", "by language reasonably and ordinarily calculated to incite persons to such action", and with the intent to cause the overthrow "as speedily as circumstances would permit." On any scale of values which we have hitherto recognized, speech of this sort ranks low.

Having accepted the position of the Court, Justice Frankfurter cannot, however, refrain from adding that the decision must be understood within the framework of existing tensions and relationships in the community: "it is relevant to remind that in sustaining the power of Congress in a case like this nothing irrevocable is done. The democratic process at all events is not impaired or restricted. Power and responsibility remain with the people and immediately with their representatives."

Frankfurter also wants to show that the question of the wisdom of the legislation is another matter. "In finding that Congress has acted within its power, a judge does not remotely imply that he favors the implications that lie beneath the legal issues." Frankfurter's hands are tied. He doesn't like the Smith Act, but judicially he cannot say so. Proceeding to quote at length from a number of authorities all warning against excesses in the handling of communist influence in American society— excesses which can damage America far more than the Communist party can—Frankfurter ends with a warning to the people of America not to be satisfied with mere judgments of judicial bodies concerning the validity of legislative acts. While the Courts are limited in what they can do, the people are free and they ought to show concern for the heart of the matter and the substance of freedom:

> Civil liberties draw at best only limited strength from legal guaranties. Preoccupation by our people with the constitutionality instead of with the wisdom, of legislation or of executive action is preoccupation with a false value. . . . Focusing attention on constitutionality tends to make constitutionality synonymous with wisdom. When legislation touches freedom of thought and freedom of speech, such a tendency is a formidable enemy of the free spirit. Much that should be rejected as illiberal, because repressive and envenoming, may well be not unconstitutional. The ultimate reliance for the deepest needs of civilization must be found outside their vindication in courts of law. . . . The mark of a truly civilized man is confidence in the strength and security derived from the inquiring mind. We may be grateful for such honest comforts as it supports, but we must be unafraid of its uncertitudes. Without open minds there can be no open society. And if society be not open the spirit of man is mutilated and becomes enslaved.

True, one should refrain from nourishing excessive illusions about the influence of the Supreme Court. One can speak of it as the central pivot of American constitutionalism, and one should not underestimate its moral prestige, but both public and private life can bypass the bench of the Supreme Court. Decisions affecting the future of the country may not be subject to any Supreme Court control. The Court may speak for freedom, but in a hundred ways the private activities of men may move against freedom and the pressures, the discriminations, the repressions, the imposed conformities, the injustices that flow from these private actions may never reach the Court.[38] Though the Court is supreme, there are limits to its power.

Nevertheless, Justice Frankfurter was too pessimistic in measuring the potentialities of the Court. He was right in calling attention to other areas of public responsibility, but he underrated the strength of the moral leadership the Court can provide and has indeed provided many times in determining the course of events and in shaping public opinion. The very fact that the Court is "unrepresentative," in Frankfurter's meaning of the word, may indeed be one of the Court's main sources of authority.

This has been shown in a number of decisions rendered by

[38] What happened in the case of the so-called Attorney General's list of subversive organizations may be recalled. The list was issued in 1947. In 1951, the Court (in *Joint Anti-Fascist Refugee Committee* v. *McGrath,* 341 U.S. 123), speaking through Justice Burton with the support of Douglas, Black, Frankfurter, and Jackson (Vinson, Minton and Reed dissenting), cast serious doubts on the validity of the list. In a concurring opinion, Black held that "the executive has no constitutional authority, with or without a hearing, officially to prepare and publish the lists challenged by petitioners," for these lists punish for belief in violation of the First Amendment. Frankfurter maintained that the petitioners had been denied "due process . . . perhaps the most majestic concept in our whole Constitutional system," for "designation has been made without notice, without disclosure of any reasons justifying it, without opportunity to meet the undisclosed evidence . . . and without opportunity to establish affirmatively that the aims and acts of the organization are innocent." And Justice Jackson said: "Unless a hearing is provided in which the organization can present evidence as to its character, a presumption is entered against its every member-employee, and because of it, he may be branded disloyal, discharged, and rendered ineligible for government service." Four years later, in lectures written for delivery at Harvard (but undelivered because of his death), Jackson had to admit:

"But the list had long been widely circulated and accepted, and despite the Court's views it has never ceased to be used in the press, in the executive department, by and before congressional committees, and even in courts to prejudice individuals in their liberty, position, and good name." (Jackson, *The Supreme Court,* p. 25).

the Court during 1956 and 1957 under the guidance of Chief
Justice Earl Warren. It may not be too much to say the
preferred-status doctrine has reasserted itself and, by avoiding in its latest version some of the asperities of the 1943–1949
period, may have established itself on firmer grounds as the
doctrine of the Court, to be applied with wisdom and prudence
to be sure, but to be used as an indispensable instrument in the
defense of human freedoms.

In April, 1956, the Supreme Court held invalid as a denial
of due process the New York City Charter provision requiring
the automatic dismissal of any city employee pleading the
protections of the Fifth Amendment against self-incrimination
when questioned by an investigating committee on his political
affiliations.[39] In the same year, speaking through Justice Harlan,
the Supreme Court supported a discharged federal employee of
the Department of Health, on the grounds that the Congress
did not authorize the President to extend the security program
to positions having no direct connection with national security.
The term "national security," the Court said, refers only to
activities directly concerned with the protection of the United
States from internal subversion or foreign aggression.[40]

In a striking series of decisions rendered in June, 1957,
the Supreme Court gave encouragement to those who had
been concerned about the manner and extent of the invasion
by governmental agencies and by the Congress of the privacy
and freedom of individuals. In a reinterpretation and more
careful redefining of what is permissible under the Smith Act,
the Supreme Court rejected (without overruling the Dennis
case) the view that mere doctrinal justification of forcible overthrow of the government is punishable per se under the Act.
The Court held that the Act did not "prohibit advocacy and
teaching of forcible overthrow as an abstract principle divorced

[39] *Slochower* v. *Board of Education*, 351 U.S. 944 (1956).
[40] *Cole* v. *Young*, 351 U.S. 536 (1956).

from any effort to instigate action to that end." [41] The Court declared secret Federal Bureau of Investigation records must be made available to the defense. If they cannot, because vital national interests have to be protected, then "the criminal action must be dismissed." [42]

The Court rebuked the state of New Hampshire for its infringement of the rights of academic freedom: "We do not now conceive of any circumstance wherein a state interest would justify infringement of rights in these fields." [43]

Finally, in a most important decision dealing with the scope and method of congressional investigations and with contempt of Congress, the Court reminded the Congress the language of its resolutions authorizing investigations must be clear. It is unquestionably the duty of a citizen to co-operate with the Congress in its efforts to obtain the facts needed for intelligent legislative action; still, the Congress must guard against abuses of the investigating process, for they may imperceptibly lead to abridgment of protected freedoms:

> The mere summoning of a witness and compelling him to testify, against his will, about his beliefs, expressions or associations is a measure of governmental interference. And when those forced revelations concern matters that are unorthodox, unpopular, or even hateful to the general public, the reaction in the life of the witness may be disastrous. This effect is even more harsh when it is past beliefs, expressions or associations that are disclosed and judged by current standards rather than those contemporary with the matters exposed. Nor does the witness alone suffer the consequences. Those who are identified by witnesses and thereby placed in the same glare of publicity are equally subject to public stigma, scorn and obloquy. Beyond that, there is the more subtle and immeasurable effect upon those who tend to adhere to the most orthodox and uncontroversial views and associations in order to avoid a similar fate at some future time. That this impact is

[41] *Yates* v. *United States*, 354 U.S. 298 (1957).
[42] *Jencks* v. *United States*, 353 U.S. 657 (1957).
[43] *Sweezy* v. *New Hampshire*, 354 U.S. 234 (1957).

partly the result of non-governmental activity by private persons cannot relieve the investigators of their responsibility for initiating the reaction . . . the mere semblance of legislative purpose would not justify an inquiry in the face of the Bill of Rights. The critical element is the existence of, and the weight to be ascribed to, the interest of the Congress in demanding disclosure from an unwilling witness. We cannot simply assume however, that every congressional investigation is justified by a public need that overbalances any private rights affected. To do so would be to abdicate the responsibility placed by the Constitution upon the judiciary to insure that the Congress does not unjustifiably encroach upon an individual's right to privacy nor abridge his liberty of speech, press, religion or assembly.[44]

It would be difficult to find in the annals of jurisprudence a more eloquent and sensitive statement than this, bringing to bear on the case all the varied strands of the problem: the need for proper sanction of legislative inquiry, the rights of the individual, the menacing and often incalculable indirect and psychological repercussions on a man's very life and happiness. This is a statement in the noblest tradition of freedom, and it has driven its point home, to judge from the anguished reactions of those at which it was directed.

The Supreme Court has not been alone in its endeavors to secure a better balance of rights; many lower federal courts have also shown increasing regard for the liberties of individuals, and in the nature of things, have often taken the lead in particularly delicate fields. In 1953, a federal court found that the government's efforts to prosecute Owen Lattimore for perjury for denying under oath he had been a "follower of the Communist line" or a "promoter of Communist interests" were invalid. The court held these phrases to be fatally vague since "they had no meaning about which men of ordinary intellect could agree." In June, 1955, a federal district court ordered the State Department to issue a passport to Otto Nathan,

[44] *Watkins* v. *United States,* 354 U.S. 178 (1957).

executor under the will of Albert Einstein. Another decision of the same Court declared the right of an American citizen to travel abroad a "natural right"; in refusing a passport the State Department must meet the tests of due process of law.

Is it possible to draw up a judicial balance sheet to measure the achievements of the Supreme Court in the field of human rights during the last generation? One may perhaps be attempted.

The press is free. The Court has protected it even when the press was involved in criticisms of courts and judges. As Justice Douglas has said, "Judges are supposed to be men of fortitude, able to thrive in a hardy climate." [45] Efforts at censorship have been rebuked when a New York State statute was held invalid in 1952 on the ground that no such vague standard as "sacrilegious" could be held compatible with constitutional requirements.

Freedom of conscience and of religion have been equally carefully protected by the Supreme Court, even in those cases where an individual's obligation to his conscience prevents his performing some of the more universally recognized duties of citizenship, such as bearing arms for the defense of the country. The Court has upheld separation of state and church and has shielded captive public school pupils against the pressures of religious bodies. Public schools cannot arrange for released time in the school premises for the religious instruction of pupils, even though the pupils may consent. The arrangement is unconstitutional and is a violation of separation of church and state.[46] Parents are, however, free in their choice of schools

---

[45] *Craig* v. *Harney,* 331 U.S. 367 (1947).

[46] *McCollum* v. *Board of Education,* 333 U.S. 203 (1948). In a learned decision delivered in 1953 by the New Jersey Supreme Court, speaking through Chief Justice Vanderbilt, the distribution of Bibles to public school pupils was declared a violation of both the federal and the state Constitutions. In what must be one of the very few judicial citations

and can send their children either to a private religious school or a public school.[47] After a short flirtation with the opposite view, the Court now holds that a state cannot require public school children to salute the flag, since this can lead to a violation of religious freedom for those children whose faith does not allow them to pay homage to such symbols.[48]

The Supreme Court has been equally sensitive to issues involving unusual punishment, cruelty to prisoners, and abuse of police power.[49]

After years of uncertainty, academic freedom and the rights of witnesses before investigating committees are once more deemed to justify a frontal defense by a Court less concerned with the reconciliation of conflicting interests than with the outright protection of liberty and fair play. And the legal boundaries of the communist problem have been redefined with the required sharpness.

RACE AND FREEDOM

One of the most striking contributions to human freedom made by the Court in the last quarter of a century must be found in its support of the American Negro. Here the trend of the Court's opinions is an even one, and it moves steadily in the

of Marsilius of Padua, the Court said: "In 1324 Marsilius of Padua in his *Defensor Pacis* denied the right of the Church to interfere in any matters which were not spiritual. He expounded the very ideas that centuries later were credited to Locke, Montesquieu, Rousseau and Jefferson. Marsilius was far ahead of his age when he claimed that no man may be punished for his religion." (*Tudor* v. *Board of Education of Rutherford,* 14 N.J. 31).

[47] *Pierce* v. *Society of Sisters,* 268 U.S. 510 (1925).

[48] *West Virginia* v. *Board of Education,* 333 U.S. 203 (1948).

[49] *Ashcraft* v. *Tennessee,* 322 U.S. 143 (1944); *Upshaw* v. *United States,* 335 U.S. 410 (1948); *Rochin* v. *California,* 342 U.S. 165 (1952); *Leyra* v. *Denno,* 347 U.S. 556 (1954). In this last case, a confession extracted by a psychiatrist was held to deny due process of law.

same direction, that of abolishing as far as it is in the power of the Court to do so the handicaps which the Negro population of the United States still has to face.

The difficult task has been attacked on many fronts. The Court has fought the cruelty and the denials of due process of law of which certain Southern states have been guilty. Torture, continuous interrogation for days on end, peonage, and brutality have led to the Court's intervention.[50] The Court has fought segregation in publicly operated conveyances, in trade-union bargaining, in the selection of juries.[51]

Repeatedly the Supreme Court has refused to sanction and to provide for the enforcement of private contracts excluding Negroes from access to certain residential zones. No one can now seek to have these agreements acquire legal validity; they are considered to be a violation of the Fourteenth Amendment.[52] While unable to prevent the type of housing discrimination which does not lead to a legal suit, the Court has effectively withdrawn from this practice the very important sanction of the law.

One of the worst forms of discrimination practiced by the Southern states has been the prevention of Negroes from exercising their right to vote. The devices and the stratagems used to achieve this purpose and to nullify federal intervention to thwart it show in a clear light the ingenuity of the white man seeking to retain his political monopoly. The Supreme Court

[50] *Brown* v. *Mississippi,* 297 U.S. 278 (1936); *Chambers* v. *Florida,* 309 U.S. 227 (1940); *Pollock* v. *Williams,* 322 U.S. 4 (1944); *Williams* v. *United States,* 341 U.S. 97 (1951).

[51] *Mitchell* v. *United States,* 313 U.S. 80 (1941); *Steele* v. *Louisville and Nashville R.R. Co.,* 323 U.S. 192 (1944); *Morgan* v. *Virginia,* 328 U.S. 373 (1946); *Henderson* v. *United States,* 339 U.S. 816 (1950); *Cassell* v. *Texas,* 339 U.S. 282 (1950); *Brotherhood of Railroad Trainmen* v. *Howard,* 343 U.S. 768 (1952).

[52] *Hurd* v. *Hodge,* 334 U.S. 24 (1948); *Shelley* v. *Kraemer,* 334 U.S. 1 (1948); *Barrows* v. *Jackson,* 346 U.S. 249 (1953).

has exposed and voided many of these schemes, thus contributing to the slow but steady increase of Negro participation in voting processes. The Court has declared invalid a Texas statute making Negroes ineligible for voting in party primaries (primaries which in the South are the equivalent of election). This was declared a denial of the right to vote guaranteed by the Fifteenth Amendment. When Texas tried to shift the task of deciding who could vote in a primary to private executive committees organized by the parties themselves, the Supreme Court invalidated that law too. The Court said Oklahoma had violated the Fifteenth Amendment when it required in a 1916 statute that, in order to be entitled to vote, a voter must either have voted in the 1914 elections or have registered in 1916 within twelve days of the passage of the law. The Court has resurrected an 1870 statute forbidding obstruction or infringement of the rights guaranteed to citizens by the Constitution of the United States, in order to chastise persons guilty of election frauds in Louisiana and to guarantee the right to vote in primary elections. Literacy tests and requirements to interpret the Constitution have been outlawed, as have efforts to have private clubs reserved to white people exercise control over the selection of political candidates.[53]

Finally, the Court has attracted world-wide attention with its unanimous 1954 opinion supporting a new doctrine of educational equality for the Negroes.[54] The Court had been gradually moving for some time toward that goal. In 1950, it had ruled out segregation in professional schools and in universities. Requiring the admission of a Negro student to the law school of the University of Texas, the Court pointed out that the state of Texas could not provide equal legal education

[53] *Nixon* v. *Herndon,* 273 U.S. 536 (1927); *Nixon* v. *Condon,* 286 U.S. 73 (1932); *United States* v. *Classic,* 313 U.S. 299 (1941); *Smith* v. *Allwright,* 321 U.S. 649 (1944); *Schnell* v. *Davis,* 336 U.S. 933 (1949); *Terry* v. *Adams,* 345 U.S. 461 (1953).

[54] *Brown* v. *Board of Education of Topeka,* 347 U.S. 483 (1954).

for Negroes in a separate school. "Few students," said Chief Justice Vinson, "and no one who has practiced law would choose to study in an academic vacuum, removed from the interplay of ideas and the exchange of views with which the law is concerned." [55]

In requiring the University of Oklahoma to admit a Negro student on an unsegregated basis, the Court said:

> Our society grows increasingly complex, and our need for trained leaders increases correspondingly. Appellant's case represents, perhaps, the epitome of that need. . . . Those who will come under his guidance and influence must be directly affected by the education he receives. Their own education and development will necessarily suffer to the extent that his training is unequal to that of his classmates. State-imposed restrictions which produce such inequalities cannot be sustained.[56]

But, with these decisions, the Court had not yet repealed its 1896 doctrine stating that the equal protection of the laws clause of the Fourteenth Amendment did indeed require equal treatment of the races but did not rule out their separation. Provided public facilities in transportation, in education, in public welfare, were equal, it was not a violation of the Constitution to have separate facilities for the white and black races.[57]

This "separate but equal" doctrine, which had dominated the American landscape for more than half a century and had provided the legal foundations of segregation, was rejected with finality and in its entirety by the Supreme Court in the Brown case of 1954.

At a time when, on important matters, the Supreme Court seemed to speak so often with divided and multiple voices, in lengthy and involved opinions, the Court spoke with one voice and with amazing brevity. Chief Justice Warren said:

[55] *Sweatt* v. *Painter,* 399 U.S. 629 (1950).
[56] *McLaurin* v. *Oklahoma State Regents,* 339 U.S. 637 (1950).
[57] *Plessy* v. *Ferguson,* 163 U.S. 537 (1896).

Today, education is perhaps the most important function of state and local governments. Compulsory school attendance laws and the great expenditures for education both demonstrate our recognition of the importance of education to our democratic society. It is required in the performance of our most basic public responsibilities, even service in the armed forces. It is the very foundation of good citizenship. Today it is a principal instrument in awakening the child to cultural values, in helping him to adjust normally to his environment. In these days, it is doubtful that any child may reasonably be expected to succeed in life if he is denied the opportunity of an education. Such an opportunity, where the state has undertaken to provide it, is a right which must be made available to all on equal terms.

Does the segregation of children in public schools solely on the basis of race and in spite of the seeming equality of facilities deny the children of the minority group equality of education? The answer of the Court is yes; the "separate but equal" philosophy must be rejected and modern scientific authority, it declared, amply supports this view.[58]

The Chief Justice pointed out that to separate Negro children "from others of similar age and qualification solely because of their race generates a feeling of inferiority as to their status in the community that may affect their hearts and minds in a way unlikely ever to be undone."

This solemn pronouncement, it must be admitted, is only the beginning of the end, and the end is not in sight. Many years

[58] It is interesting to recall the evidence quoted by the Court. This is the bibliography listed in a footnote to the decision: K. B. Clark, *Effect of Prejudice and Discrimination on Personality Development* (Midcentury White House Conference on Children and Youth, 1950); Witmer and Kotinsky, *Personality in the Making* (1952), Chapter VI; Deutscher and Chein, "The Psychological Effects of Enforced Segregation: A Survey of Social Science Opinion," *Journal of Psychology*, 259 (1948); Chein, "What are the Psychological Effects of Segregation under Conditions of Equal Facilities?", 3, *International Journal of Opinion and Attitude Research*, 229 (1949); Brameld, "Educational Costs," in *Discrimination and National Welfare* (MacIver, ed., 1949), 44–48; Frazier, *The Negro in the United States* (1949), 674–81. And see, generally, Myrdal, *An American Dilemma* (1944).

are bound to elapse before the educational handicaps of the Negro can be surmounted. The painful and bitter periodic clashes in Southern cities, the elaborate defensive plans being discussed or carried out in some Southern states, are proof of the deep roots of a problem which no country without it can fully understand. The crux of the matter, however, is that the Supreme Court has played a decisive role, within its sphere as expounder of the ultimate principles of a constitutional democracy. By exercising leadership, it has determined the moral climate around which can rally the forces that over the next generation will work for a lessening of racial tensions in America.

As the defender of freedom and equality, the Supreme Court has now acquired a position of influence and moral power in the American democracy such as it seldom had before. And on the eve of the 1958 elections, a Cleveland Negro mechanic forcefully expressed this state of affairs and clearly became the spokesman of multitudes: "You really would like to know how I'd like to vote?," he asked. "I'd like to vote for the whole United States Supreme Court, that's how I'd like to vote." [59]

[59] *The New York Times,* October 17, 1958.

The New Landscape
of American Society:
Lights and Shadows

Contemporary American society bears the imprint of the Roosevelt Revolution, of World War II, of the unexampled prosperity of recent times, and of the communist crisis which is tearing apart the world of the twentieth century. These factors are all interrelated and together have produced the shifts in the behavior, the aspirations, the mood, the substance, of the American community that are visible today.

THE WELFARE OF MAN

The Roosevelt Revolution caused a far-reaching reappraisal of the meaning of government in American society. As he views the large-scale transfer to public power of a wide range of affairs, the man in the street now accepts government as a more important factor in his daily life, government intervention as a matter of necessity, and the restrictions and guidance imposed by Washington as a natural part of his life. Government is not yet considered with the suspicious enmity typical of older nations. Government is part of the stream of life, an associate and partner whose increased strength is due to the decreased strength of individuals no longer professing, as their forefathers did, unlimited confidence in their unaided power.

This does not mean the trend to advance specific and multiple claims against government has not become part of the contemporary American climate. Government supports millions of Americans: veterans, pensioners, farmers, homeowners. Many programs of public economic assistance are always present in the daily routine transactions in which the citizen engages. Reliance on government, not as a partner in a common endeavor, but as a substitute for private effort is, of course, to be expected when government expands the scope of its responsibilities. This is still, however, only a small part of the bigger phenomenon of the association of man and public authority in a joint attempt to face the difficulties of the present.

The Roosevelt Revolution has placed within the reach of a majority of that third of a nation described by its leader as ill-clad, ill-fed, and ill-housed, the means of satisfying the requirements of a more tolerable and even more comfortable life. It has pushed strongly upward the millions who already were on the threshold of middle-class comfort, and has produced an urge for better living and for luxury which strikes foreign observers as an almost frightening manifestation in a world which by and large still struggles under the strains of poverty.

Here the Roosevelt Revolution and World War II became jointly responsible for the forward movement in the welfare of the American people. Building upon the renovated foundations of the financial and economic worlds, exploiting the tools of equality, organization, and opportunity offered by New Deal legislation, America completed the passage from deep depression to full employment with the help of the strenuous mobilization imposed by the war. The recovery became a boom, calling forth once again the traits of risk-taking, of hard work, of adventure, inherent in the American people. The war multiplied the beneficial consequences beginning to flow from the New Deal. There was a more favorable framework of social and labor legislation, new equality of opportunity between whites and Negroes and between old-stock Americans and recent immigrant groups, and new geographic and technological frontiers had opened up. Americans could, after the war, replace the waning demand for military goods with a fresh and increasing demand for private goods. This sustained buying was the basis for the exceptionally high level of capital investment industry was induced to make in order to satisfy the "needs" of the consumer.

These needs could not always properly be described as essential. Often the need was not there at all: the urgent intervention of producers and their advertising agencies was required to create it, while certain categories of consumer demand closely bordered on waste. Nor were these needs satisfied by a reasonable utilization of assets already available to the consumer. One of the major characteristics of the American economy in the last ten years has been the present commitment, on a large scale, of expected future income. Undoubtedly, some of the economic difficulties America experienced in 1957 and 1958 were due to the manipulations of public taste and expectations in which manufacturers of goods, aided by the ubiquitous agents of the "communications world", have engaged with reckless abandon.

It would be wrong to consider only these negative aspects of American prosperity and to base on them the familiar charge of American materialism; one should see it for what it fundamentally was, a strong effort to realize the benefits of a newly acquired freedom—a complex freedom made up of freedom of movement, freedom from fear, freedom from insecurity. Ultimately, what the New Deal did was to remove, to a considerable extent at least, the anxieties peculiar to American civilization, whose uncertainties could more cheerfully be borne in the empty and undeveloped spaces of the nineteenth-century prairie and the small urban community than amid slums and smokeless factories. The New Deal provided relative personal security. This was extended by the excitement of the war and made to appear even stronger by the honeyed words of industrialists and publicity men, amid the prosperity of the late forties and early fifties.

The attempt on the part of the masses to realize the ideal of luxury had sound justification both in the conditions of life in America and in what may be considered the normal, even if distant, aspiration of man in a democratic society. There is nothing improper in owning a house, in having some independent means of transportation, in equipping one's household with a few basic mechanical contrivances, and in aspiring to satisfy one's curiosity about the outside world. Before the frontier of crass and vulgar materialism is reached, there are vast intermediate open spaces which can be filled with the comforts an industrial society must be expected to produce. Across these intervening spaces the American people marched at a brisk pace in the years after 1945.

Some statistical data may best of all provide a broad description of the new economic landscape of the United States.

A striking redistribution of income has taken place. The unhealthy trend of the years between 1914 and 1929 when the disposable income received by the highest 5 per cent of the income earners increased from 32 to 35 per cent of all income has now been reversed. By 1939, the highest 5 per cent of income earners got only 27 per cent of the total, by 1952 only 16 per cent.

At the other end of the scale, families with personal incomes of less than $2,000 a year (expressed in constant dollars with a 1950 purchasing power), declined from 41 per cent of all families in 1929 to 19 per cent in 1953–1954. The nonfarm families owning their home were 44 per cent of the total in 1940 and 60 per cent in 1956.

The remaining areas of poverty are due, for the most part, to special causes. In 1956, approximately 12 per cent of all nonfarm families had a money income below $2,000, while about 22 per cent of all farm families had money incomes below $1,000. The National Planning Association points out, however:

> A closer look at the nonfarm families having less than $2,000 a year income underlines these differences between the poverty of the past and that which remains in the United States. The heads of over half of those families were not working owing to illness or physical handicaps, old age, or inability or unwillingness to find employment. The heads of almost 35 percent of these families were 65 years of age or older. In other cases, the heads of families were widows, or divorced or separated wives—often with children to support—who lacked the time, training, or ability to obtain full-time employment or standard rates of pay. Many low-income urban families were composed of recent migrants from economically less developed parts of the United States (particularly Puerto Ricans), who possessed few of the skills required for ordinary urban occupations. Thus, the main reason for poverty found in urban areas today is the difficulty of finding suitable employment as a result of particular personal handicaps of various kinds.[1]

Of decisive significance in the solution of the problems of poverty and insecurity has been the spreading of private and public insurance and pension programs, practically nonexistent in the pre-New Deal days.

PRIVATE AND PUBLIC INSURANCE AND PENSION
PROGRAMS, 1940-1956 [2]
(*Number of individuals covered, in millions*)

	1940	1945	1950	1956
Old-Age and Survivors Insurance	35.4	48.3	46.4	68.9
Unemployment Insurance	25.1	29.0	34.8	38.9
Private Pension Plans	3.7	5.6	8.6	16.5

---

[1] Gerhard Colm and Theodore Geiger, *The Economy of the American People*, National Planning Association, Washington, 1958, pp. 97–98. And see John K. Galbraith, *The Affluent Society*, Boston, 1958, ch. xxiii, "The New Position of Poverty."

[2] *Ibid.*, p. 101.

These changes toward economic equality and security came as the mobility and restlessness of the American people reached a new high. Some of the most notable population shifts in the history of the United States have taken place since 1932. Many were direct consequences of the New Deal. New York City has received and attempted to absorb half a million Puerto Ricans, most of them with limited professional and English-language skills. The industrial cities of the North and of the Middle West have had to face the consequences of an unprecedented northward migration of Negroes. The farms of America have continued to do their job even though by 1956 they accounted for only 10 per cent of the total labor force of the country, against 22 per cent in 1930. The welfare state, the AAA, the farm security programs did not, in the United States, stem the tide of modernization and the urge to move on to better opportunities.

Population movements and industrial expansion went hand in hand in many areas. The South has enjoyed an industrial and development boom which has transformed its appearance. In the Tennessee Valley, per capita personal income was in 1929 half the average American income. By 1956 it was only 30 per cent below that average. But the rest of the South has also shared in the shifts of industrial activities: Florida, Georgia, the Carolinas, Louisiana have seen the rise of great industrial enterprises in paper, chemicals, oil, natural gas, and consumer-goods industries. The Southwest and the West have relived some of the epic moments of the frontier days, first as a result of the war, later as a result of the development of natural resources and reliance on obvious natural advantages.

A democratic America held together by the ties provided by an invigorated national government was making better use on a larger scale than ever before of its favorable opportunities and assets. As the people learned to look at government with different eyes and expectations, so they acquired a fresh confidence in themselves and in their country. In many ways, and contrary to anticipations, the welfare state caused a rebirth in the spirit of adventure. Since ultimate risks were diminishing, greater immediate risks could be accepted.

The very immensity and intensity of these social and economic transformations have exacted a price the full extent of which is still concealed. The new cities (for the sprawling suburbs now circling the older industrial centers may well be classified as cities, since they have attracted the services, the playgrounds, the schools, the churches, the shopping centers that are the components of urban aggregates) have been thrown up in haste, often without planning and regard for the decencies and aesthetic values that might have been saved had more thought and intelligence been brought to bear on their growth. Efficiency and use of modern techniques have not always produced comfort or durability in the millions of houses that have been built. The speed in the circulation of individuals and groups as they go after still better opportunities has caused an instability in personal living and relationships that must be a source of serious concern.

There is no doubt these upheavals and movements have, however, been a primary cause of the prosperity and economic advance of the United States. Nor is there any doubt that we must view the present condition of man in the United States as the combined result of public policy and of individual reactions to it. Public policy has been so fruitful because it has not met with a private mood of hidebound cynicism and of reluctance to give up the present because of the veil masking the future.

A NEW SETTING FOR THE AMERICAN NEGRO

Writing in the initial years of World War II, Gunnar Myrdal said that "the Negro problem is not only America's greatest failure but also America's incomparably great opportunity for the future." [3]

Myrdal's book remains the classical study of the American Negro on the eve of the transition from the pre-New Deal to the post-New Deal period. Fifteen years later, if the opportunities for the future are still certainly great, the handling of the Negro problem can no longer be called America's greatest failure.

The judicial hammering away at the discriminations, restrictions, and repressions imposed by law or private action, culminating in the Supreme Court decision of 1954 on education, has already been examined. Gradually the legal bulwarks of past anti-Negro behavior are disappearing, and public opinion in most parts of the United States will not for long support practices that contradict the rule of law.

The judiciary has not been alone. The New Deal exploited the opportunity war brought for further economic advances and for the decrease of discrimination against the Negroes. On June 12, 1941, Roosevelt asked for action to deal with discriminatory practices in the employment policies of industries having government defense contracts:

> No Nation combating the increasing threat of totalitarianism can afford arbitrarily to exclude large segments of its population from its defense industries. Even more important is it for us to strengthen our unity and morale by refuting at home the very theories which we are fighting abroad.
>
> Our Government cannot countenance continued discrimination against American citizens in defense production. Industry must take the initiative in opening the doors of employment to all loyal and qualified workers regardless of race, national origin, religion, or color. American workers, both organized and unorganized, must be prepared to welcome the general and much-needed employment of fellow workers of all racial and nationality origins in defense industries (PPA, 1941, 216).

[3] Gunnar Myrdal, *An American Dilemma, The Negro Problem in Modern Democracy,* New York, 1944, p. 1021.

This request was followed by an Executive Order of June 25, 1941, establishing the Committee on Fair Employment Practices. The Committee was to receive and investigate complaints of discrimination in violation of the policy of the United States "that there shall be no discrimination in the employment of workers in defense industries because of race, creed, color, or national origin" (PPA, 1941, 234). To give it greater power and prestige, Roosevelt issued another Executive Order on May 27, 1943, under which the Committee became an independent body within the Executive Office of the President and with more detailed and stronger jurisdiction and enforcement powers. The Committee was authorized to receive and investigate complaints, to conduct hearings, make findings of fact, and take steps to obtain elimination of discrimination.

Due to a combination of wartime necessity and of steady federal government pressure, Negro civilian employment increased, between April, 1940, and April, 1944, by one million persons. In 1940 Negroes comprised only 2.5 to 3 per cent of all workers in war production; by November, 1944, war industries reported that 8.3 per cent of the workers were nonwhite. "In addition to the rise in total number of Negroes, the number of Negroes working as skilled craftsmen and semiskilled workers increased from half a million to one million during this four-year period" (PPA, 1943, 228, 231).

During the five years of its operation, the FEPC intervened to settle by negotiation nearly five thousand discrimination cases. Strikes caused by racial differences were also settled with its assistance. The moral significance of direct federal government intervention cannot be overestimated. Myrdal clearly saw the great significance of the President's position:

The Executive Order [of 1941] and the President's Committee represent the most definite break in the tradition of federal unconcernedness about racial discrimination on the non-farm labor market that has so far occurred. That represents something of a promise for the future. Even if the government should temporarily release its control of the labor market after the War, it is quite possible that there will be some kind of continuation of these efforts." [4]

Myrdal's prophecy proved correct. When the work of the FEPC was terminated on June 30, 1946 (even though this did not mean the end of nondiscriminatory clauses in government contracts), some states were ready with legislation to fight discrimination. New York was a typical example of the great industrial states setting up public agencies to cope with the problem of race conflict.

Not so long ago a Negro leader summed up the changes of the recent past: "No man would have dared prophesy the great changes which have occurred in the past ten years. In whatever light we view the social scene today, it cannot be denied that a century of progress, based on past standards, has been telescoped into a decade." [5]

The condition of the American Negro has changed, not only because a vast array of judicial decisions, federal executive orders, and state legislation has been set in motion in his interest, but also because of the northward trek that has altered beyond recognition the historical distribution of the Negro population within the United States.

Up to the eve of World War I, 90 per cent of the Negro population lived in the South. Today only 60 per cent does; most of the rest is settled in the industrial states of the North and of the Middle West. The Negro population of the South increased by about 10 per cent between 1930 and the present; in the Middle Atlantic and Middle Western states, the District of Columbia, and the Pacific Coast, it nearly tripled, rising from a little over two million to six million. Thus, the Roosevelt Revolution has also witnessed, and in large part been the

[4] *Ibid.*, p. 416.
[5] New York State Commission Against Discrimination, *Article One,* New York, 1955.

cause of, a major shift of the Negroes away from their traditional homeland in search of employment and a new life.

Awareness is spreading among many of the defenders of white supremacy and of segregation that they are fighting a losing battle and that the pressure of events is moving against them. On the other hand, the Negro has to face for the first time many of the complexities so far the prerogative of the white man. Insecurity may be nearly as hard to bear as discrimination. The Negro problem has thus become more complicated as it is now affected by conditions that were not part of the customary American vision of the Negro.

The South has been more directly concerned with the crumbling legal structures. The South has to carry out with "all deliberate speed" the Supreme Court decision ending school segregation. It is the South where community segregation at all levels is being eroded and where the fundamental psychological readjustment needed to bring about new relationships between the races has to be carried out. As the pressures increase and with them the feeling of a way of life under siege, tensions also increase. Little Rock and other episodes of school violence illustrate the moment of crisis which seems to precede all great social changes.

The Negro is in a better position to deal with the hazards of the present because his economic welfare has sharply increased, his job opportunities have widened, his education has improved (only 4 per cent of all Negro youth between the ages of 14 and 24 are now illiterate), and he has in the last generation acquired a mobility from which he had historically shied away, or which was precluded to him.

This migration is an impressive phenomenon. It has been a movement toward freedom and the dignity of man. It has been stimulated by the war, made tolerable by the new federal policies, supported after the war by the prosperity of the country.

The Negro has not been alone in his drive on Northern cities. Half a million Puerto Ricans have come to the mainland, settling chiefly in New York. The American cities which for a while did not have to contend with fresh waves of European immigrants have had to contend with fresh waves of internal immigrants. The problems created by the new population movements were as predictable as they were inevitable. At best only marginal housing became available as the new urban dwellers took over the occupancy of slum or near-slum areas abandoned by the more prosperous members of the New Deal middle classes. Job opportunities were not of the best, and the Negro and Puerto Rican lacked the protection seniority had built up for the older members of the working classes. In cities like Detroit, or in the steel centers, job opportunities were of the best as output mounted rapidly in such basic goods as steel and automobiles. But if his earnings were comparable to those of his white co-workers, the Negro had to share with all concerned the risks of cyclical and seasonal work as well as of technological change.

Here then is a new set of problems facing the Negro today: prejudice and discrimination within industrial communities quite different from the classical white community of the South, and fears arising not out of dim recollections of a past way of life but out of the immediate conflict of interest, of the competition for work and the struggle for survival.

If the white man can be said to be losing confidence in the theories of racial superiority, special care will have to be taken in the future to see that the Negro will retain confidence in the operation of a democratic political and economic system. In the South, the aspiration of the Negro was and remains that of achieving a position of equality and of mutual tolerance and respect. In the North, he has on balance gone a long way toward achieving those goals, but he may be coming face to face with new disabilities imposed on him not because he is black but because he arrived late and because the productive system itself presents unfamiliar risks.

By giving the Negro the legal instruments with which to carry on his fight and by making possible the mobility that has lifted 40 per cent of his people out of their traditional and limited surroundings, Roosevelt's America has done much to redeem its pledge for a new democracy. Changes in people's minds, however, are slow and subtle, and the cruelties of the impersonal economic system are far from being mastered. The greatest burdens and difficulties still lie ahead.

CORPORATIONS AND TRADE UNIONS

The position and strength of many individual Americans were changed during the Roosevelt Era. The meaning, role, and scope of some of the more important agencies of corporate or group life were altered as well. Principal among them were the corporation and the trade union.

Legally, the corporation does not appear to have undergone any change. Most of the forms continue to be the same. Its private nature cannot be doubted. The corporation is still organized to provide a useful impersonal instrument for the attainment of a variety of private ends. In the economic field where private industrial, banking, financial, and research corporations dominate the scene, the chief purpose is still gain for the personal profit of the owners.

Yet it would be a mistake to assume that behind the apparently unchanging façade things go on as before. This is not the case, and indeed the façade itself is being remodeled.

New conditions and restraints are imposed by the laws under which the corporation has to operate. The corporation must today share its profits equally with the federal government. Through taxation, the government has become the equal partner of the owners of the business, successfully advancing a fiscal claim that would have been considered fanciful a generation ago.

The corporation has to share with its owners—the stockholders—and with its creditors—the bondholders—a range of information until recently usually kept secret and even today seldom revealed in other countries. This is due in part to the legal requirements of federal legislation. The SEC imposes full-disclosure and publicity procedures that have helped to bring the conduct of the American business system into the open. In part the change is due to the attitude of the new classes in whose hands rests to a large extent the responsibility for the corporation's administration. Since most of their members are managers and not owners (in any case not substantial owners), they have less reason than the owner-managers of the past to suppress information from the stockholders and the public. Exposure to the glare of the multitude does not affect any of the managers' vital personal economic interests. It may, rather, strengthen their position by making the community at large aware of their administrative skill. As an "outsider," the current president of General Electric can philosophize about electricity or reveal the plans and future hopes of his company as the elder Rockefeller could not possibly have done in any public discourse about Standard Oil, his very own child which was to be defended with all available means, including secrecy.

The corporation has to deal with its workers through an intricate set of relationships whose terms are fixed mostly by law. At key points, such as collective bargaining, recognition of trade unions, hours of work, standards of employment, strike and lockout procedures, the limits and content of the corporation's freedom are defined by law.

The modern corporation has also changed, as it has adjusted to the new American political and economic climate. Its life is affected not only by the uncertainties caused by the technological revolution so much in evidence throughout the world, but also by those resulting from government policies. They may be due to evolving government views on the use and conditions of sale of certain raw materials, like oil and natural gas. The conservation measures of the government may interfere with the private corporations, plans, and the government's ideas as to what the public interest requires from the point of view of prices charged to the consumer may limit the freedom of management. The corporation is seldom allowed to forget its social responsibilities.

The modern American corporation has also found out that the traditional reliance on Wall Street's banking and financial houses as the main source of their new capital requirements was misplaced or no longer needed or no longer adequate, since in the age of the New Deal the economic might of the United States has increased much faster than the might of Wall Street—hence the growth of strong tendencies to financial autonomy and self-sufficiency within the corporation. Autonomy has meant chiefly the use of internal resources of the corporation itself, principally profits. The data reported by Berle are astonishing, as they indicate that, in effect, between 1946 and 1953, only a little more than 3 per cent of the 150 billion dollars of investments made by American business came from risk capital, freely volunteered as such.[6] Independence from Wall

[6] "In November 1953, the economists for the National City Bank made an excellent brief study of the use and sources of capital. . . . They calculated that in eight years (1946 to 1953 inclusive) an aggregate of 150 billions of dollars had been spent in the United States for capital expenditures, namely, modernizing and enlarging plant and equipment. . . . Sixty-four per cent of the 150 billion came from 'internal sources,' that is to say, receipts of the enterprises which had been accumulated and not distributed as dividends. Included in this figure (about 99 billion) were (1) retained earnings and (2) reserves set aside for depreciation, depletion, and amortization on past debt. Retained earnings were, of course, far and away the largest proportion. Of the remaining 51 billion, or 36 per cent of the total, one-half was raised by current borrowing, chiefly represented (directly or indirectly) by bank credit. This accounts for approximately 25½ billion. Eighteen billion, or 12

Street means reliance on internal resources. Reliance on internal resources means relieving the stockholders of any immediate and large share in both profits and responsibility.

This is certainly one of the trends contributing to the formation of the image of the corporation as a public body, as an agency engaged in the productive process and deriving substantial profits from it, but not distributing them to the owners: rather retaining them to add to its power and usefulness and for the benefit of the community. The corporation has become a device used to force savings on the reluctant American capitalist. He sees the profits to which he thought he had a legitimate claim channeled in increasing proportion into the maintenance of quasi-public institutions.

The basic decisions are as a rule reached by managers who, when depriving stockholders of fatter dividends, stress their duty to both country and village, as well as their role in the defense of liberty and of the free world. In the hierarchy of values the managers are setting forth, the maintenance of the integrity of the enterprise in difficult times, the recognition of the scope of the technological revolution currently under way, and the claims of workers and government always occupy a high position, even though the reality is often masked by continuing attacks against government taxation and restrictive

per cent of the total, was raised by issue of bonds or notes. . . . Six per cent, or 9 billion, out of the total of 150 billion was raised by issue of stock. Here, and here only, do we begin to approach the 'risk capital' investment so much relied on by classic economic theory. Even here a considerable amount was as far removed from 'risk' as the situation permitted: without exact figures, apparently a majority of the 9 billion was represented by preferred stock. Probably not more than 5 billion of the total amount was represented by common stock—the one situation in which an investor considers an enterprise, decides on its probable usefulness and profitability, and puts down his savings, aware of a degree of risk but hoping for large profits. There is substantial evidence, which need not be reviewed here, that this is representative of the real pattern of the twentieth-century capitalism. The capital is there: and so is capitalism. The waning factor is the capitalist." A. A. Berle, Jr., *The Twentieth Century Capitalist Revolution*, New York, 1954, pp. 37–39.

legislation, and by a spirited defense of private property and of the rise to power of the small stockholders, pictured as the backbone of the new "people's capitalism."

Community and public pressures have reached the point at which managers cannot any longer dismiss the new competing claims of the Roosevelt Era, in spite of their verbal smoke screens. The general climate of the times has deeply affected the thinking of the businessman. Throughout the period following World War II, the language used by the industrial managers of the United States has reflected the temper and policies of the New Deal. Full employment, sixty million jobs, expanding economy, markets for the masses—these are the goals of the business community. In this respect, the mood is different from that of a Henry Ford. Today, the economic calculations of the nonowner-managers are predicated upon the continuing discharge by government of the major social and economic responsibilities established since 1932. The last decade has seen a measure of industrial expansion which cannot be explained except through the belief that American society will advance with the aid of active government support. In the calculations of the corporations, therefore, the factor of public policy has intruded itself to a degree unprecedented in American history; it has made the corporation dependent upon the successful application of that policy.

Not the least of the fields in which a change has occurred is corporate concentration and monopoly. On the eve of the New Deal, Adolf Berle and Gardiner Means published a book that painted a dramatic picture of the power in the hands of a few corporations.[7] They found the two hundred largest corporations in the United States controlling nearly one-half of the corporate wealth of the country and 22 per cent of all national wealth. These two hundred corporations (they included forty-

[7] A. A. Berle, Jr., and Gardiner C. Means, *The Modern Corporation and Private Property,* New York, 1932.

two railway companies and fifty-two public utilities, but excluded banking, insurance, and financial corporations) had been growing since 1909 at a faster rate than the rest of the economy. Berle and Means estimated that if the 1909–1929 rate of growth continued, the two hundred largest corporations would by 1950 control 70 per cent of American corporate wealth, and more if the trend exhibited during the middle twenties (from 1924 to 1928) continued. Alongside this alarming prospect was the control of these dominant corporations by few individuals. "Production is carried on under the ultimate control of a handful of individuals. . . . Approximately two thousand men were directors of the two hundred largest corporations in 1930. Since an important part of these are inactive, the ultimate control of nearly one-half of industry was actually in the hands of a few hundred men."

A generation later, it is possible to say the apocalyptic forecast of 1932 has not been fulfilled. As the Kaplan study indicates, the trend has been in the opposite direction.[8] If railways and public utilities are eliminated from the Berle and Means list (for these very good reasons: railways are today both bankrupt and regulated—these two traits rather than their size being their chief characteristic—and public utilities, while profitable, are regulated and subject to a degree of public control which aims at preventing, as we have seen, excessive and uneconomic concentration of power), the assets of the 106 remaining largest corporations represented in 1929 about 30 per cent of aggregate industrial corporate assets. Twenty years later, in 1948, the 106 leading industrial corporations accounted for less than 27 per cent of those assets, a 10 per cent decline in relative strength, quite at variance with the 40 per cent increase which should have been expected on the basis of the lowest of the Berle and Means estimates.

[8] A. D. H. Kaplan, *Big Enterprise in a Competitive System,* Washington, 1954.

The Kaplan inquiry also points to a fairly continuous process of change in the composition of the top one hundred corporations. Size is no guarantee of security against the varied political and economic forces that keep the top one hundred, as well as the lower echelon of units, in a state of constant turmoil. The laws of the New Deal, the war, and the new opportunities and requirements of a peacetime economy, have kept the American corporate world in flux and aware of the limited power of the giants. They have made it susceptible as well to the public influences at work against the steady widening of concentrated industrial power forecast a generation ago.

The successful pressure against undue concentration has been maintained in multiple ways.

There has been some new-fashioned trust-busting, carried out with the help of World War II. The case of the Aluminum Company of America (Alcoa) is an example of government-induced elimination of industrial monopolies. Before the war, Alcoa enjoyed a monopoly in the production of the metal. Its power was enhanced by the control exercised by the chief owners of the company on the other dominant international producer, Aluminium Ltd., a Canadian corporation. Here was power absolute, world-wide, and in the classical capitalistic tradition, concentrated into the hands of a few families owning a decisive proportion of the shares of the two companies.

The federal government moved in 1937 to disband the company in order to create competition in the aluminum field. Upon the outbreak of the war, as aluminum became very scarce, the government started to build new plants to satisfy war demand. For the most part, new corporations were induced to come forth to take over the management of the new plants. After the war, as the government sold or leased these facilities to private companies, the competitors of Alcoa were favored. In the end, twenty years after the start of the antitrust suit against Alcoa, the original conditions had been basically changed. Now Alcoa was producing only a relatively small percentage of total American output and at least five new producers were actively competing with the original monopolist. In 1957, the twenty-year-old government antitrust suit was ended. As the Court said, with notable economy of language but with finality, the facts failed to reveal any basis for retaining jurisdiction.

The federal government had not restricted itself to setting up strong domestic competitors against the monopolist. It had also taken steps to end the tie-up between the Canadian and American companies. The owners found themselves faced with this dilemma: Although free to decide which of the two companies they wished to continue to control, they would have to sell their holdings in the other company. The decision made by the controlling families was to retain their ownership in Alcoa. Under court supervision a plan was devised for the sale, over a period of years, of their holdings in the Canadian company. The plan has now been carried to its practical completion and millions of shares worth hundreds of millions of dollars have been liquidated, and one of the foremost examples of international concentration of industrial and financial power in the hands of a few persons has been ended.

A similar story can be told for the many government-built and-owned plants in such new fields as synthetic rubbers and chemicals, nitrogen and plastics. In every instance the new plants have been sold among as large a number as possible of competitive industrial corporations. Throughout, as in the case of the public utilities holding companies, the New Deal's purpose was to maintain the maximum possible flexibility in the economic system. It used the dislocations and upheavals of war to demonstrate the invalidity of the law so dear to the heart of the Marxists that, since war is the finest flower of capitalism, it will be managed so as to advance the interests of the dominant and most predatory capitalistic elements. Whenever possible, the war was used instead as an instrument of policy against dangerous private interests, and to support the aspirations of the newcomers, of the outsiders, of the experimenters.

The counterpart of the corporation is usually the trade union. And in few areas were the repercussions of the New Deal more drastic than in the field of labor. Almost overnight, the American workingman found himself. Freed by the Roosevelt Revolution from the fears and restrictions of the past, the industrial workers who, outside of certain traditional and skilled fields, had remained largely unorganized, set up unions of their own choosing. Within ten years of the passage of the National Labor Relations Act of 1935, trade-union membership had increased from 4 to 15 million. It now stands at 18 million, while 100,000 collective labor contracts of immense variety and complexity, the object of constant negotiation and renovation at the hands of specialists and technicians, provide the stuff out of which their daily lives are made.

The transformation has indeed been amazing and in the short period of a quarter-century trade unionism in America has come of age, for the first time placing in the hands of the worker instruments of power that have given him a well-defined place within the system and a shelter within which his isolation and insecurity could be diminished.[9] As trade unionism made its appearance as a major element in the public policy and structure of American society, it acquired characteristics peculiarly American.

There is, first of all, the efficiency and discipline of most trade unionism. In managing their own trade-union affairs, Americans have brought to them the sense of commitment,

[9] Frank Tannenbaum, *A Philosophy of Labor,* New York, 1951, has some interesting ideas on the revival of "status" at the expense of "contract."

responsibility, and serious work that they often bring to their other community and organizational efforts.

Trade-union leaders, entrusted with great power, came at once into close touch with one of the most important New Deal regulatory agencies, the National Labor Relations Board, with its primary tasks of investigating complaints of unfair labor practices by employers and administering secret elections to determine what union should represent the workers in a plant. The rise of the trade unions coincided with the emergence of the complex public procedures connected with union recognition, collective bargaining, and drafting of labor contracts. And major trade unions began very early to consider themselves as an integral part of the productive system.

The historically wide chronological gap between "revolutionary" and "formalized" trade unionism was greatly reduced in the United States, as the new trade unionism quickly developed a class more like that of statesmen than of rabble-rousers. Research into labor and industry problems was soon accepted as essential. Trade unions showed inventiveness and initiative in adjusting their claims to the transformation of technology and economic life. The collaboration of John L. Lewis' miners union with the coal producers is a remarkable example of this. The pioneering initiatives of the steel and automobile workers' unions helped industry in coming to terms with such concepts as long-term contracts and guaranteed annual wages that are unique contributions of American trade unionism to our industrial society. The French communist leader, Pierre Hervé, only one among several Marxists expressing themselves in similar fashion, recognized in 1955 in his *La Révolution et ses Fétiches,* that the exchange of ideas between American labor and management was producing results that the European Marxist labor movement ought well to take into account. No more singular tribute to the strength and originality of the American labor system could be expected.

In part, these achievements have been possible because by and large American labor has remained nonpolitical. The truth of this statement is not invalidated by the fact that most labor leaders are Democrats, many of them New Dealers, very few of them are ready to support even "modern Republicanism," and that, on balance, the American labor movement has supported Democratic administrations and candidates, and has generally or specifically been hostile to the Republican party. The American trade-union movement is nonpolitical because its activities have been concentrated on the task of improving the conditions of work and security and the standards of living of its members; because, notwithstanding the obvious fact that a large percentage of trade-union members is made up of Republicans and Democrats voting along party lines, no division on political lines has occurred; because, in spite of occasional exceptions, no labor candidates as such have ever been backed by the trade-union movement. This has not prevented unions from expressing their opinions on candidates at election time, but this intervention has primarily tended to be related only to the candidate's position on specific labor matters.

The issue deserves some further clarification. To be elected as the direct representative of an interest group is not the same thing as being elected because of its support. That this is so can best be seen by considering the election in Europe of spokesmen of labor unions who, usually, are nothing else besides, and the election in the United States of those candidates who enjoy the broad support of organized labor but who are a great many other things besides. No society can possibly prevent some of its more important interests—and labor is one of them—from making political choices. The danger to pluralistic and free democracy arises when large interests advance exclusive claims to the obedience of those they elect. Today we can still say that society must be deemed happier where no such monopolistic claims are made.

The workingman in the United States can make some careful political choices, as the issues are precisely defined and as he senses the weight of his role in the political process. He will want his representatives, among other things, to be ready to support the specific legislative items which in the normal evolution of political life, appear to him to be necessary. As American society moves toward higher forms of industrialization and its institutions and legislation recognize to an ever greater extent the inevitable consequences of that process, the political influence of the classes which are the backbone of the system, will increase. To decry the so-called usurpation of political power by labor means in effect to believe that America should not be what it is.

The role of the European workingman is, for the moment, rather different. He is still on the defensive and he can see that often the management of public affairs in his country is not what it should be if the full promise of an industrial civilization is to be realized. Therefore his political choice will be more narrow and belligerent than that of his American counterpart; his premise will still be a revolutionary one. He will want his representatives to be his direct agents fighting without compromise and in his exclusive interests.

The European workingman needs slogans and definite party labels. The American workingman looks at the concrete details of the issue and does not care about party affiliation. He is ready to vote for the best man.

All of this leads to interesting results in the turnover of the political elite. In a slow-moving political world, the European workingman finds himself, in effect, deprived of the possibility of selecting fresh leaders as the years go by. The slogans remain unhappily the same, the party is the same and the same old men will get his vote. In the United States, the turnover rate is higher, as the programs are fulfilled and as issues change from election to election and as the voter is able to identify in the candidates of either party the man he wants, depending on circumstances. The so-called "upset," which is a typical and frequent phenomenon in America, is proof of the relevance and freedom of the electoral process. On the European political landscape, there are fewer upsets, as the same tired faces appear year after year to "defend" the interest of the "proletariat." When they do occur, they are proof of the failure or manipulation of the democratic process and of the presence of near-revolutionary conditions.

Hence the final paradox: the nonpolitical behavior of the American labor movement has led to a more meaningful and decisive share in the political life of the country by the American worker. The extreme forms of political commitment to which European labor movements have been driven, have, on the other hand, been barren of results, tending to isolate the worker politically and to deprive him of real freedom.

If the job of setting up the intricate network of collective relations that lie behind the worker has been well completed, difficulties, inevitable in an undertaking of this scope, have not been avoided altogether. Until recently, widespread rivalries and competitive recruiting campaigns have been part of trade unionism. They have now been reduced as a result of the merging of the two leading trade-union groupings in America, the American Federation of Labor and the Congress of Industrial Organization, the former representing the older tradition of skilled trade unionism, the latter the more direct fruit of the mass organization of the less skilled workers achieved in the New Deal years. The legal support the Wagner Act has given to the trade union properly certified by the National Labor Relations Board for purposes of collective negotiation, has placed into the hands of labor organizers strong weapons with which to put pressure on the workers to join the union and to maintain discipline. Even if the workers themselves often like the elements of compulsion of union life, forced membership and payments of dues do create serious issues of individual freedom.

Finally, the meteoric rise of trade unions has created un-exampled opportunities for corruption and personal power. This has been particularly true in those fields where the ethics of the employers themselves left much to be desired. There is no corruption in the great industrial trade unions that organize the workers in the basic industries of the United States—for example, coal, steel, automobiles, engineering. There is corruption, in varying amounts, as has been revealed in a series of congressional investigations in those industries where competition is desperate, the chances of survival for the entrepreneur limited, the difficulties of operation extreme, the climate within which the industry carries on unfavorable. This is true of industries that operate in thousands of small urban establishments, susceptible to the pressures and vicissitudes of life in large cities. Food, trucking, transportation, service trades, retail shops—these are the unhappy, often unprofitable, and harassed segments of our economic system in which the pettiness, the ruthlessness, the lack of public responsibility exhibited by many employers, usually because of their unsteady economic health, are matched by similar behavior on the part of the workers. These are the areas of employment into which the latecomers, the poorer, the more marginal groups among American workingmen have been pushed. The workers here are more subject to worry concerning their future, and thus to blackmail, than workers in the basic industries. Both a restaurant or laundry owner and a restaurant or laundry worker may have to submit to humiliations to which it is impossible to submit a steel master or a steel worker. Hence it is not surprising that the rise of trade unionism in these areas has given rise to some corruption and violence which have tended to make trouble for the entire labor movement.

Considering the problem in its entirety, the transformations the rise of trade unionism has brought about in American society is remarkable. John Galbraith speaks of the union's new countervailing power; Clark Kerr refers to the shift from monism to pluralism.[10] It is certain that for the first time the American worker is fully represented in the reaching of decisions of vital concern to him. The industrial corporations, a generation ago largely alone in their sphere of action, now find themselves confronted by the dual power of the new federal government and of the new trade unionism. A fresh equilibrium has been introduced in the operation of the industrial system. The American worker has, together with notable material benefits, acquired a sense of participation which is one of the essential elements in the life of a democracy.

As trade unions have grown in importance, they have acquired as the corporations have, the characteristics and responsibilities of public bodies. Their policies and procedures have become the object of public scrutiny. The way in which the power inherent in union leaders is exercised has become a matter of lively public concern. Trade unions have entered full maturity, and as mature bodies they are expected to behave in a manner different from that of their youth. Power—personal, direct, and unaccountable—was of no particular consequence in the days of the barricades, when the labor movement had not acquired the universality it now possesses. Power exercised within the framework of a detailed system of public policy, of labor contracts affecting the totality of the workers of a given industry where the union shop prevails, removed by at least a generation from the days of crisis of the early New Deal, becomes power derived from public bounty and must be, therefore, power regulated, properly administered, and controlled in the interests of all those who are directly or indirectly concerned with it. But the exercise of trade-union power is not

[10] John K. Galbraith, *American Capitalism*, Boston, 1952; Clark Kerr, *Unions and Union Leaders of Their Own Choosing*, New York, 1957.

only of concern to the outsiders, to the third parties, to the community: it matters increasingly to the insiders, the union members themselves. Both problems of freedom and problems of professional pride are involved here.

The problem of freedom is often the opposite of what it was a generation ago. The freedom of the worker was then the freedom to join the union of his own choice. This was the overwhelming issue as the unorganized workers rushed to seek the status that the industrial climate of the pre-New Deal era has so often denied them. Today's freedom is no longer to be vindicated against hostile employers as in the 1930's, but sometimes against the trade unions themselves. Certain unions suffer from the same human weaknesses concerning attitudes toward race relationships as do the other segments of society, and the Negroes may be the victims of discrimination at the hands of their co-workers as cruel as any they have known from the general community. Also significant in today's discussions is the freedom not to join, a freedom usually translated into the so-called "right to work" and written into the statute books of a number of states. There is the question, finally, of the right of the worker to sue a union for damages if his freedom of movement and of employment has been interfered with.

What must be remembered is the frame within which these debates are taking place. In the early days of the New Deal, it was clear what the stand of employers on behalf of the "freedom" of the worker meant. It was an appeal to freedom motivated by the desire to prevent the rise of a strong trade-union movement. It was therefore proper to take a dim view of it, since this was not the freedom the overwhelming majority of the workers wanted.

Today another world has been born, and in the face of a strong union movement the careful qualifications and discriminations that have been introduced or may still have to be introduced in labor legislation are justified, because the fundamental freedom of the worker to organize is no longer challenged. While thirty years ago many American workers had to be rescued from the antisocial behavior of the industrial classes, there is today a minority of workers to be protected against the excessive claims of the trade-union movement itself.

Another problem also affects the internal life of trade unionism. It is the result of the contradictions between the increasing professionalization of the American worker and the tendency of the large industrial unions to support labor contracts that reflect greater uniformities, rather than greater particularities.

In the United States, as in other advanced technological societies, the claims of those possessing special or unique skills are made with greater and greater energy and persuasiveness with every passing day. Skills are not acquired to be disregarded, nor is expensive technical education to be wasted. On-the-job training and added skills are not to be thrown away in a morass of uniformity. The special demands for recognition, position, pay, and security advanced by special groups have to be recognized.

On the other hand, mass unionism is based on mass democracy concepts and on the need of equal treatment for the broadest possible groups. The task of job and skill classification is an uncommonly hard one that may force on union leaders a rearrangement of internal procedures, in so far as trade unionism denies the recognition of special interests and claims. The difficulty is: There appears to be a lag between mass unionism and the professionalization of the workers, with a consequent rise in internal tensions that may become a serious threat to vested labor interests and stir up the seemingly placid waters of some of the larger unions.

The issue of internal democracy is another problem confronting trade unions. Will it be solved by generic appeals to a generic concept of democracy which may well have no place in trade-union life?

Existing legislation, as found in the Taft-Hartley Act, says a union may enjoy the legal advantages accruing from access to the processes of the National Labor Relations Board only if it has filed with the Secretary of Labor a list of its officers with their salaries and a detailed statement of its constitution, including the procedure for the election of officers. There is no requirement concerning the method or the periodicity of election of officers. The law as it stands is incapable of guaranteeing trade unions "democracy." It is because of this that for many years proposals have been advanced, aimed at strengthening the law to ensure the election by secret ballot of the officers at stated and fairly frequent intervals. This is, in itself, a desirable practice that should be effectively instituted where it does not exist. The issue of union "democracy," however, has wider implications.

It should be noted, in the first place, that arrayed against the trade union stands the industrial corporation. The question of the extent to which democracy exists in the management of the affairs of an industrial corporation is not a simple one to answer. Public control and accountability are, of course, not democracy. A corporation must have as public a record as possible. Its accounts must be above doubt; the owners of the corporation must be kept informed as to the risks they are running, yet the unseating of a board of directors, or a change in top management are equally important matters that cannot usually or readily be solved by obviously recognizable and quickly effective democratic processes. Quite often the change is carried out by a coup d'état or perhaps no change is possible for all practical purposes. There are large corporations which are examples of autocratic and self-perpetuating rule, but against which no charges of misdoing or violation of the interests of the owners can properly be leveled.

In the second place, the issue of democracy in a trade union is unlike that of democracy in a political community, which requires both free elections and the confrontation of opposite views on the political battlefield to give victory to the view which wins the support of the majority. The evolution of the power process within a trade union is mainly toward the election of the best leaders capable of protecting the interest of the members. In principle, within a trade union (and apart from the possibility of the kind of conflict that communism brought to some American unions), there is no basic confrontation of different issues, but a gradual groping toward the realization of what are the usually clearly defined interests of the group. The interests and purposes of the steel workers, though changing ones, will always be capable of more narrow and univocal definition than the interests and purposes of the American people. Therefore, union democracy cannot be defended on the basis of the need for the rotation in power of men with different ideas and programs, because, within trade unions, the problem is essentially the continuous maintenance of the best in power. Repeated election of the same leaders is not proof of lack of democracy. While the thought of Walter Reuther occupying the White House for thirty years is unbearable for many, the thought of Walter Reuther managing for the same length of time the affairs of the United Automobile Workers of America can be an appealing one. Though it may be said that the best tend to become corrupt and have to be eliminated, the defense against trade-union corruption requires not democracy in the political sense, but merely the presence of appropriate procedures whereby the officer guilty of specific charges may be removed.

These concepts have to be stated, because too often the businessmen who speak in favor of union democracy are not concerned about the welfare of the union or the regular election of officers, but are interested chiefly in the possibility of removing from positions of command able trade-union leaders who have become dangerous opponents. The appeal to democracy can be a rhetorical device which conceals a wish to weaken the prestige and negotiating power of the enemy.

In conclusion, however, let it be understood that trade unionism in America has entered a new phase, one in which it will have to reconcile itself to a wider measure of public inspection, and to adopt the model practices of such unions as those of the automobile and the steel workers. Too often, the recollection of past strife and dangers, of exposed positions, not to mention the pressure of personal advantage and gain, conspire to render the behavior of trade unions less admirable and public-minded than it should be. The issue cannot be pushed aside by the reflection that sometimes this happens in response to direct invitations to collusion by the employers themselves. This is a problem an organized community, with a production system such as the American one, must face.

AMERICA AND COMMUNISM

The issue of communism exploded with startling suddenness in the midst of a society in full expansion and confident of having within its reach, if not the stars, certainly most of the benefits of democracy. The American reaction to communism must be understood within the specific framework of American conditions.

Let there be no doubt as to the outlines of the communist problem seen from the United States in the late 1940's and early 1950's. There was first the Soviet refusal to co-operate in what to the American people appeared eminently reasonable, altruistic, and peaceful programs for the reconstruction of Europe. From the Monetary Fund and the World Bank, to the European Recovery Plan and the proposals for the international control of atomic energy, the Soviet answer was uniformly negative. In 1948, the Prague coup convinced the United States that Russia was bent upon the aggressive expansion of its already large sphere of direct European influence. Events in China, climaxing in the Korean aggression, further persuaded the American people that here was a total danger to freedom to which total resistance was needed. Russia in those years presented her cruelest face to the outside world, and Stalin successfully lifted whatever remaining doubts lingered in people's minds about the nature of Soviet expansionistic policies.

Until then, few had paid much attention to the Soviet Union, fewer still to theoretical Marxism. During the thirties, the shape of Soviet affairs was vaguely known to a handful of urban intellectuals who at times tended to build dreamy visions of Russia as a land of plenty and full employment to be contrasted with the stillness of deserted American factories. The New Deal erased that vision, but the war, of necessity, conjured up for the masses a new picture of a friendly and powerful ally. The threat perceived after 1948 hit America with singular force; suddenly, the policies of the Soviet government appeared aimed at denying to the United States the fruits of victory and of peace. More, they seemed aimed at destroying the foundations of the American system.

That system had become an effective one in the governance of men, of their lives, of their economic activities, of their security. America had never been happier or more convinced that after its many tribulations it was on the high road to freedom and plenty, that through its own hard work and a renovated government it was in a position both to help the rest of the world to recover its bearings after the destructiveness of war and to keep domestic conditions in balance. With reason, the United States could say that it had made long strides toward the solution of some of the worst problems of an industrial society. The expectations for the future were high, and the present, too, looked all right.

Few in the United States could contemplate communism

with the detachment, the cynical look, the eager anxiety, or the definite approval of the European accustomed to ideological disputations and placed in the midst of largely unresolved political and economic tensions. When the European intellectual flirts with communism, he does so out of a long habit of play with Marxism and with problems and contrasts that, given the state of affairs in his country, appear to him to be better understood within the context of the Marxist tradition. He is pondering difficulties, real and immediate, which he may think communism might solve. His over-all evaluation of communism, ranging from parallelism to complete acceptance, is related to a totally or nearly totally unsatisfactory appraisal of conditions at home.

The reaction of the majority is dictated by considerations of expediency and relativism and by the knowledge that, conditions being what they are, a certain amount of tolerance is required. Governments also are far too conscious of their weaknesses and of the problems looming ahead to take firm positions, except for purposes of rhetoric or of foreign policy. In practice, the tendency is toward accommodation and a live-and-let-live attitude, for, after all, the future is dark.

In America, the attitude was different. What was to be defended against total evil was total good. The country had emerged from a long series of readjustments and had written on its statute books an imposing variety of reforms. It stood at the end of prolonged war, conscious of its strength, of the basic fairness of its internal arrangements, ready to help the world. This was certainly too confident a view of American power, of the readiness of the world to accept American leadership, and of the extent to which domestic problems had finally been liquidated. Compared to Europe, however, the United States could justifiably claim for itself a greater inner fire and achievement of social justice than many other countries. The reaction to the dangers of a communist blight on the American dream as it was coming near fruition was harsh and uncompromising. This situation of understandable psychological stiffening of a people convinced of the essential worth of its way of life, under which liberty was being reconciled with social coherence, was exploited skillfully by some adventurous politicians-at-large who succeeded in establishing a strong base of operations for themselves.

The American reaction to communism in the late forties took place against the background of a second essential factor, equally absent from European calculations. Tied to the belief that the American community had reached a stage of democratic freedom and integration worth defending was the belief that, since America had become the sole possessor of a new and devilish weapon of destruction, every effort was to be made to secure the continuation of this monopoly.

No serious attempt has been made to study the moral and political consequences of the American possession of the "secrets" of atomic power. It was the tragic destiny of the United States, as the strongest power of the wartime coalition, to be the first developer of atomic power and the first user of that power through the atom bomb. In 1946, the United States offered the world, in a series of proposals going back to a report prepared at the direction of Dean Acheson by a committee which included David E. Lilienthal and J. Robert Oppenheimer, a plan for the international control of atomic energy. In spite of certain cumbersome features, the plan was a most generous offer, by a power having at that time the undoubted monopoly of atomic weapons, to share with the rest of the world the future development of the atom for peaceful purposes. The proposal was found unacceptable by the Soviet Union. As the appalling scope of the destructive power of the atom bomb dawned on the American people, the conviction then grew that steps were required to insure the absolute security of the United States against the absolute destruction that would come from an atomically armed Russia.

We see at work here a series of factors which, it should be realized, had not until that time been present in the estimates and thoughts of any other people on earth. At the same moment in history, the American people were confronted by the consequences both of a new position of world responsibility and of their monopolistic control over the most disruptive force ever discovered by man. At that same time, the Europeans found themselves in the contrary condition of atomic outsiders, in the midst of weak democratic processes and of sharply reduced international power. From the point of view of the United States, the interaction of these factors produced a series of negative results. The vastness of the international power of the United States did not always go with the experience needed for its successful maintenance. The power given the United States by the atom bomb, and now felt by the people to be vital to their security, came at a moment when scientific innocence concerning atomic energy and weapons and the problems they raised, including the chances of retaining atomic "secrets," was inevitably widespread. Mistakes were made in the handling of the problems of power and of security, but it is not legitimate for anyone to forget the readiness of the United States in 1946 to solve with imagination the awful problem of the bomb, nor the unprecedented nature of the issues confronting the country. It was a lonely position of absolute power the United States occupied in those years. When the attempts to share it failed, the repercussions were bound to be grave.

In the debates of those years, the intellectuals, who had had such a large role in the formulation of the ideals of the American government in the heroic years of the New Deal, were in a weakened position. The inventiveness that had presided over the first fifteen years of the New Deal was no longer there. In part this was due to the fact that much that needed inventing had been invented. Governments alternate between periods of intense activity and periods of peaceful management. The primary task as the end of the twenty-year Roosevelt Revolution approached, seemed to be to administer as well as possible the many new, and at times not even completely developed, institutions of government. The intellectual was less wanted. It was not difficult for the country as a whole to separate itself from some of the values Roosevelt's brain trust had attempted to inject in the discussions of public policy.

Furthermore, the intellectual, with his sensitive antennae and continuous preoccupation with the future, appeared to be involved in confused speculations about the nature of science, the impossibility of secrecy, the fearsome consequences of the ultimate development of atomic energy for war purposes. To many Americans, the intellectuals engaged in these exercises came close to treasonable activities, as they were ready to give up, without compensating gains, positions of strength and security which, with some effort, were thought to be capable of indefinite preservation.

We must count, among the achievements to the credit of the Roosevelt Revolution, the increased participation by the people in political life, as the New Deal succeeded in awakening large numbers of hitherto politically indifferent or inactive Americans to the significance of politics—people who had never voted because they were too poor, because they lived at the margins of American society, because they didn't care; Negroes who had been disenfranchised; recent immigrant groups —by the millions these people had entered political life. And almost at the beginning they found themselves baffled by issues of a complexity quite beyond their power to grasp. Mass democracy is difficult to manipulate and to control under the most favorable conditions. These difficulties became all too clear when American mass democracy was suddenly confronted by questions of life and death and by a scientific revolution whose meaning escaped even the most sophisticated and educated members of the community.

*

The federal government played a crucial role in determining the course of events. It was committed in the field of foreign policy to strong resistance to communism. In Europe, the American government had taken the lead in a plan of European reconstruction aimed to solidify the political and economic institutions of that continent against the temptations of communism. The Marshall Plan first and the North Atlantic Treaty later were evidence of a joint economic and military program against the expansion of the Soviet Union. In Asia, Truman had not hesitated to commit the military forces of the United States, under the jurisdiction of the United Nations, in outright physical resistance to communist aggression against Korea.

This firm posture of the Truman administration against communism abroad was easily translated into an equally firm posture against the potential threat of communism at home. In the process, the subtleties and wide range of American action overseas, which went from support of European federalism and reconstruction to combat on the battlefields and which took into account the multitude of different problems posed by the rise of communist power, were lost. To an uncomfortable extent, domestic protection against communism was seen as a fight against disloyal public servants and citizens ready to do incalculable damage to the security of the country if given half a chance. Black-and-white slogans were summoned to do their duty, and the ensuing irrational rigidities were accepted without excessive qualms.

The Executive Order issued by President Truman on March 21, 1947, prescribing procedures for the administration of an employees' loyalty program in the executive branch of the government, fed the fires of procedures incompatible with the American tradition of freedom. Until then, security programs for the removal of civil servants from public office required the existence of reasonable grounds for belief that the person involved was disloyal to the government. This placed the burden of proof on those who were challenging the loyalty of the employee. The Truman Executive Order of 1947 changed this standard to one of reasonable doubt as to the loyalty of the person involved. It is far simpler to doubt loyalty than to prove disloyalty.

Writing in 1955, Dean Acheson makes this handsome admission:

> These practices had their root in the President's Executive Order, 9835, of March 21, 1947. This order and the Act of August 26, 1950, upon which rests the present Executive Order, 10450, of April 27, 1953, were adopted under a Democratic Administration. I was an officer of that Administration and share with it the responsibility for what I am now convinced was a grave mistake and a failure to foresee consequences which were inevitable. That responsibility cannot be escaped or obscured. It is true that these measures had strong bipartisan and popular support, indeed insistence, behind them. It is true, also, that the present Republican Administration, and particularly Attorney General Brownell, has continued, defended, and expanded the most harmful aspects of the loyalty program long after their destructive and corrosive consequences were plainly apparent. This does not absolve the Democratic Administration, but it should crowd the mourner's bench.[11]

By 1950, President Truman, alarmed at the course of events, was attempting to stem the tide of proposed legislation and of increasing congressional usurpation of executive prerogatives. Addressing the Federal Bar Association in Washington in April, 1950, Truman expressed the hope that his Executive Order would be carried out with fairness and restraint, and said that loyal government employees should be protected against accusations which were false, malicious, or ill-founded.[12]

[11] Dean Acheson, *A Democrat Looks at His Party,* New York, 1955, pp. 126–27.
[12] *Ibid.,* p. 128.

But the administration was on the defensive at that time, as politicians and the press were mounting charges against it and its predecessors of wholesale surrender, even of treason, in the face of the communist conspiracy. If Russia was strong and China had been lost, the New Deal was indubitably to blame. This being the case, there could be no doubt at all that the New Deal was nurturing with care thousands of spies in public office, busy day and night betraying America's interests and security.

During the fateful summer of 1950, Truman sought to stop proposed congressional legislation, but in vain. He protested in a special message of August 8, 1950 against the Internal Security Bill, which, he thought, was weakening basic American liberties. He vetoed on September 11, 1950, a bill amending the Nationality Act of 1940, which, the President said, in attempting to reach persons who seek the overthrow of the government through association with communist-front organizations, jeopardized basic rights of naturalized citizens.

On September 22, 1950, he vetoed the Internal Security Bill which, while intended to protect the security of America, did, in effect, assist the Communists in their efforts to create domestic dissensions and to discredit as hypocrisy American efforts on behalf of freedom by making a mockery of the Bill of Rights.

And what kind of effect would those provisions have on the normal expression of political views? Obviously, if this law were on the statute books, the part of prudence would be to avoid saying anything that might be construed by someone as not deviating sufficiently from the current Communist-propaganda line. And since no one could be sure in advance what views were safe to express, the inevitable tendency would be to express no views on controversial subjects.

The result could only be to reduce the vigor and strength of our political life—an outcome that the Communists would happily welcome, but that freemen should abhor.

We need not fear the expression of ideas—we do need to fear their suppression.

Our position in the vanguard of freedom rests largely on our demonstration that the free expression of opinion, coupled with government by popular consent, leads to national strength and human advancement. Let us not, in cowering and foolish fear, throw away the ideals which are the fundamental basis of our free society.[13]

The President's veto was overridden the same day by overwhelming congressional majorities (286 to 48 votes in the House of Representatives, and 57 to 10 votes in the Senate).

The United States had entered on a most difficult phase of its domestic history,[14] from which it emerged about four years later with the approval by the Senate on December 2, 1954, and by a vote of 67 to 22, of a resolution censuring the Senator from Wisconsin, Joseph McCarthy.

During those four years, great damage was inflicted on the United States by the uncontrolled reactions of both public bodies and individuals to the threats, imaginary and real, of communism.

Government agencies, at all levels, felt impelled to issue security and loyalty rules. In the words of the Commission on

---

[13] Quoted in *ibid.*, pp. 127–28.

[14] Acheson describes it vividly: "Furthermore, it was not realized at first how dangerous the practice of secret evidence and secret informers, how alien to all our conceptions of justice and the rights of the citizen, even though he was also an employee. Experience proved again how soon good men become callous in the use of bad practices. Familiarity breeds more than contempt, it breeds indifference. What was, at first, designed for cases which it was thought would be serious, sensitive, and rare, became commonplace and routine. Now in cases involving no secret agent or sensitive position, a person may be branded as of doubtful loyalty and dismissed on evidence by persons whose identity not even his judges know and whose words, summarized for them, are withheld from the defendant. Nor is this practice restricted to cases involving the employer-employee relation between the government and the defendant. It can apply also to private employment. . . ." *Ibid.*, pp. 128–29.

Government Security established by Congress in 1955 to "fill an urgent need for an objective, nonpolitical and independent study of the innumerable laws, executive orders, regulations, programs, practices, and procedures intended for the protection of the national security," there grew up "a vast, intricate, confusing and costly complex of temporary, inadequate, uncoordinated programs and measures" [15] which clearly defied intelligent and fair administration.

In a study published in 1955 in the *Bulletin of the Atomic Scientists,* Ralph S. Brown made the following estimate of the number of employees exposed to some existing loyalty or security test:

	(*in thousands*)
Professions, including teachers	1,600
Managers	300
Government and military	7,200
Manufacturing, construction, transport, utilities	3,500
Total	12,600

As Brown writes, "Taking the total labor force at around 62,000,000, this means that one person out of five, as a condition of his employment, has taken a test oath, or completed a loyalty statement, or achieved official clearance, or survived some undefined private scrutiny."

Another estimate, prepared by Senator Harry Cain, concluded that directly or indirectly the livelihood of 20 million Americans was affected.[16]

Worse still were the trends and the attitudes of mind generated by the security programs, the blunting of the classical lines separating the branches of government, the usurpation of

[15] Report of the Commission on Government Security, Washington, 1957, p. xiii.
[16] Both estimates quoted in Acheson, *op. cit.,* pp. 164–65.

judicial power by legislative bodies, the quest, in George Kennan's words, "for security within the walls of secular uniformity."

The absence of leadership from the White House made itself felt. Roosevelt had dealt effectively with some of the earlier raids of the House Un-American Activities Committee. In 1938, he was much disturbed to realize that "a Congressional Committee charged with the responsibility of investigating un-American activities should have permitted itself to be used in a flagrant, unfair, and un-American attempt to influence an election" (PPA, 1938, 559). And in 1940, addressing himself to the same Committee, he had made it clear that though it could investigate, it could not "conduct the administrative functions of Government under the Constitution" (PPA, 1940, 577). Truman, though a good fighter, did not have the strength required to insist on certain fundamentals in the enforcement of the loyalty program, and his leading policy-makers were handicapped by fantastic accusations of past surrenders to international communism.[17] Eisenhower was initially too un-

---

[17] That the Soviet government should first have published two letters addressed by Roosevelt to Stalin on April 1 and April 5, 1945 (Roosevelt died on April 12, 1945), must surely be counted as one of the ironies of history. In the first of these letters Roosevelt wrote as follows:

> I cannot conceal from you the concern with which I view the developments of events of mutual interest since our fruitful meeting at Yalta. The decisions we reached there were good ones . . . so far there has been a discouraging lack of progress made in carrying our . . . political decisions . . . particularly those relating to the Polish question. . . . You are aware of course that the commission which we set up has made no progress. . . . Your Government appears to take the position that the new Polish Provisional Government of National Unity . . . should be little more than a continuation of the present Warsaw Government. . . . I must make it quite plain to you that any such solution which would result in a thinly disguised continuance of the present Warsaw regime would be unacceptable and would cause the people of the United States to regard the Yalta agreement as having failed. (*New York Times,* February 12, 1958.)

The State Department still regards this letter as a "classified" document, even after its publication by Moscow. Had it been published ten years

certain about his proper role in the scheme of government to take any effective position until 1954, when he did contribute to the general revulsion of public opinion against McCarthyism.

The spread of McCarthyism in the body of American society, facilitated by these governmental weaknesses, assumed pre-occupying proportions. Not only was communism bad, in all its implications and manifestations, but nonconformism of any kind was to be avoided, too. There was widespread fear of new ideas, or reluctance to express clearly even such ideas as were contained in the Constitution of the United States. In an address at Washington University in St. Louis on February 19, 1955, the Chief Justice of the Supreme Court, Earl Warren, felt com-pelled to recount the following episode, which he must have considered typical of the climate of the times:

> A few days ago I read in the newspaper that a group of state employees . . . charged with responsibility for determining what announcements could be posted on the employees' bulletin board refused to permit the Bill of Rights to be posted on the ground that it was a controversial document. It was reported that the alter-cation became intense, and that only after the Governor in writing vouched for its non-controversial character was the Bill of Rights permitted to occupy a place along the routine items of interest to the state employees. And this happened in the United States of America on the 15th day of December, 1954, the 163rd anniver-sary of our Bill of Rights, declared by proclamation of President Eisenhower to be Bill of Rights Day.
>
> It is straws in the wind like this which cause some thoughtful

---

ago, as it should have been, and had the stand taken by Roosevelt in the last days of his life against Soviet policy been known, perhaps something of the confusions, misapprehensions, and downright mistaken notions entertained by American public opinion on the faithfulness of their leaders in defending American interests and ideals would have been dissipated. The conflict between the Soviet Union and the United States would have appeared in its proper light as a conflict between two rising world powers, and American difficulties as not necessarily due to the treacherous inclinations of public servants. But throughout the long night of McCarthyism, Roosevelt was described as a weak and blind dupe of the Russians.

people to ask the question whether ratification of the Bill of Rights could be obtained today if we were faced squarely with the issue.

Under the lash of McCarthyism, an exceptional timidity developed in dealing with the political and intellectual problems of contemporary life. If communism was the prototype of evil, the forces fighting communism were by definition beyond reproach and beyond criticism. If the Catholic Church was a leader in the world-wide struggle against communism, the Church, its institutions, and the propounders of its doctrines, were to be immune from attack, for to attack Catholic doctrine meant to weaken the common defense against communism. This timorous state of mind was revealed in examples that are bound to leave one stupefied at the insidious spread of the disease.[18]

[18] An extreme instance of this is to be found in the *New York Times* of April 9, 1950. The *New York Times* is not only the best newspaper in America, it is also an uncommonly stubborn, intelligent, and tireless defender of freedom, of democracy, of tolerance, of open discussion; it not only prints the news, but, on balance, all the news and more news than any other newspaper in the world. It also shows an extraordinary sensitivity to the problems of survival of free societies in the twentieth century. Yet, this is what happened: The Book Review Section of the *Times* published a review of Lionel Trilling's book, *The Liberal Imagination.* The author of the review, Philip Toynbee, had this to say about the book:

> The supreme interest of this particular critical oeuvre is that Trilling makes his perceptive and even affectionate attack on the cultural aridity of liberal democracy from inside that political citadel. We are all too familiar with the facile and vitriolic attacks on liberal and democratic culture made by Roman Catholics and members of the political right. Their furious partisanship, their tiresome love of paradox, has produced little criticism of importance.

This was a mildly polemical statement, largely true, perfectly defensible, and of a type that one usually expects to find in any literary journal in which the discussion of books is not reduced to mere summary or automatic praise. Yet, on the editorial page of the *Times* of the same day the following notice appeared, entitled "A Correction":

> In today's issue of the Book Review, in a review by Philip Toynbee of a book by Lionel Trilling, 'The Liberal Imagination,' there appears a reference to Roman Catholics that obviously should not have been

*

Why did these things happen? At the beginning of this discussion, some of the broad underlying reasons for the American attitude toward communism were noted. But further comment is needed to understand the particular forms of American behavior, specifically what many recent European critics of America have considered to be the primitive childishness of certain manifestations of individuals, groups, and public bodies.

What is so often forgotten is a chief trait of American society, one particularly important in this connection—its pluralism. American society has always expressed itself with a phenomenal multiplicity of views. The developments of the last generation have not hampered the continued strengthening of this basic pluralism in spite of the rise of a federal government far more powerful than in the past. Group life has been stimulated. Vocal middle classes have multiplied their numbers. More leisure has encouraged organized activities of all kinds. Education has extended its boundaries: the voices of innumerable school boards throughout the land cannot be stilled. Indeed, they are more widely heard as new social groups, who have just emerged into the limelight, are sharing in their administration and in the determination of their policies.

Traditional forms of political pluralism have persisted and have perhaps even increased within such institutions as the Congress. In the absence of party discipline and of effective party whips, it is impossible to prevent a member of the Senate from speaking his mind and from organizing around himself a practically unassailable area of power and influence which he

made. Every reviewer has the right to express his opinion and that opinion is his rather than the opinion of *The Times*. The editor, however, has the responsibility to delete statements that are inaccurate or offensive. That responsibility should have been exercised in this case. Unfortunately, it was not and the offending sentence was not detected until after the press run of the Book Section had been completed."

can use to articulate his views and to acquire publicity and prestige useful for his re-election.

It would be idle and unreasonable to expect a pluralistic society of this kind not to express itself sometimes, or even often, in ways that appear to offend common sense, the weight of evidence, the normal standards of decency, or to show contempt for the processes of a rational mind, particularly on such issues as communism, in the age of the atom bomb.

If, merely for the sake of the argument, one were to say that such multiple and varied exhibitions of folly and ignorance by public officials or by school administrators do not take place in Europe, the fundamental reason in most instances will not be that there are no public officials or school administrators in Europe capable of error or foolish behavior. The reason will be that they are gagged, unable to speak their petty and ignorant minds, not authorized to go against the official line established at the center. The reason will be that the man at the center does not care or finds it impossible to express himself. The silence of fear and not of wisdom rules over the land. On the other hand, contradictions, errors, absurdities, and a babel of voices are part of the price of freedom. The price has to be paid. What matters in the end is what happens to the society paying that price.

Next to pluralism, the increased power of slogans should be mentioned, a trend for which social engineers, public relations men, advertisers, and psychologists and motivational experts in the service of business, are to a large degree responsible. It has by now become almost unfair to criticize these members of American society, so cruel has been the recent exposure of their doings. But it is still necessary to point out the extent of their role in some of the more troublesome complications of American life—a role that goes from the widespread acceptance of frozen and meaningless ideas about property and free enterprise to the cynical attempt to foist a religious revival on the

American people through advertising and vulgar public pressure, from the sedulous and now even invisible fostering of consumption desires and wants beyond the real need of the American consumer, to the deadening of aesthetic values and tastes. The defense of American values and traditions in the hands of groups who never cared for them since they were busy upsetting them, has had a deleterious impact on the public mind. The overwhelming financial difficulties any private citizen will encounter before he can make a fresh contribution to public debate with the publication of a new paper or journal of ideas have added to the manipulative power of the slogan-makers. Here we have frightening examples of the soporific possibilities inherent in the technological instruments of our civilization and of their negative repercussions on society, when they are too often used in a uniform and uncontradicted manner.

The result has been a weakening of the defenses of a free and inquiring mind. Too many people seem to accept as sensible the alternative propounded by a famous businessman addressing himself to the nonconformist: "You are either a Communist or a thinker." In this atmosphere, McCarthy and his stooges, satellites, and frightened followers of all kinds had a freedom of movement and acquired a hearing that went beyond their power and far beyond their effective influence on American society.

For the mistake of the world at large was to assume that as these weaknesses of modern American society stood revealed, no strong defenses could be detected. But those who were close to the heartbeat of America thought otherwise, and their optimism is gradually being justified. Indeed, the rally from the confusion and sickness of the early fifties has been quick and even more successful than could have been anticipated.

Pluralism itself provided one of the best defenses. Just as it had facilitated the expression of points of view that have been judged in this analysis to be immature and grievously opposed to the American tradition of freedom, so it permitted at the same time the manifestation of opinions of a more mature kind and more in keeping with that tradition. No one, anywhere, was in possession of total power over the United States. For every school board that imposed censorship, that indulged in extravagant statements on the problems of the day or that fired innocent teachers for alleged disloyalty, there were a hundred that stood firm on the essentials of educational and intellectual freedom. For every university that was guilty of repression of academic freedom, for every board of trustees that made a defense of capitalism a test of admission to the faculty, there were ten that maintained unaltered the strongest practice of academic freedom, whose faculties continued to speak with the voice of reason and independence and where research on the broadest range of issues went ahead without fear. No less important was the fact that all the great universities, all the institutions properly entitled to be called universities, were unaffected and unafraid and, except for insignificant episodes, remained bulwarks of liberty of thought and of inquiry.

In brief, the essence of the history of those years can be summed up by saying that, confronted by new issues posing entirely new threats, American society engaged in a debate and a course of action which, if veering at times toward dangerous directions, in the end maintained the fundamental framework of a free society.

Nor should the role played by institutions in the recovery of freedom be forgotten, those institutions which in other countries have often proved to be empty shells, mere shadows, incapable of affecting events and of contributing to the orderly growth and renovation of public life. As of today, American institutions stand vindicated.

The intervention of the Senate in bringing to an end the career of Joseph McCarthy was decisive. Following the introduction, on June 30, 1954, of a resolution to censure the Senator from Wisconsin, a Senate Select Committee was appointed to study the censure charges. The committee reported unanimously on November 8, recommending censure. The committee found the conduct of McCarthy toward one of his witnesses, "in reprimanding him and ridiculing him, in holding him up to public scorn and contumely and in disclosing the proceedings of the executive session in violation of the rules of his own committee, was inexcusable. Senator McCarthy acted as a critic and judge upon preconceived and prejudicial notions." The committee found that in dealing with government documents, Senator McCarthy "manifested a high degree of irresponsibility towards the purposes of the statutes and executive directives prohibiting the disclosure to unauthorized persons of classified information." The Select Committee felt compelled to conclude: "the conduct of Senator McCarthy in inviting federal employees to supply him with information, without expressly excluding therefrom classified documents, tends to create a disruption of the ordinary and constitutional functioning of the executive and legislative branches of the government, which tends to bring both into disrepute. Such conduct cannot be condoned and is deemed improper." The Committee recommended, on these and other specific charges, which went to the core of the Senator's malpractices, the censure of McCarthy by the Senate.[19] On December 2, 1954, on a roll-call vote of 67 to 22, the Senate adopted the resolution.

The vote liquidated Senator McCarthy. It may be said that the Senate waited too long and that when it acted it did so out of self-interest. What matters is that it acted effectively and that in defending itself it defended the survival of the constitutional system. The role played by the Supreme Court has already been described in some detail in Chapter V. Its restate-

[19] *Report of the Select Committee to Study Censure Charges,* United States Senate, 83rd Congress, 2nd Session, Washington, 1954.

ment of the principles and methods of freedom helped immeasurably in bringing about a more balanced view of the position of America in the minds of citizens preoccupied and uneasy about the course of events.

It has been fashionable in many quarters of the globe to cry "fascism" and to write off America from the roster of free nations because of McCarthyism. But no country can be described as a fascist country only because it may have "fascists" in its midst. (This is quite apart from the question of what is the proper description of McCarthyism.) When pressure groups triumph, when institutions no longer fulfill their original purpose, when public power falls into the hands of factions, when all the train of consequences are set in motion that lead to the ultimate destruction of freedom, then we may have fascism or some fresh variety of it. When a country comes to grips with its own difficulties, however, when institutions soon reassert their purpose within the constitutional framework, when reason prevails, when at the end of many painful experiences, those opposed to the unconstitutional elements in their midst gain the upper hand, that country may perhaps be described as a constitutional democracy going through an agonizing reappraisal of itself, in full view of the world—but not as a fascist country.

One of the heartening phenomena of recent years has been the maturing of public opinion, the reconciling of the views of the man in the street with the requirements of the difficult age in which he lives, the downgrading of "secrets" as a result of a wider appreciation of the nature of the scientific process.

In an investigation published in 1955, Samuel S. Stouffer perhaps best summed up the contemporary mood of America when he wrote that less than 1 per cent of those questioned considered communism their chief source of concern:

Great social, economic, and technological forces are working on the side of exposing even larger proportions of our population to the idea that "people are different from me, with different systems of values, and they can be good people, too." This would seem to be a necessary condition to tolerance, but not the only condition. It should be a first step to the recognition that it is good for a country both to respect the civil rights of people whose ideas challenge cherished traditions and to preserve a free market place of ideas even if they seem dangerous. And that the country can and must do this, while still standing firm against its enemies from within and without. In this book we have seen some of these great forces at work.[20]

POLITICAL LIFE

Paradoxes abound in American party life. The New Deal caused a readjustment of party alignments and strength of such depth that Samuel Lubell could write: "the toppling of the dominance held by the Republicans for nearly three-fourths of a century can be considered as the Third American Revolution." [21] America saw as well in the course of the last generation an extraordinary quickening and extension of citizen participation in political life. But in 1952, as the end of the New Deal era came and the Republicans once again took over the government of the country, the political mood of the United States appeared to change. Intensified political interest was translated into more diffused demands of the electorate on parties and into a convergence on a broad central area of moderate conservatism. The flames of the Third American Revolution were extinguished by its accomplishments.

The picture of American party politics, given in 1893 by James Bryce in *The American Commonwealth,* was altered by the New Deal in many of its premises. A powerful national government, an efficient administration, the setting in motion

[20] *Communism, Conformity and Civil Liberties, A Cross-Section of the Nation Speaks Its Mind,* New York, 1955, pp. 220–21.

[21] Samuel Lubell, *The Future of American Politics,* New York, 2nd ed., 1956, p. 3.

of policies with national repercussions, reduced to smaller proportions the influences of some of the historic elements of
American political life, such as regionalism, professionalism,
urban machines, and political bosses. These factors could not
guide a political life played against a continental background
and concerned with much larger issues.

The New Deal brought with it unprecedented group mobility, the economic expansion of the South and of the West,
the northward shift of millions of Negroes. It led to prosperity
and to the rise of large new middle classes, to the building of new
satellite cities surrounding the older centers. The recent immigrant group for the first time acquired a full vision of their
power and of their possibilities as great numbers of them entered economic and political life.

The New Deal made all aware of the role that an active
central government can play. This brought about an awakening
of the interest of millions who had until then refused to look
at political life as a meaningful exercise of man's capabilities.
The political parties, and above all the party supporting the
Roosevelt Revolution, gained tremendously in the process.

As the turmoil increased, as old systems and privileges
crumbled, and the influence of the New Deal began to pervade
the life of the nation, elections acquired higher dignity as
manifestations of political beliefs and as moments of political
decisions essential to the welfare of all. The increase in the
number of voters in presidential elections from 29 million in
1924 to 61 million in 1952 (without any change in suffrage
law and far out of proportion to the increase in population)
is a unique phenomenon in the history of a modern democratic
state: American democracy came fully of age with the New
Deal.

Both parties flourished, the Democratic party far more than
the Republican.

DEMOCRATIC VOTE IN ELEVEN NORTHERN
AND WESTERN STATES
(*thousands of votes*)

STATE	1924	1952
Connecticut	110	482
Pennsylvania	409	2,146
Michigan	152	1,231
Illinois	577	2,014
Wisconsin	68	622
Minnesota	56	608
California	106	2,198
Ohio	478	1,600
Massachusetts	281	1,084
New Jersey	280	1,015
Washington	43	493

REPUBLICAN VOTE IN ELEVEN SOUTHERN STATES
(*thousands of votes*)

STATE	1924	1952
Virginia	73	307
North Carolina	191	558
South Carolina	1	168
Georgia	30	199
Florida	31	544
Tennessee	131	446
Alabama	43	149
Mississippi	8	113
Arkansas	41	177
Louisiana	25	307
Texas	130	1,103

What these figures[22] show is that the urban population of the

[22] Adapted from E. E. Schattschneider, "United States: The Functional Approach to Party Government," in *Modern Political Parties*, S. Neumann, ed., Chicago, 1956, p. 211.

United States, its industrial workers, its recently naturalized immigrants, the beneficiaries of the new prosperity and of the industrial growth of California, voted in extraordinary numbers to support the New Deal, and were in 1952 still committed to the Democratic candidate, Adlai Stevenson, who best represented a continuation of that tradition. But the New Deal had also shaken the rigid and torpid political positions of states traditionally Democratic but where only small percentages of the population ever voted. From this shakeup the Republican party gained, especially in the Southern states.

The New Deal was therefore responsible for giving fresh vitality to both political parties. Perhaps one may better say that the New Deal succeeded in multiplying the interest of all American citizens in party life and in the role of parties. The New Deal was a process of mass political education and resulted in the acceptance by the mass of citizens of their duties under a democratic party system.

It is at this point that some of the paradoxes alluded to a moment ago begin to make their appearance.

In Europe, the entry upon the political stage of roughly similar groups of factory workers and of urban dwellers, which occurred in the course of the last seventy-five years in answer to new political and voting rights, has led to sharper political tensions and difficulties, to a deepening of party conflicts, to increased claims by the parties on government, to growing organizational rigidities within the parties, to attempts to impose party discipline and programs on the elected party representatives. It cannot be doubted that the democratization and universalization of political life in Europe has tended to place in the hands of parties weapons which have shifted the balance of political power and the nature of constitutionalism. Marxist and Christian-Democratic parties, to mention two of the main beneficiaries of this process, have tended to become demanding organizations, whose presence is keenly felt as they press forward their policies and aspire to dominate political life to the very end of the institutional process. In brief, the more political participation has widened and political life has become democratized, the more party divisions, rigidities, and intrusions have increased, to the detriment of the classical structure of parliamentary power. Contemporary events in Europe show only too well that these are some of the root causes of the crisis of constitutionalism.

The opposite is true of the United States. The swelling of political participation and the strengthening of parties, underlined by the data just shown, have resulted in a relaxation of party conflicts, a moderation of party programs, a convergence of community goals toward a generically middle-of-the-road common ideal.

As the war ended, Henry Wallace thought this could not, or should not, happen. He felt the time had come to give some institutional strength to the revitalized parties. In a political speech made on March 18, 1946, he expressed the belief that both the Republican and Democratic parties should impose party discipline, and that, for example, members of the Democratic party should support the administration foreign economic policy, or be put out of the party by not being allowed to run again on the Democratic party ticket. Testifying before a congressional committee on April 10, 1946, Wallace restated his views in a more prudent way: "I said at the March 18 meeting that I believed completely in the two-party system, but that if we were to get action on major issues some way must be worked out so that the voters know what they are voting for. I suggested that a party might make a party issue of perhaps three or four or five points." The Wallace attempt to impose a rigid programmatic party discipline, even if limited to a few key issues, failed, and since then the chances of imposing even feeble discipline on party life have been diminishing steadily.

The reasons for this are complex, purely American, directly

linked to the final impact of the New Deal on American society.

Parties are not in America the instruments of government they have tended to become in Europe. Parties are useful for local purposes, they are essential for the screening and nurturing of leaders, they are all-important as the vehicles through which the process of selection of the national leaders and of the legislators is accomplished every two or four years. But America has acquired a sufficiently realistic and common-sense view of what are the tasks of government not to nourish any illusions as to the aptitude of parties to engage directly in governing activities. Parties are indispensable elements in the democratic process, but they have, as such, no decisive role to play when it comes to governing. The members of Congress are ideally seen operating within a framework of independence from party pressures, even though they are not imagined as capable of forgetting party interests, or even less the interests of the groups or the communities that have contributed to their election and are likely to do so again in the future. Party discipline in the sense of a steady discipline imposed from an outside party organization upon the legislators as they attempt to exercise responsible congressional functions is not tolerated. Even mere advice by nonelected party leaders is viewed with suspicion.

The same applies to the relationships of parties to the White House. The President is far too strong and independent a figure who, once elected, enters upon an immense inheritance of power which cannot by any stretch of the imagination be related to party affairs. He is, indeed, the leader of the winning party and has to perform certain chores in that connection. But the President is the president of the whole country and has responsibilities which are defined by the Constitution and not by party statutes. What he has to do and the policies he will support are evolved in the light of considerations and of data analyzed by the President as a constitutional agent of the community and not as a party agent.

The parties themselves are aware of this state of affairs. The claims they put forward are modest. They are satisfied with minor or merely resplendent bestowals of patronage benefits. Their official spokesmen will limit themselves to the utterance of simple platitudes on the life and goals of the republic. No more pathetic figures exist in American political life than the two chairmen of the national committees of the Republican and Democratic parties. Most of the time they are exchanging polemical attacks against each other to which the country pays no attention whatsoever, for it is generally understood that what they say is unlikely to have the slightest effect on the business of government. Party organizations come to life only at intervals, during the months preceding national electoral campaigns. At other times the relationship between the President and his Cabinet and party administrators is erratic and mostly for the public record. The President relies too much on the autonomous sources of his power to have to yield to the requirements of the party machine. In the United States today, the influence of party stops at the front doors of the offices of government. What goes on at the back doors is, with some unhappy exceptions in the field of patronage, of no great consequence.

To this basic phenomenon of the inability of parties to penetrate the areas reserved to the operation of constitutionalism, a second must be added, probably temporary in its nature: the gradual fading of the black-and-white contrast that separated Democratic and Republican parties at the beginning of the Roosevelt Revolution. By 1952, the ultimate goal of Roosevelt's vision had taken substantial shape—the vision of a nation at peace with itself, prosperous in its economy, strong in its instruments of government, having achieved a broad democratic base and eliminated many areas of privilege and of private action contrary to public policy; a nation in which the common good was no longer a distant ideal and in which its citizens would become increasingly anxious to defend what they had within a multiple framework of free community life.

The reaction against the Democratic party in 1952 was, of course, not against the New Deal or its basic advantages and readjustments of the balance of domestic affairs. It was the expression in part of a desire to improve the performance of government by bringing to power a new group of men, in part of the desire for a stronger hand that would bring the Korean War to a close. The American people felt also that the Republicans, as the official conservative party, could be relied upon to a greater extent to preserve the existing order, one under which so many benefits had accrued and were accruing to its members. The New Deal suffered the fate of successful revolutions, and the opposition was entrusted with the task of maintaining the revolution's conquests.

The danger of the situation is that the beneficiaries of the revolution may misconstrue the cause and the policies that have brought about the advantages they are so anxious to preserve. The New Deal meant movement, experimentation, constant inquiry into the maintenance of a proper balance between economic forces, the searching for new policies, and the taking of initiative in dealing with crises. It was because of this flexibility and this readiness to take risks that the New Deal succeeded. It did not succeed because of caution, avoidance of conflict, fear of upsetting vested interests.

The new conservatives may be bent upon doing the opposite. The millions who as moderates occupy the middle plateau of American conservatism—those whose pressure has watered down the fighting spirit of the Democratic party of the thirties while forcing on the Republicans a reluctant acceptance of the social reforms of the New Deal—show an inclination to forget the conditions and the hard work which caused their present state of well-being.

These masses of both young and middle-aged Americans

who appear so imbued with a conservative outlook in politics have been described by some as anxious above all to retain their improved and lofty social status, by others as pseudo-conservatives who do not really know what their status is, by still others as materialists who confuse conservatism with the retention of economic gains. All these elements to which may be added conformism, shock reaction to communism, and the increased habit of living by slogans, account for some of the present aridity of American political life, for the seeming paradox of a nation with the highest political participation ever achieved in history but ready at the same time to relax in the comfortable attitude that as long as things go well, there is no need to look for coherence or hard-driving leadership in the national government.

Can the United States have reached this nirvana at a moment of history when the expectation of paradise on earth was never less justified, and attained a state of self-satisfied complacency and a belief in the protective quality of great principles at a time when those principles are not operative as they were in the past? Americans would then be fighting for the status quo at a time when the status quo is no longer defensible and when revolutions in science and in the balance of world power are bringing about relentless pressures toward revolution on a world scale.

But the chances are that this convergence of political attitudes toward a blurred golden mean, in an age which is far from being golden itself, will not last. The success of the New Deal, great as it was, was never complete and its drive will have to be renewed. The illusions of security and of permanent well-being are still often illusions in a world in which the adaptation of United States interests to world conditions is proving more and more difficult. The disparity between the higher aspirations of society and the surrounding reality may be seen in a cruder light as the years go by. The material benefits en-

joyed by many members of the community may look less attractive in the midst of a political society which has—in the
fierce light of the heightened competition among world powers
—recently had to admit the existence of a number of deficiencies in its midst.

Quite likely, sharp reactions are already under way. If
McCarthyism had been due to the rise of the new American
middle classes brought about by the New Deal, then McCarthyism should still be part of the contemporary American scene;
but it is not, although the middle classes continue as strong as
before. It seems clear that the political sensibility of the American people is beginning to react to what are proving to be
only temporary molds of thought. The reaction may soon
bring to the fore large unresolved issues on which the two major
parties will once more have to take different stands. Too
often what is called the lack of issues separating the two major
political parties is due to sheer laziness or to fear of excessive
public exposure. The issues of today are as important as the
issues of the thirties—issues of foreign policy, education, race
relationships, improvements of health and urban planning, the
proper goals of industrial policy, of the roles of production
and consumption, the mastery and uses of atomic energy.

When the time will come—as it soon will—to reopen the
now half-closed book of political debate, the reawakening of the
fires of battle between ideas and between parties should lead to
political struggles and decisions that will not only redound to
the further advance of democracy and of freedom in the United
States, but should also take place under conditions that promise
a better informed, a more satisfactory, a better balanced political
game. America has changed. America is not only promises
and principles. It is also an effective reality, a country that
moves within a sturdier framework of institutions and of political wisdom than was true a generation ago. This is the lasting
accomplishment of the Roosevelt Revolution.

Reflections on Tocqueville

THE INSTITUTIONS OF GOVERNMENT

The temptation, at the end of our journey, to go back to Alexis de Tocqueville's *Democracy in America,* is irresistible. This famous book, appearing near the beginning of the life of America as a nation, has been, ever since its first appearance in 1835 and 1840, a landmark and reference point for all those engaged in the difficult task of trying to find out the secret of what makes America go.

There is no reason whatever why the temptation should be resisted. The scope and the insight of Tocqueville's analysis remain unmatched. The point of view from which he sought to understand America—the relationship between democracy and freedom—is the fundamental one that should concern us today, and the era with which this book has been concerned, the Roosevelt Revolution, had more to do with the issues of democracy and freedom than any other in American life since the Civil War. It seems therefore proper and necessary to come to whatever conclusions are possible, in the course of some reflections on what Tocqueville's vision was of the American continent more than a century ago and on the relevance and significance of that vision for our generation.

As those who have read *Democracy in America* will agree, a more descriptive title might have been "Democracy *and*

329

America." For we find in Tocqueville's pages two basic efforts: the first, describing and analyzing American institutions; the second, understanding the democratic drive and its influence on the future. It was Tocqueville's preoccupation with democracy that impelled him to cross the Atlantic to find out how the democratic process was operating in the New World and what were the chances of the survival of freedom. If today we still retain a vital interest in what Tocqueville said, this is due at least as much to his interpretation of democracy at work and the lessons it contains for the future of mankind, as it is to his picture of America in the 1830's.

We are struck by the immense range of materials and of aspects of human behavior taken into account in Tocqueville's *Democracy*. Legal patterns and traditions, political factors, social and group phenomena, moral qualities and religious fervor, custom and principle, economics and the Constitution —everything is considered in order to arrive at a full knowledge of the United States. The constant relating of the institutional to the moral and social approach gives depth and life to his treatment.

The larger issues are not forgotten in the discussion of concrete constitutional details. In trying to find out why, as he thought, the House of Representatives is a body remarkable for its vulgar elements and why the Senate seemed to enjoy a monopoly of intelligence and talents, Tocqueville felt the answer lay in the direct popular election of the House. The time would come when America, "would be obliged more frequently to introduce the plan of election by an electing body, or run the risk of perishing miserably among the shoals of democracy."

What has happened since 1835, of course, has been the opposite. The Senate, too, is now elected by direct universal suffrage and yet it has retained the special prestige Tocqueville attributed to it. The reason then for the decay of parliamentary assemblies need not or cannot only be brought back to the operation of the electoral process. In the case of the Senate, more significant causes inherent in its structure and position within the constitutional system have counteracted the possible deleterious consequences of direct election. There is the smallness of the body, the difficulty of access to it, and the stern process of selection that this imposes. There is the continued presence of federalism that invests the senators with special dignity even though their specific roles in its maintenance may not have been conspicuous. There is the accretion of responsibility enjoyed by the Senate as a result of a specific mandate in the field of foreign policy. This has kept the Senate in the limelight and given it a chance, for evil or for good, of playing a part in the history of the country. There is, finally, the marked resistance of American legislative assemblies to the claims of parties pretending to act as the monopolistic representatives of mass democracy. In Washington, avenues of control of the constitutional process have been firmly blocked against the advance of extraconstitutional forces.

Tocqueville's dislike of the direct elective process extended to the election of the President. Here, "the most weighty argument against the election of the chief magistrate is that it offers so splendid a lure to private ambition and is so apt to inflame men in the pursuit of power that when legitimate means are wanting, force may not infrequently seize what right denies." This has been a danger minimized to the vanishing point by the abiding influence of certain beliefs in law and freedom to which Tocqueville himself ascribes a great role. But he was right in saying that the period which precedes the election of the President must always be considered one of national crisis.

On balance, however, Tocqueville was inclined to attribute a relatively small importance to these factors, because the powers of the President of the United States he found to be "temporary, limited and subordinate," and his influence on

public business "no doubt feeble and indirect." The President
has little wealth and little glory to share among his friends,
and his influence was too weak for the successful rule of a
party to depend upon his elevation to office. Interestingly
enough, he was writing these words during the second Jackson administration.

America contradicted Tocqueville by going in the contrary
direction. Surely one of the most striking features of the
presidential office as it stood at the end of the Roosevelt
Revolution was its conjunction of responsibility and power and
its combined reliance on the constitutional system and depend-
ence upon public opinion, a rare combination in this age of
totalitarianism or of pseudodemocratic governments.

Roosevelt brought this long-range historical development,
a continuing one in spite of the number of inevitable setbacks
and interruptions, to a new peak. Never before had the assumption of the inherent powers of the President been so
complete, or had such frank consequences been drawn from
their application. Nor had any leader in American history,
governing through the successive emergencies of domestic and
international crises, been able to win the confidence of the
people in four successive elections.

The very success of Roosevelt created fears, and rightly
so, about the continuation of the Presidency in its traditional
form, and led to the later amendment of the Constitution which
limits tenure to two successive terms. The wisdom of the amendment remains to be tested, for the writing off of the President
after his second election, implied in the present system, is
bound to weaken his effective influence during the second half
of the eight-year period. There are unfortunately already enough
gaps in the continuous operation of the American government
(chief among them the protracted electoral campaign), to add
to them the potential disability flowing from the lack of attention politicians will pay to anyone whose career is known to

come to an end on a fixed day without any chance of reprieve.

The belittling of the role of the President, which could still be defended in the 1830's in spite of the great leaders who had occupied the White House by that time, was only one aspect of Tocqueville's failure to see what was happening to the federal government. The first volume of *Democracy in America* was published in 1835, the year in which Marshall died. Yet there is scarcely a hint that he sensed the significance of Marshall's work. Of the Federalist party, even though he calls its accession to power a "most fortunate incident," he has this to say: "Whether their theories were good or bad, they had the fault of being inapplicable, as a whole, to the society they wished to govern." He had seen the development of the nullification movement in South Carolina on the issue of the tariff, but there were more enduring forces at work which made for a strong union and which Tocqueville did not see. Thus, reluctantly it is true, he came to the conclusion that the federal government was constantly losing strength, retiring gradually from public affairs and narrowing its circle of action, and that unless some extraordinary event occurred, the government of the Union would grow weaker and weaker every day. This being so, he could write that "the Federal Government scarcely ever interferes in any but foreign affairs, and the governments of the states in reality direct society in America." These words were written fifteen years after *McCulloch* v. *Maryland,* and ten years after *Gibbons* v. *Ogden,* the great Marshall decisions that established the foundations of the powers of the federal government in the economy and commerce of the United States.

Only in the case of Congress could the question of a relative over-all weakening of power be raised today. It is indeed a serious question, even though one cannot say Congress has failed to fulfill its constitutional mission. During the last twenty-five years, the Congress has performed its legislative responsibilities well. From the passage of the vast range of New Deal and Fair Deal statutes to its reorientation in foreign affairs and the enactment of radically new legislation in this field, the Congress has acted at least as well as any other parliamentary body, and better than most.

The fact remains that often the Congress has come to life only under the steady application of executive pressure, and that this pressure, especially in foreign affairs, has had at times to be so vigorous that the laurels belonging to the Congress for what it did are modest at best. If, in order to secure legislative action, crises have to be manufactured and decisions are possible only after painful and protracted debates likely to alienate friends and delight foes, then the liabilities incurred in the process are to be taken into account in evaluating the role of Congress.

There is, too, the failure of Congress to deal effectively with such sensitive areas of domestic policies as education and minorities problems. Here the ideals of federalism may have been a drawback, for they have transformed the Congress into the stubborn defender of points of view and legal positions that sooner or later will have to be modified. Mass democracy and mass education (as, earlier, mass production) have created tasks which go beyond the power of the states and the localities to solve. The new co-operative federalism that has been successfully applied in economic areas will have to be extended to the school problem too, and yet the Congress has failed to act on most of the proposals that have been made to it in this field. As far as the Negro problem is concerned, the Congress has allowed the Supreme Court to assume the leadership and force the issue of equal and nonsegregated education for all.

Finally, the rise of the administrative state with its quasi-legislative powers vested in the new independent regulatory commissions, has reduced the scope of congressional action. Here the Congress is to be praised rather than blamed for having accepted one of the transformations which are evidence of the birth of a modern state.

Any balanced assessment of the position of Congress is a complex one. In part, we see a strong hesitation to move forward in new directions, unaided. In part, we see the acceptance of bigger responsibilities by the Executive, and the adaptation to the new exigencies of the administrative and welfare state. Perhaps one can say that the Congress had abdicated some of its old powers and has not entirely lived up to its new obligations. This in the end is due to the general decline of parliamentary bodies in the twentieth century and to the impossibility of realizing under today's harsh conditions the bright promise of James Bryce's prophecy on the extension of classical parliamentary government. But for the United States the central issue is the greater claim to power put forth by the Executive and the fact that after the shift took place the spirit of the Constitution was left intact.

There is yet another general criticism that Tocqueville made about American political life. It is the little continuity he saw in it. "As soon as a party has become dominant," he writes, "all public authority passes into its hands; its private supporters occupy all the offices and have all the force of the administration at their disposal."

"As the most distinguished members of the opposite party cannot surmount the barrier that excludes them from power," he further adds, "they must establish themselves outside of it and oppose the whole moral authority of the minority to the physical power [of the majority] that domineers over it."

This was true enough in Tocqueville's time, as he viewed the spoils system then coming into its first bloom. But even then, above and beyond the noise of battle of politicians engaged in murderous competition for jobs—visible under both Jefferson and Jackson and fundamental in American history—was the willingness of each party, when gaining power, to take over and carry on many of the policies of the party which had preceded it in office while adding the new ones which the times and the electoral mandate demanded.

This is a process which has since then been refined and intensified, as part of a generalized transformation of political conditions in many countries, and has been continued after the Roosevelt Revolution, not only as a matter of tradition but as a matter of necessity. The scope of the transformations of American government and society from 1932 to 1952 has been so great, because of the unprecedented nature of the problems of those years, that a basis for the operations of the American government has been established which it is impossible to disregard. Continuity is a must for governments taking over after the end of a period of changes such as were witnessed during those twenty years. If, after 1952, the forward march of certain programs was halted and even some backward steps were taken (TVA, public power), further advances were made elsewhere (as in most of the programs of the welfare state and in minimum-wage standards), while in still other areas (public control over private economic activities and checks over the financial world) essentially the same policies were followed.

This does not mean that a different administration will not bring about important consequences in the spirit with which laws are managed, or in the way in which the country is led to contemplate its future. The point is that the Roosevelt Revolution established the conditions which will guarantee the continuity of policy of which a great nation stands in need, without preventing the changes which it may legitimately want to introduce. Standards of government and of administration have been built within a modernized whole which will survive in spite of verbal warfare. This of course had been true even before Roosevelt's days, as it has been true in the other great Anglo-Saxon democracy where the application of rational considerations to political life has not been a too rare occurrence in modern times.

FREEDOM AND DEMOCRACY

In taking up institutional items alone, we would miss the core of Tocqueville's *Democracy in America,* for the issues of presidential power, federal government, and continuity pale by comparison with the question: How can freedom survive in a democracy? And to this question we now turn.

Of Tocqueville, Sainte-Beuve said that he started thinking before he learned anything. It is certain that from his earliest youth, and a quarter of a century before the publication in 1865 of his other great work on the causes of the French Revolution, he had arrived at the most important conclusion of his life with regard to the unfolding of history. This was that the world was witnessing a leveling process. For centuries, under the impact of ever stronger central governments, the barriers of institutions and of customs which had sheltered groups and individuals against the direct pressures of the state, had been crumbling. Also, as a result of the urge toward equality, the balanced hierarchies of society had been disappearing. The intermediate bodies of parliaments, of estates, of the nobility, of provincial governments, had lost their meaning and become obsolete or had been destroyed.

Tocqueville had no illusions about the advance of the equalitarian movement, to him the essence of democracy. Equality of status was the basic fact of modern times everywhere in the Western world. Democracy, conceived as equality, was both inevitable and desirable, in spite of the longings of Tocqueville for the aristocratic societies of the past. But there was no surrender in his mind of the power of man to determine the course of history: "It is true," he says, "that around every man a fatal circle is traced beyond which he cannot pass; but within the wide verge of that circle he is powerful and free; as it is with man, so it is with communities. The nations of our time cannot prevent the conditions of men from becoming equal, but it depends upon themselves whether the principle of equality is to lead them to servitude or freedom, to knowledge or barbarism, to prosperity or wretchedness."

This, then, was the problem to which Tocqueville addressed himself: the problem of the survival of the individual, with his rights, in a democratic society where the essential doctrine was that of the rule of the majority, of a majority which, no matter how formed and by what issues, viewing itself as the *major pars* in numbers and in wisdom, would strive to assert itself and to stamp out the minority.

With Europe seething with unrest, with France starting on its journey of moral corruption under the July monarchy and unable to find the pivot around which to hinge her political system, Tocqueville saw the need of starting an inquiry into the sources of strength and weakness of the greatest of the democracies operating under ideal conditions, American democracy. For here he might find the answer to the question uppermost in his thoughts.

Once possessed of the answer, Tocqueville imagined himself ready to advise his countrymen and to help a democratic France and Europe to follow the path of freedom rather than that of despotism. This, then, was his objective.

With this in mind, how did American democracy appear to Tocqueville?

In America, as in Europe, the pressure of the majority was becoming stronger. Most of the state constitutions were fostering the absolute sovereignty of the majority with artificial means. Elected for brief terms, legislators were laboring under the weight of direct mandates from the electors. Laws were uncertain and short-lived, and so were the constitutions, subject to continuous change. "This omnipotence of the majority," continues Tocqueville, "and the rapid as well as absolute manner in which its decisions are executed in the United States, not only render the law unstable, but exercise the same influence upon the execution of the law and the conduct of the administration. As the majority is the only power that it is important to court, all its projects are taken up with the greatest ardor; but no sooner is its attention distracted, than all this ardor ceases."

Tocqueville thought that, as a result, the individual would suffer and often be left without any redress for wrongs suffered. He foresaw the danger of tyranny because public opinion, legislative powers, and executive powers were each only different manifestations of the same majority which had inflicted the wrong. But he was underestimating the ultimate power of the federal judiciary in taking over the protection of the rights of freedom, and one can lament his readiness to envisage the coming about of a multitude of petty tyrannies before which the federal Constitution and government would be helpless, in spite of his noble vision of the federal Union.

Developing rapidly in a country in which democracy was flourishing was a new and harsh aristocracy, identified by Tocqueville as the aristocracy of industry. The danger was that this business class would first impoverish and debase the men working under it and then abandon them to the charity of the public. Tocqueville had no doubt concerning the vigor with which the industrial classes would pursue their goals of innovation and expansion. Nor did he have any doubts of the means they would use in order to gain their objectives, nor, finally, of the way with which they would meet the difficulties they were creating. He thought that the American experience would differ little from the European one in its human consequences, and that the trail of the industrial revolution would often be one of despair, even though he saw in the United States a greater participation of the people in industry and a greater co-operation between the poorest and the most opulent members of the commonwealth. This spirit of adventure and of risk-taking is exposing Americans to "unexpected and formidable embarrassments. . . . As they are all more or less engaged in productive industry, at the least shock given to business all private fortunes are put into jeopardy at the same time, and the state is shaken."

Tocqueville remains one of the earliest critical commentators of our industrial age to have seen the problems of business controls over the community, and the dangers of the probable failure of the industrial classes to accept the responsibilities that went with power and to which earlier aristocracies had submitted. To have also suggested that America would face greater hardships than other countries because of the urgency that manufacturing and industrial activities had assumed in the country represents a remarkable feat of prophecy.

Most of the trends forecast by Tocqueville came true in the next century. The rise of America's industrial power was indeed phenomenal, and the state was "shaken" in 1929. The vitality of American democracy which Tocqueville had felt joined hands with constitutionalism to subdue the industrial monster to the medium of constitutional principle, to use Harold Laski's words. And this may well be listed as one of the permanent accomplishments of the Roosevelt Revolution.

For our time, there is added significance in the broad outlines of American economic policy since 1932. It is the demonstration of the irrelevance of the theories and practices of the Soviet revolution in the affairs of an industrialized society. The demonstration was not an easy one nor was its success expected with confidence by everybody. There have been many and persistent voices in the West bent upon proving our indebtedness to Russia in so far as planning and state intervention were concerned. The belief that the Soviet pattern of action had to be applied in times of trouble was an ingrained one. It took John Maynard Keynes's eloquence and theoretical constructions and Franklin Delano Roosevelt's practical political manipulations to provide proof of the inapplicability of the Soviet experience to the West and to give evidence of the bottomless gap between the enforced-slave drive to industrialize a peasant society at full speed and regardless of cost, and the delicate task of assuring the continued free growth of a highly industrialized nation, some of whose means of production were idle.

What stood out at the end of the 1932–1952 period was that the United States could face its day of reckoning, not with verbally simple and fetching formulas such as expropriation or nationalization, or forced savings, or directed labor, or central and total government planning and investment, but with other policies, less easily reducible to ideological generalizations, but which succeeded in effect in reconciling tradition and contemporary realities, the ideals of individual and of community action, those of free and public enterprise.

Government intervention was limited and selective. It aimed at freeing, not freezing, economic life. It fought private monopolistic rule over the welfare of man (what Roosevelt called "private socialism") and replaced it, to some extent at least, with the more distant benevolence of public oversight. It showed by example what private activity should be, and faded away when private business was ready to do the job. It moved into the higher financial reaches to restore to capitalism the freedom and responsibility it had lost. It demonstrated that a strong public hand did not mean exclusion of private efforts. It viewed under a fresh light the old disputes about property rights and, against the Marxist doctrine, it made clear the possibility of bringing to private property a sense of its duty to the community at large, without interfering at all with its formal structure. Property could be chastised and yet kept alive.

In the contest of Keynes versus Marx, the New Deal sided with Keynes (perhaps without realizing it) and sent Marx tumbling down. It has been difficult ever since to put Marxism together again as a revolutionary doctrine within a mature industrial society. The fact that in the United States some large private economic enterprises do exist and that they certainly do move toward forms of "social" exercise of their functions does not vindicate Marxism at all. For too many other conditions of freedom and types of individual and group activities are in being as countervailing factors. American economic life has not become a narrow, one-way, street. Communist theoreticians know this to be true and are giving increasing signs of restlessness when looking at the "unexplainable" developments of the American economy. Instead of the unbearable tensions that ought to be present at this moment of history, preceding as it does in the Marxist mythology the final catastrophe of the capitalistic system—instead of the one supreme, commanding, will that Marx envisaged as a necessity in a system of such complexity, America shows narrowing social cleavages and all the characteristics of a pluralistic society.

But even in 1835, in spite of the difficulties to which he was pointing, Tocqueville was confident that in America democracy would not suffocate freedom. Democracy had indeed been successful, while at the same time freedom had been able to maintain itself. Customs, legal habits, decentralization, and physical conditions account, in Tocqueville's judgment, for this happy combination.

Customs, which Tocqueville takes to mean the whole moral and intellectual condition of the people, include religion. "In France," he writes, "I had almost always seen the spirit of religion and the spirit of freedom marching in opposite directions. But in America I found they were intimately united and that they reigned in common over the same country." The principal reason for this different state of affairs Tocqueville finds in the separation between state and church prevailing in America: "In Europe, Christianity has been intimately united to the powers of the earth. Those powers were now in decay, and Christianity, as it were, is buried under their ruins. The living body of religion has been bound down to the dead corpse of superannuated polity; cut but the bonds that restrain it, and it will rise once more."

This is a simplification which does not do justice to the variety of historical experience which has often led in Europe to relationships between state and church different from those which could more easily be established in the United States. But Tocqueville's reasoning on this point is sound. It stresses the necessity of separation of temporal and ecclesiastical powers as well as the significance of moral factors in the maintenance of political institutions, implying, we might add, a doctrine of equality which, instead of being expressed in equality of status, is founded on a concept of moral equality before the law.

No great changes have occurred since the days of Tocqueville. Church and state are still separate. The leaders of the American community are thus enabled to pay homage to the spiritual values of the majority, while maintaining a careful distance from ecclesiastical entanglements. Separation of church and state has served the cause of religion very well indeed throughout most of the history of the United States as a nation, while in Europe, up to recent times, the fierce and righteous detachment of political power from religious values went hand in hand with pitiful entanglements between church and state at the bread-and-butter levels. In America, disestablishment made spiritual solidarity possible. In Europe, concordats fed vulgar laicism.

The possibility, however, of new trends should not be overlooked. The first is that the churches, or some of them, instead of being satisfied with the independent and mutually respectful existence of church and state, may insist on a more active recognition by government and governmental leaders of the values and principles they defend, and seek from political power a more precise knowledge of them and continued public declarations of ecclesiastical viewpoints. No open alliance between the two powers need be envisaged, to be sure, but a more specific recognition of the metaphysical in policy-making might be sought. It is not farfetched to say that the tendency to express national goals in religious terms, which has recently begun to appear in the declarations of public men, indicates a search for a greater solidarity of the earthly and of the divine. That this search can be seriously fruitful, for instance, in the field of foreign affairs, where it has been most in evidence, must be doubted.

There might also be a shift in the balance of power within the various religious bodies that fill the American scene. Pluralism, here too, has meant much for the maintenance of tolerance, of a living body of religious beliefs, and for their acceptance by great numbers of people. This is one of the factors that explains the greater influence of religion in American life compared to the countries where that pluralism does not exist.

Finally, there is the danger that religion in America might suffer from the bureaucratization, the formalism, which has imprisoned it between church walls elsewhere. When those masters of mechanization and organization, the business leaders and advertising men and television network executives, try to take the lead in the defense of religion, then it is time to take alarm and to feel that, as religion becomes linked to the powers of the earth, it may well end by being buried under their ruins, as Tocqueville said.

Custom extends to the press and the school: universal education, the finest flower of democracy, a free press, the stoutest foundation of freedom.

America shares the Anglo-Saxon tradition that has held freedom of the press the key to all other freedoms. Tocqueville finds freedom of the press well entrenched in the United States. He then writes: "The more I consider the independence of the press in its principal consequences, the more am I convinced that in the modern world it is the chief, and so to speak, the constitutive element of liberty. A nation that is determined to remain free is therefore right in demanding, at any price, the exercise of this independence."

That the American press is still free today is certain. It could also be said with justification that, with the British press, it is the freest in the world.

The reasons why the American press is free today appear to be these. In the first place, it has not the slightest fear of government. Governmental power is viewed with unconcern. Fair play in dealing with government policy goes with readiness to tell the truth and to present the news in such a way as to permit the public to understand their meaning. News is not suppressed or given out cryptically in order to save somebody's face. Politicians in power are not given special consideration. Rather, they must suffer the constant inquiry and investigation of newspapermen. Statements of public officials are not received with awe and treated at their face value as if they were gospel truth, but are merely viewed as a set of sentences to be taken apart, analyzed, and interpreted to find out what they mean in effect.

In the second place, the press is free because of the aggressiveness and enterprise and search for news on the part of many of the tillers in the vineyard. The profession of newspaperman requires skills and intelligence of a high order. Scientists and economists are needed to find out what is news, to relate scattered and obscure items and make them newsworthy. What is news today was not news a generation ago. The American press has kept pace with the revolution of our age. The

American press insists on feeding, to probably restive readers, great quantities of very difficult stories on scientific and technical matters. This is as it should be.

In the third place, the American press is free because it is a profitable enterprise that does not need subsidies. As a commercial operation it stands on its own feet and, in spite of the large volume of advertising it must carry in order to do so, it has successfully defended its independence against advertisers' pressures.

Finally, the press is free because no government power dares to interfere from the outside with the operation of a newspaper nor does any police authority dare to prevent the sale of any newspaper. The simple constitutional imperative that there shall be no law abridging freedom of the press has been observed.

These are principles whose broad validity seems to be unchallengeable. But the total effectiveness of the press may be diminished in other ways.

The newspapers answering fully to the description just given are not as many as the interests of the American people, or the range of the problems facing it, would require. There may be more great newspapers in the United States than in any other country. Among them would have to be included not only papers known throughout the world, but also many local papers run with independence and intelligence and a concern for truth that are altogether admirable. Even so, they are too few and they are read by too few people, as the geographical barriers of the American continent interpose practically insuperable difficulty to the national readership of the papers that really matter. There are vast reaches of the United States from which the *New York Times* is absent and where the local substitutes are inadequate. Many educated, interested, politically "conscious" citizens are deprived of access to the kind of information they need and are anxious to get.

There is the danger of uniformity of interpretation and discussion for which both the chain and the columnist, the latter especially a peculiar phenomenon of the American press, can be called responsible. In part, both the chain and the columnist are related to the economics of American journalism, still based, because of the vastness of the continent and of local requirements which cannot be disregarded, on nearly two thousand dailies. It is cheaper to pay one writer for one article to be printed in five hundred newspapers than it is to pay five hundred writers to do five hundred different ones. There may be benefits in the system, whenever a very able newspaperman can be persuaded to do the job. But there is greater danger in the diffusion throughout the land of the formless and banal thoughts and illiterate prose of mediocrities. The chain will also result in standardization of news and of editorial comment and when in any city—beyond the reach of other papers—only a chain newspaper is published, that city suffers a loss of freedom.

There is the trend to widen the meaning of news so as to include in newspapers information which is not news at all. If a greater and greater percentage of the available space is taken over by pieces on fashion, love, high society, bridge, cooking, mental hygiene, and comics—most of them sent out as canned items by a few syndicates—then the newspaper as an institution devoted to its primary original purpose, the political life of the community and the discussion of ideas, will be gone.

The economic structure of the press also has a bearing on freedom. In common with other segments of American economic life, newspapers have been driven to mechanized and more complex production processes. Not all of them can carry on with thinner profit margins. The survivors, and especially the weaker among them, engage in a frantic quest for revenues, with advertisers contributing in a damaging manner to the scramble by their fatuous insistence on circulation. This means, in varying combinations, the debasing of taste, the running after vulgar public inclinations, and the cramming of nearly all available space with advertising. These are days when the reading of even the best American newspaper becomes a disheartening adventure, as its pages are nothing but a catalogue of merchandise, with a few dead stories planted here and there in a sea of announcements and displays which are often but a caricature of real life. It seems inevitable that those laboring under such mounting financial worries should behave timidly—and timidity is not a virtue in the journalistic craft. No less important, the freedom of entry into the field has been sharply curtailed, as the costs of starting a new paper have become prohibitive.

Freedom of the press is a tender plant. To be free, a press must have enough freshness and authenticity, enough devotion to its original mission, sufficient variety of voices and freedom of movement, to do its job well. Press freedom shines brightly in America, and in some respects more brightly than ever, but the stuffiness and institutionalized rigidities that are making their appearance cannot be dismissed lightly, for a great deal is at stake.

Custom also includes education: "An American should never be led to speak of Europe. . . . But if you question him respecting his own country . . . his language will become as clear and precise as his thoughts. He will inform you what his rights are, and by what means he exercises them; he will be able to point out the customs which obtain in the political world. You will find that he is well acquainted with the rules of the administration, and that he is familiar with the mechanism of the laws."

How well did Tocqueville identify one of the chief merits of the American democratic educational system: the sense of civism and responsibility which is strongly instilled in its members. And how much of it has continued to be true, even under today's conditions of mass education, when new issues, disturbing in their implications and in the problems they pose, have risen.

One should first be clear as to what America has undertaken. This is nothing less, in principle, than the education, up to the age of about twenty, of all American youth.

This was not quite true, notwithstanding Jefferson's dream, in the past. Education for most was limited to younger age groups. College education was reserved to the few who could afford it or who wanted it, or who satisfied the stiffer admission requirements then prevailing.

But within the last generation we have seen not only a tremendous expansion in the number of boys and girls going to secondary schools, but a universal craving to enter the magic world of college life. New conditions of life, the experience of war, a sense of freedom, the higher security and welfare of the American people, the coming of age of recent immigrant groups, a fresh realization of what college education contributes to help meet the new opportunities of a smoothly working economic system, all of these factors are at the origin of the revolution in American higher education. As the older private universities could no longer satisfy the multitudes clamoring at their doors, state colleges and universities, throughout the land, undertook to bear most of the burden of higher education. Even in the East, state universities—until not so long ago the typical culture fruit of the prairies and the Western mountains—were called upon to face the incredibly large numbers of students. A new university world has sprung up, run by the people and for the people, ready to admit anybody with a minimum show of good will and literacy and offering new concepts of education to the startled consideration of those who remember the waning traditions of the past.

Nearly four million students will soon be crowding America's universities and colleges, most of them doing so at public expense. The United States is the first country to have given such wide practical translation to the theoretical conclusion that universal education is necessary in a democratic state.

One can visualize the day when no one who wants and deserves to go to college will be unable to do so. Already the frustrations and class antagonisms showing up when one child goes to school while his neighbor does not, have tended to disappear. Scholarship assistance has diminished the waste of talents fostered by poverty. The broad sweep of liberal arts colleges—of education for education's sake, without regard to diplomas, degrees, or professional interest—has given a fresh lift and sense of purpose to the young men and women busy all over the country in the daily routines of their lives.

There is impressive moral intensity in a policy which sets out to treat everybody on equal educational terms and which, with unprecedented speed, attempts to extend to all the privileges of school up to adulthood. This is a binding and universal experience which gives a unique democratic flair to American society and makes life in America one of relationships among equals, easy-going and cheerful, free from patronizing attitudes, the result of years of growing up shared in common.

It is only when one tries to measure the scope of the commitment and the high conceptions upon which it is based, that one can evaluate the difficulties which the experiment has had to face, its shortcomings, and the troubled issues to which it has led.

The means placed at the disposal of such a plan could not possibly have been adequate from the beginning. It has, therefore, suffered from a shortage of physical facilities and even more of brains. For, in a paradoxical twist, the democracy which has placed the highest value on universal and free education has also placed the lowest value on the services of those who are responsible for it.

One of the main reasons for this state of affairs, as far as the United States is concerned, is that education is a local matter. Even a large state university is a local affair. Secondary schools are under the jurisdiction of school boards that are primarily municipal in outlook. Each of the scores of thousands of units into which the system is divided, is, in a real sense, both the beginning and the end. This has meant educational freedom and diversity. There is a price that must be paid for freedom. The problem is to reduce it as much as safety permits. Each independent educational agency has tended to look at its problems on the reduced scale of its small world—a world in which today's necessity of increased efforts to secure a sound and discriminating education often finds but a pale and tired reflection. Delay and confusion have arisen in deciding what students ought to be taught in a mass-education experiment and what criteria, based on intelligence and skills, ought to be applied in the educational process.

One tendency has been to teach everything, since everybody has to be taught. An educational system, universal in its numerical scope, became universal in the subjects taught. Hence the dilution and multiplication of subject matters in American schools. With the increasing numbers of students, the practical-minded have overwhelmed the theoretical-minded by a decisive margin. Practical subjects have tended to clutter the curriculum to the disadvantage of the classical fields. If democracy means equality, it must mean equality of effort spent on all the pupils. If democracy means freedom, the educational system must be built on foundations of student autonomy and liberty of choice. A democratic educational system was thought to be incompatible with the creation of elites as well as with the imposition of programs of study from above. In the ensuing confusion, able students have felt lost in a sea of mediocrity and the aimless wandering of the others in search of the line of least resistance has led to wasted time and effort.

On these democratic premises, important distinctions are nevertheless beginning to appear. The older private colleges and universities have, for instance, become the champions of the so-called higher values of pure scholarship, with only the ablest students admitted within their sacred walls under a carefully organized program of study and research. Special programs for gifted students have been set up. These institutions have thus become the aristocracy of the educational system, while the larger and better financed state universities, for the most part prevented by law from adopting too selective policies, are seen as the representatives of mass culture. This is not a healthy development, as it leads to invidious comparisons and to an uneven tug of war between private and state universities. The private universities have tradition on their side but not much in the way of new weapons with which to defend themselves. The state universities have access to unlimited tax funds and the more skillful and enterprising members of the academic profession have not been slow to understand that, with some eloquence, they could, in the name of democracy and the future of the country, obtain money from state legislatures in larger amounts than they could by appealing to foundations or private donors. More public assistance to private universities appears unavoidable.

There is a final and most difficult test of the universality of the educational system of American democracy: obedience to the rule of law as defined by the Supreme Court since 1954 in *Brown* v. *Board of Education*. It is one that will have to be met over a period of time, the length of which will depend on the wisdom and courage of the political leadership of the United States. Much will have to be left to local customs and decision. But much of the essential guidance and drive must be provided by government, to uphold the doctrine of equality of which the Supreme Court has become the reasoned and eloquent proponent.

*

This is the same Supreme Court in which Tocqueville had already placed such high expectations. As he moved from custom to legal habits, Tocqueville pointed to judicial power as the protector of freedom in American democracy.

The complexities of the common law, he found, placed lawyers on a higher pedestal than their fellow men; the reliance on precedents further removed them from any intercourse with simple mortals: "The French codes are often difficult to comprehend, but they can be read by everyone; nothing, on the other hand, can be more obscure and strange to the uninitiated than a legislation founded upon precedents. . . . The French lawyer is simply a man extensively acquainted with the statutes of his country; but the English and the American lawyer resembles the hierophants of Egypt, for like them he is the sole interpreter of an occult science."

Sitting on the benches of the courts of justice, the judges transform them "into the visible organs by which the legal profession is enabled to control the democracy. [The judge's] legal attainments have already raised him to a distinguished rank among his fellows; his political power completes the distinction of his station and gives him the instincts of the privileged classes."

For the American judge, as Tocqueville was aware, is armed with political power as a result of his ability to declare laws unconstitutional. He is therefore continually interfering in the political processes of democracy. Tocqueville recognizes that this is the result of the greater validity given to the principles embodied in the Constitution of the United States, and declares that this tradition "forms one of the most powerful barriers that have ever been devised against the tyranny of political assemblies." And later, speaking of the Supreme Court, in an incisive anticipation of what was to be the Court's role, he says: "The peace, the prosperity, and the very existence of the

Union are vested in the hands of the seven federal judges. Without them the constitution would be a dead letter; the executive appeals to them for assistance against the encroachments of the legislative power; the legislature demands their protection against the assaults of the executive; they defend the Union against the disobedience of the States, the States against the exaggerated claims of the Union; the public interest against private interests, and the conservative spirit of stability against the fickleness of democracy."

Today much of the color of American life still comes from the legal system, from the way in which the courts function, and above all from the behavior of the Supreme Court. If anything, the Supreme Court stands today on an even higher pedestal as the symbol both of constitutionalism and of democratic aspirations to equality and freedom. The ground covered in the long years between 1835 and 1958 has been a difficult one, with more complications than Tocqueville could foresee. There were times when the very existence of the Union seemed to be threatened by the stand taken by the Supreme Court. At other times, the conservative spirit of the Court seemed to be fighting not the fickleness of democracy or the brutal weight of majorities, but the considered political decisions of government acting for the common good.

We have seen, in our judicial analysis of the Roosevelt Revolution, the double task of the Court in the maintenance of a free constitutional system. The first was the adapting of its social and economic views to the needs of the revolution, which could thus move forward without doing damage to the constitutional system itself. The second was that of the defense of human freedom, of individual rights and of equality among the races, a role enabling the Court to fulfill the highest duty that any institution can perform in a democracy, the protection of minorities and of individuals who might otherwise be left helpless by the high tide of majority rule.

The Court has done all this without in the end being only what Tocqueville expected it to be, the defender of the status quo. The tyranny of political assemblies has diminished with the passage of time. For the time being, the Court finds that the use of the instrument of review of legislative acts has lost much of its earlier significance, and is paying greater attention to the ways of administrators, to the interference of executive power with rights, to the reluctance of the states and local agencies to comply with the fundamental constitutional principle of equality.

This does not, however, alter the essence of the problem, and in different ways and causing different reactions, judicial power, respect for procedure, and recognition of the independence of the courts are still there as Tocqueville saw them to give to the advance of democracy in America the special orderliness it possesses.

Democracy and freedom can also live together in America, because America has refused centralization of administration, all too readily accepted in Europe as the inevitable consequence of the uniformity imposed by democratic leveling. The diffusion of political authority, Tocqueville writes, contributes in two ways to the maintenance of really free democratic institutions. First, the local bodies form "so many concealed breakwaters, which check, or part, the tide of popular determination. If an oppressive law were passed, liberty would still be protected by the mode of executing that law; the majority cannot descend to the details . . . of administrative tyranny." Secondly, the local bodies are the training grounds of citizens, where the members of the political community first realize what is individually at stake for them in the political game.

These points have been among the better understood of Tocqueville's political thought; but let it be added here that it is of good omen for the future to realize they are still widely accepted today, notwithstanding the disabilities they sometimes impose when national policies founder on the rocks of localism. A new co-operative meaning has been added to them during the Roosevelt Revolution, when they have emerged from the twilight of rigid taboos, to be re-examined successfully by the more perceptive among public administrators, struggling with the same questions facing Tocqueville—problems of how to bring about some participation of both insiders and outsiders in the making and carrying out of decisions, of how to make distant and massive national power locally intelligible.

AMERICA AND UTOPIA

In his ideal balance sheet, Tocqueville gave physical conditions last place. America's wild forests would not alone guarantee that it would become a Utopia. If democracy could retain freedom only where open spaces predominate, there would be little hope for mankind, in an overcrowded world and a fast disappearing wilderness. But Tocqueville puts on record his admiration for the American who "fearlessly braves the arrow of the Indian and the diseases of the forest," who is "unimpressed by the silence of the woods" and "the approach of beasts of prey," and who, confronted by a boundless continent, "moves onward with a passion stronger than the love of life."

The energy of man, confronted with great spaces of the physical world to conquer, is transferred to the political realm, where a ceaseless agitation influences all social intercourse. "I am not sure," Tocqueville adds, "that, on the whole, this is not the greatest advantage of democracy." It is true that a single despot may perform what he undertakes better than a democratic government. "Democratic liberty is far from accomplishing all it projects with the skill of an adroit despotism. It frequently abandons them before they have borne their fruits . . . but in the end it produces more than any absolute government; if it does fewer things well, it does a greater number of things. Under its sway, the grandeur is not in what the public administration does, but in what is done without it, or outside of it. Democracy does not give the people the most skillful government, but it produces what the ablest governments are frequently unable to create: namely an all-pervading and restless activity, a superabundant force and an energy which is inseparable from it, and which, under however unfavorable circumstances, may produce wonders. These are the true advantages of democracy."

Democracy, then, was good, and it was here to stay. And as a result of the historical process he had unraveled with such perspicacity, Tocqueville knew that it would have been idle to imagine a return to traditional absolutism were free democracy to fail. Princes were called tyrants, but religion, local autonomies, and traditions limited their powers. "Princes had the right, but they had neither the means nor the desire of doing whatever they pleased." With the flattening of the intermediate structures of the old regimes, under the urge toward equality and uniformity, a new oppression, which the traditional concepts of despotism and tyranny would be inadequate to define, would arise, were the balance lost between freedom and democracy.

Tocqueville offers a memorable description of democratic despotism:

> Above this race of men stands an immense and tutelary power, which takes upon itself alone to secure their gratifications and to watch over their fate. That power is absolute, minute, regular, provident, and mild. . . . For their happiness such a government willingly labors, but it chooses to be the sole agent and the only arbiter of that happiness; it provides for their security . . . manages their principal concerns, directs their industry, regulates the descent of property, and subdivides their inheritances. . . . Thus it every day renders the exercise of the free agency of man less useful and less frequent, it circumscribes the will within narrower range and gradually robs a man of all the uses of himself.

. . . The will of man is not shattered, but softened, bent, and guided; men are seldom forced by it to act, but they are constantly restrained from acting. Such a power does not destroy, but it prevents existence; it does not tyrannize but it compresses, enervates, extinguishes, and stupefies a people, till each nation is reduced to nothing better than a flock of timid and industrious animals, of which the government is the shepherd.

The question was how to avoid this destructive and all-pervasive tyranny over men, for which we have today found a name.

Contemporary American democracy is not Utopian and is not totalitarian. It is planted in common sense, in the realm of the possible, in freedom.

America is not Utopia. The confidence in the political process often shown by these pages has not been meant to convey the belief that all is well with America and that somehow the American people, presumably endowed with higher rational faculties, have been able to do what other peoples have failed to do—that Americans have at long last embarked upon the journey to which everybody aspires, to that never-never land of milk and honey and diamonds described by eighteenth-century travelers.

Utopia could not be born in the middle of the twentieth century, amid the ugliness of our industrial civilizations, the terrors of the atomic age, and the desperate confrontation of the old Western way of life with the new ways of life of the East. It can hardly even be conceived as a distant image, in times filled with dismay and waiting. The present itself in the United States is complicated and critical enough to make one feel that the country is still a long way this side of Utopia.

There is the sadness of the cities, showing so clearly the failure of man to relate growth to beauty. There is the bitterness of race relations as the two camps see sweeping change approaching, but are not yet prepared to accept its consequences. There is the impersonality of large areas of human activities with its dampening effect on man's freedom; the cumulative accretion of power to the bureaucracies, both public and private, managing them; the weight of the use of public funds for nonproductive purposes.

There is still poverty, more shocking because we do not seem to know what to do about it. The poor are no longer the submerged one-third of the 1930's, but their far smaller clusters appear irreducible and pose a challenge which is still beyond the comprehension of the country. There is the problem of what to do with what we produce. And there is the appalling gap between aesthetic values and material gadgets, essential social needs and the way in which the economic effort of the country is spent.[1]

There is the all too visible leveling of habits, the conformity and the aiming at the average. Even though the rich are not very noticeable in the sea of prosperity, they still have great privileges and power as well as the ability to control their own affairs regardless of the interests of others.

It is conceivable, as Robert Hutchins has suggested, that large numbers of Americans, spoiled by industrialism and success, no longer want to be, or can be, free. It is true, as Arthur Schlesinger has said, that there is a surfeit of official piety.

But America is not today, nor is it likely to become tomorrow, a totalitarian democracy, nor a garrison state, nor a police state. America is a democratic and individualistic society which, showing the ugly scars of modern mass-production civilization, has retained faith in the human beings that make it up. As constitutionalism, defined as the regulated application of humane and rational faculties to the task of guiding the political community toward common goals in an atmosphere that will recognize the supreme moral values in-

[1] On the economic issues confronting the United States today, see the persuasive book by John K. Galbraith, *The Affluent Society*.

herent in the individual, declines elsewhere, it still retains the upper hand in the United States.

What we have witnessed since 1932—a time of despair and gloom, a time when by all contemporary evidence the political processes the West had applied during its period of growth and expansion in the preceding centuries appeared doomed—has been the recovery and use of power by democratic leaders who, without rigid ideology and tyranny, yet with a broad conception of the needs of the times, have succeeded in renovating the historical heritage of the United States while maintaining freedom.

What we have seen in the United States has been the systematic and inventive search for solutions to the difficulties of industrial mass democracy, a search intended to realize the ideals of community without collectivism, the ideal of freedom without anarchy, the advantages of technology without the loss of humanism. The managers have had their day in the United States. But they have been kept in check and have not taken over the country.

What the Roosevelt Revolution has done has been to keep the door open so as to permit to our generation a chance to decide in liberty what we must do. The United States can today do so, on a higher platform of welfare and happiness and real freedom than ever before. When we look around us, we see throughout the world peoples whose doors toward the future are controlled by irresponsible elites now making all the decisions. America is still free, I believe, to choose among alternatives and to make up its mind to a large extent as to what it wants. In 1932, there was a strong chance that this would not be possible for long. The Roosevelt Revolution, having brought together common action and individual liberty, has preserved that freedom. This is bound to be the verdict of history.

INDEX

Academic freedom, 242–43, 247, 248, 259, 262; and McCarthyism, 309, 313–18

Acheson, Dean, 119, 120 *n.*, 302, 308 *n.*, 309 *n.*; quoted, 306, 308 *n.*

Adair v. *U.S.* (1908), 44, 207 *n.*

Adkins v. *Children's Hospital* (1923), 46, 207 *n.*

Adler v. *Board of Education* (1952), 242 *n.*, 248 *n.*

Administrative agencies, 137–40, 334–35; court review, 224–27

Affluent Society, The (Galbraith), 272 *n.*, 359 *n.*

Advertising, 270, 314–15, 347–48; and religion, 344

Age of Reform, The (Hofstadter), 81 *n.*, 92 *n.*

Agricultural Adjustment Administration (AAA), 13, 84, 273; and Supreme Court, 110, 111, 115, 209–11

Agriculture Department, 169, 188

Allen, Frederick L., quoted, 27–28

Aluminium, Ltd., 286–87

Aluminum Co. of America, 286–87

American Capitalism (Galbraith), 294 *n.*

American Commonwealth, The (Bryce), 319

American Communications Assn. v. *Douds* (1950), 252

American Dilemma: The Negro Problem in Modern Democracy (Myrdal), 266 *n.*; quoted, 274–75, 276–77

American Federation of Labor (AFL), 10, 292

American Federation of Labor v. *American Sash Co.* (1949), 43 *n.*

American Individualism (Hoover), 73

American Presidency, The (Rossiter), 124 *n.*, 126 *n.*; quoted, 121 *n.*

Antitrust policies, 92–93; and NIRA, 13, 81–84. *See also* Monopoly

Ashcraft v. *Tennessee* (1944), 262 *n.*

Assembly, freedom of, 232, 233, 248, 250

Atomic bomb, 3, 60 *n.*, 302–03

Atomic Energy Commission, 137, 169

Attlee, Clement, 68

Bail, right to, 248

Bailey v. *Drexel* (1922), 44–45

Banking, 30–33, 49, 122

Barnhart, Edward N., 237 *n.*

Barrows v. *Jackson* (1953), 263 *n.*

Beard, Charles A., 34

Berle, Adolf A., Jr., 80 *n.*, 282, 284–85; quoted, 282 *n.*, 285

Big Change, The (Allen), quoted, 27–28

Big Enterprise in a Competitive System (Kaplan), 285–86

Bill of Rights, 201–03, 311–12; "new," 94; and due process, 206; preferred-status doctrine, 233–38, 240. *See also* First, Fifth, *and* Tenth Amendments; *and under* Assembly, Press, Religion, Speech, *etc.*

Black, Hugo L., 219, 236 *n.*; quoted on preferred-status doctrine, 235; libertarian views, 241, 242, 244, 248–49, 253, 257

Blackstone, William, 232

Board of Trade v. *U.S.* (1942), 225 *n.*

Bonus army, 54

Borah, William E., 47

Boulder Dam, 98

Bowles v. *Willingham* (1944), 225 *n.*

Brain trust, 80 *n.*, 129, 130

Brameld, Theodore A., 266 *n.*

Brandeis, Louis D., 47; dissents, 210, 211; and "sea-change," 221

Brinegar v. *U.S.* (1949), 241 *n.*

British Labor party, 68

Brookings Institution, 27–28

Brown, Ralph S., quoted, 309

Brown v. *Board of Education of Topeka* (1954), 264 *n.*, 265–66, 352

Brown v. *Mississippi* (1936), 263 *n.*

Brownell, Herbert, Jr., 306

Brotherhood of Railroad Trainmen v. *Howard* (1952), 263 *n.*

Bryan, William Jennings, 81

Bryce, James, 319, 335

Budget, Bureau of the, 126, 133

Budget balancing, F.D.R. on, 66

Bulletin of the Atomic Scientists, 309

Burnham, James, 138

Burns, Arthur F., 130

Burns, James M., 84 *n.*, 87 *n.*, 89 *n.*; quoted, 58 *n.*, 65 *n.*

Burton, Harold H., 257